The Columbia Guide to
American Indians of the Northeast

Kathleen J. Bragdon

COLUMBIA UNIVERSITY PRESS   NEW YORK

COLUMBIA UNIVERSITY PRESS
Publishers Since 1893
New York   Chichester, West Sussex

Library of Congress Cataloging-in-Publication Data
  Bragdon, Kathleen Joan.
  The Columbia guide to American Indians of the Northeast / Kathleen J. Bragdon.
    p.   cm. — (The Columbia guides to American Indian history and culture)
  Includes bibliographical references and index.
  ISBN 0–231–11452–4 (cloth : alk. paper)—0–231–11453–2 (pbk. : alk. paper)
    1. Indians of North America—Northeastern States—History.   2. Indians of North
  America—Canada, Eastern—History.   I. Title.   II. Series.
E78.E2   B72   2001
974.004'97—dc21   2001047341

Columbia University Press books
are printed on permanent and durable acid-free paper.
Printed in the United States of America

c   10   9   8   7   6   5   4   3   2   1
p   10   9   8   7   6   5   4   3   2   1

CREDITS

Frontispiece: Photograph by the author.
Figure 1: John Smith, *A Map of Virginia, with a Description of the Countrey, the Commodities, People, Government, and Religion* (Oxford: J. Barnes, 1612).
Figure 3: Henry R. Schoolcraft, *Notes on the Iroquois, or, Contributions to the Statistics, Aboriginal History, Antiquities and General Ethnology of Western New York* (New York: Bartlett and Welford, 1846).
Figure 5: Roger Williams, *Key Into the Language of America* (London: Printed by Gregory Dexter, 1643). Image of title page is taken from Joseph Constantine Pilling, *Bibliography of the Algonquian Language* (Washington, D.C.: Government Printing Office, 1891).
Figure 6: John Smith, *The Generalle Historie of Virginia, New England, and the Summer Isles*, 1624 (London: Printed by I.D. and I.H. for Michael Sparks, 1808–14).
Figures 9, 11, 13, 15, 16, 19: From Thomas L. McKenney and James Hall, *The Indian Tribes of North America* (Philadelphia: D. Rice and A. N. Hart, 1849–54; reprint, Edinburgh: J. Grant, 1933–34).
Figure 10: Photograph by the author.
Figure 12: From John Frost, *Indian Wars of the United States, from the Discovery to the Present Time* (Philadelphia: J. B. Smith, 1855).
Figure 14: Photograph by the author.
Figure 17: George Catlin, *Manners and Customs of the North-American Indians* (London: Printed by C. Adlard, Bartholomew Close, 1841?).
Figure 18: Courtesy of the National Anthropological Archives, Smithsonian Institution, Washington, D.C.

To my parents-in-law,
Ruth and Marley Brown,
with respect and admiration

Contents

Acknowledgments

James Warren, editor for Columbia University Press, encouraged me to write this book, and without his help it would not have reached completion. He is not, however, responsible for any errors, all of which are mine. Hank Lutton, a graduate student in the Department of Anthropology at the College of William and Mary, assisted with the illustrations and in writing the encyclopedic sections, for which I am very grateful. The National Foundation for the Humanities and the College of William and Mary provided research time and funds to pursue this and other projects. My parents, George and Patricia Bragdon, have encouraged me all along, but especially in the final stretch, and my husband and colleague, Marley Brown, and my son, Marley Brown, have been loving and generous throughout.

Introduction

The Columbia Guide to American Indians of the Northeast is an introduction to the broad field of scholarship concerning the Eastern Woodlands region and its indigenous peoples, as well as a guide to research on a number of more specialized topics within the same field. Many different native communities and polities have lived in this vast area, both now and in the past; their histories and cultures well repay closer investigation.

Since scholars from several disciplines have written about the native peoples of the Northeast, especially historians and the practitioners of an interdisciplinary approach known as ethnohistory, this volume also reviews their complementary and contrasting contributions to the scholarship on the region and its people.

Descriptions of native peoples of the Northeast date back to the Norse sagas, and several important historical sources for the study of their cultures and economies predate the European settlement of eastern North America by a century or more. Increasingly, scholars move the "contact period" for the region back in time, as linguistic and archaeological evidence show traffic in European goods along trade routes stretching from Newfoundland to North Carolina and westward to the Great Lakes as far back as the sixteenth century A.D. At the same time, the volume of scholarship about the Northeast and writings by native people themselves has increased dramatically in the past two decades, resulting in a large body of new work. While much of the historiography of the Northeast has been based on documentary sources, the data from languages and archaeology increasingly available for the Northeast require the skills of disciplines such as anthropology and linguistics. Ethnohistory, the field of study that specializes in reconstructing past lifeways from a variety of historical and ethnographic sources, is especially useful in the Northeast.

As a region with a long history of contact, conflict, and accommodation between Indians and non-Indians, the Northeast is important both historically and theoretically. Indian events in New England and elsewhere were central to colonial history. Many of the policies later applied in federal Indian policy were initiated, in early form, against Indian peoples of the Northeast. Seminal works in anthropological and historical scholarship have events and peoples of the Northeast as their subject.

Today the Northeast is also the locus of great controversy. Federal recognition, gaming, land claims, and repatriation programs there are all foci of debate. Archaeological evidence fuels new scholarly argument over the traditional prehistoric timelines for the origins of agriculture, the rise of complex societies, the role of women, and the contributions of Native Americans, especially the League of the Iroquois, to forms of American government. Increasing demands for Indian sovereignty also raise questions about who should write their history and conduct archaeology on the past remains of their people.

This book is organized into four parts. Part I is an overview, which summarizes the cultures and histories of the native peoples of the region. This section is targeted especially at readers new to the historical and ethnographic literature concerning the Northeast culture area, and provides an overview of broad historical trends, cultural patterns, and the distribution of indigenous peoples across the landscape. Interpretive issues of interest to contemporary scholars are briefly reviewed here, to be taken up in more detail in part IV, to which they are also cross-referenced. Part II consists of an encyclopedic listing of people, places, and events significant in the Northeast culture area. Although not exhaustive, it covers a wide range of topics and provides an accessible guide to peoples, polities, and events mentioned elsewhere in the text.

Part III is an annotated timeline of significant historical events relating to native people in the Northeast. This list puts the history of the Northeast into a wider perspective, and underlines the fact that while various native peoples encountered European newcomers at different periods, their "contact" experiences had much in common. At the same time, the timeline makes clear that patterns in the native history of the Northeast are also unique to that region.

Part IV, a resource guide to research and theory, discusses a number of topics of current or enduring interest as they are reflected in the scholarly literature, with an annotated review of sources for the beginning or experienced student. In general, only the most comprehensive and/or most recent publications concerning each research subject are included. Exceptions are the most important primary sources and the "classics" in the literature on the Northeast, regardless of their date of publication. This section is divided into primary sources, including archaeological data and human remains and their analyses, documentary sources, early linguistic records, and ethnographies; secondary literature, organized by topic; and a brief survey of general reference works and selected media, museum, archival, and electronic research resources.

While many other important books and encyclopedias take the Northeast as their subject, this volume seeks to organize information and discussion for the reader who wishes an introduction to the scholarship concerning the native people of the region as it is now constituted. Rather than being presented as if they were undisputed, therefore, most research issues in the final section are discussed in terms of pros and cons, with references to the scholarship on both sides of each debate. Readers are invited to address these issues themselves through further research avenues suggested in the narrative, or by making use of the references provided in the resource guide. The Northeast is the scene of vibrant cultural revival today and continues to be the focus of important scholarly research. This volume is only one place to begin its exploration.

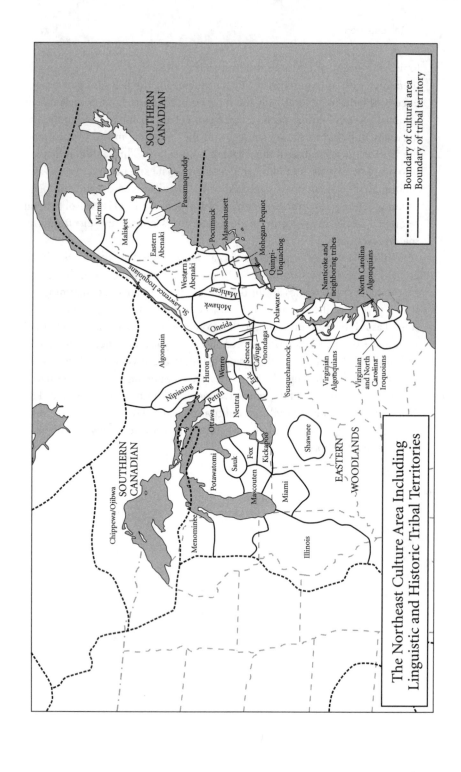

The Northeast Culture Area Including Linguistic and Historic Tribal Territories

- - - - Boundary of cultural area
——— Boundary of tribal territory

SOUTHERN CANADIAN

SOUTHERN CANADIAN

EASTERN WOODLANDS

Micmac
Maliseet
Passamaquoddy
Eastern Abenaki
Western Abenaki
Pocumuck
Massachusett
Mohegan-Pequot
Quinpi-Unquachog
Mahican
Mohawk
Delaware
Oneida
Onondaga
Cayuga
Seneca
Erie
Susquehannock
Nanticoke and neighboring tribes
North Carolina Algonquians
Virginian Algonquians
Virginian and North Carolina Iroquoians
St. Lawrence Iroquoians
Algonquin
Nipissing
Huron
Wenro
Petun
Neutral
Ottawa
Chippewa/Ojibwa
Menominee
Potawatomi
Sauk
Fox
Kickapoo
Mascouten
Miami
Shawnee
Illinois

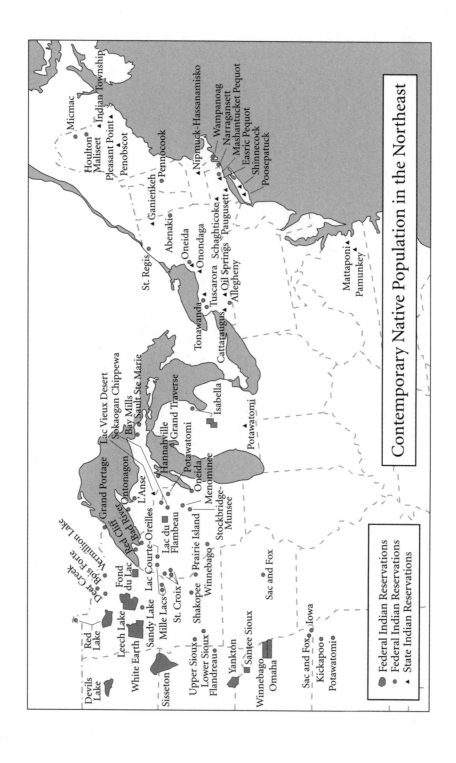

Contemporary Native Population in the Northeast

Federal Indian Reservations
Federal Indian Reservations
State Indian Reservations

Devils Lake
Red Lake
Leech Lake
White Earth
Sandy Lake
Sisseton
Upper Sioux
Lower Sioux
Flandreau
Yankton
Winnebago
Omaha

Deer Creek
Bois Forte
Vermillion Lake
Fond du Lac
Red Cliff
Bad River
Ontonagon
L'Anse
Lac Vieux Desert
Grand Portage
Sokaogan Chippewa
Bay Mills
Sault Ste Marie

Lac Courte-Oreilles
Mille Lacs
St. Croix
Shakopee
Prairie Island
Winnebago
Lac du Flambeau

Sac and Fox
Iowa
Sac and Fox
Kickapoo
Potawatomi

Santee Sioux

Hannahville
Grand Traverse
Potawatomi
Oneida
Menominee
Stockbridge-Munsee
Isabella
Potawatomi

St. Regis
Abenaki
Oneida
Onondaga
Tonawanda
Tuscarora
Oil Springs
Allegheny
Schaghticoke
Paugusett
Cattaraugus

Ganienkeh
Pennocook
Micmac
Houlton
Maliseet
Indian Township
Pleasant Point
Penobscot

Nipmuck-Hassanamisko
Wampanoag
Narragansett
Mashantucket Pequot
Easric Pequot
Shinnecock
Poosepatuck

Mattaponi
Pamunkey

The Columbia Guide to
American Indians of the Northeast

Part I

The Northeast: An Overview

1   Overview of the Northeast Culture Area

Chapter 1 summarizes the geographical extent of the Northeast culture area, its present and historic native populations, and the cultural adaptations of the native peoples of the region. A sketch of northeastern prehistory is provided, along with a short summary of northeastern spirituality. Native communities and tribal divisions are also briefly described by subregion and language family.

The Region Defined

Boundaries and Ecology

The Northeast is home to native peoples of many languages and cultures and, as a region, is defined more by tradition than by commonalities of speech, technology, or worldview (with exceptions—see below). The *Handbook of North American Indians* defines the Northeast as that region bordered on the north by the lower edge of the boreal forests that extend from Alaska to eastern Canada, with its western border following the line between the woodlands and its people and the prairies, occupied traditionally by the mounted bison hunters of the historic period and their semisedentary forebears (Trigger 1978a,1). The northeastern culture area conventionally includes all coastal Algonquian speakers from the Micmac and Maliseet-Passamaquoddy in the far Northeast to those who occupy what are now eastern Virginia and North Carolina. The region also includes the Northern Iroquoians, but not the southern Iroquoian-speaking Cherokees of western North Carolina, Tennessee, and Georgia. Also included within the conventionally defined boundaries of the Northeast are the peoples of the Ohio Valley and most of the natives of the Great Lakes (see Map 1).

Ecologically, the Northeast is also a region of great contrast. Harsh winters and early frosts in the northernmost reaches of the area made the adoption of agriculture there impractical, while among the coastal Algonquians of the temperate Mid-Atlantic, two crops of corn, beans, and squash a year could be harvested (Rountree 1989). Abundant maritime resources—saltwater fish, shellfish, and sea mammals—enriched the diet and governed the subsistence efforts of many coastal people, while people of the Great Lakes depended on freshwater fish, many kinds of waterfowl, and wild rice. The region is spanned by many large and navigable waterways and, in the early historic period, was traversed by numerous trails. People of the Northeast were well traveled and knowledgeable about groups living at some distance from them (Tanner 1989).

Languages

The people of the Northeast were and are speakers of languages from three major language families: Algonquian, Northern Iroquoian, and Siouan. Algonquian languages included those of the eastern Algonquian subfamily, such as Narragansett and Unami, and the central Algonquian languages, such as the Menominee and Ojibwa. The Northern Iroquoian languages included those of the Six Nations, as well as the St. Lawrence drainage area. Other Iroquoian speakers in the region were the Tuscarora, Meherrin, and Nottoway, who lived on the Virginia–North Carolina coastal plain (Boyce 1978, 282). Siouan languages are represented by the Winnebago of the Great Lakes region and the Siouan speakers of western Virginia and North Carolina, about whom little is known (Goddard 1978a; Alexander 1971, 307). (In part IV, section 2 ["Primary Sources and the Northeast"], see "Language, Language Contact, and Early Linguistic Studies"; "Pidgins, Jargons, and Creoles"; and "Language Loss.")

In the eighteenth and nineteenth centuries, speakers of some of these languages emigrated voluntarily or were forced from their original home-lands, in some cases out of the Eastern Woodlands altogether. In particular, the Shawnee—Algonquian speakers who, in the protohistoric period, prob-ably lived in what is now southern Ohio—were subject to many relocations; most of their descendants live today in Oklahoma (Callender 1978, 622). Other Algonquian speakers, most notably the Unami and Munsee Delaware, after being exiled from their original homelands in what is now eastern New York, Pennsylvania, and New Jersey, eventually settled in Kansas, Oklahoma, and Ontario, Canada (Goddard 1978b, 224, 234).

Today, eastern Algonquian languages are represented only by Maliseet-Passamaquoddy, Micmac, and small numbers of Unami and Abenaki speakers. Northern Iroquoian languages, with the exception of the St. Lawrence languages, Susquehannock, and the central Algonquian languages, still have living speakers. Winnebago, the only language of the Siouan family currently spoken in the Eastern Woodlands, still has more than 1,000 speakers. Table 1.1 summarizes data on language survival in the Northeast as of 2000.

Population Prior to the Twentieth Century

Although population estimates for native North America in the protohistoric period have generally been conservative (e.g., Mooney 1928), recent reevaluations suggest that, prior to the epidemics that swept through North America during the period of European exploration and settlement in the fifteenth through the seventeenth centuries, native population was somewhere between 250,000 and 400,000 in all areas of the Northeast. Table 1.2 summarizes these figures from a variety of sources (Dobyns 1983; Henige 1986).

The epidemics, which included devastating outbreaks of smallpox, yellow fever, bubonic plague, and hepatitis, decimated Indian communities throughout the Northeast, reaching inland communities before any Europeans themselves arrived. Both Cook (1970) and Snow and Lanphear (1988) suggest that losses of up to 90 percent were sustained in some communities. The native population of Patuxet, for example, located on or near the site of Plymouth Plantation on the southern shore of Massachusetts Bay, was completely wiped out in the epidemics that swept through southern New England between 1617 and 1619 (Heath 1969, 51).

Population density in the protohistoric period was also variable. The colder regions in the north and northeast were sparsely inhabited, with densities of only 12–29 people per square kilometer (Snow 1980, 34). Temperate coastal regions and those of the St. Lawrence, as well as the territories of the Northern Iroquoians, were very densely settled, probably ranging between 200–2,400 people per hundred square kilometers (Snow 1980, 34; Heidenreich 1978, 369).

Native populations in the Northeast continued to decline during the colonial period and in the nineteenth century, as warfare, dislocation, and the continuing vulnerability to European-introduced diseases took their toll (Bailyn 1986; Kelly et al. 1987). Those Indians who survived came to occupy limited areas of their once vast territories, established permanent "towns," or were settled onto reservations. During this period, however, many native

TABLE 1.1 Native Languages and Their Speakers in the Northeast (c. 2000)

Language	Number of Speakers	Status
Abenaki-Penobscot	20, all aged	Nearly extinct
Cayuga	380 out of 3,000, Cattaraugus Reservation, Canada	Nearly extinct in U.S.
Lumbee		Extinct
Mahican		Extinct
Maliseet-Passamaquoddy	1,500 out of 3,000, Maine, New Brunswick	
Massachusett (Wampanoag)		Extinct
Meherrin		Extinct
Miami		Extinct
Menominee	50 out of 3,500	Nearly extinct
Mesquakie (Fox)	800 out of 2,500, Kansas, Nebraska	Nearly extinct
Micmac	2,000 in Boston, 10–100 in New York City, 6,000 in Canada	
Mohawk	3,000 out of 10,000	
Mohegan/Pequot		Extinct
Nanticoke		Extinct
Nottoway		Extinct
Ojibwa, Eastern	8,000 out of 26,000	
Oneida	250 out of 7,000, Canada, New York, Wisconsin	
Onondaga	100 out of 1,500, including Canada	
Potawatomi	500 out of 7,500, including Canada	
Powhatan		Extinct
Quiripi/Unquachog		Extinct
Seneca	200 out of 8,000, including Canada	
Shawnee	200 out of 2,000, Oklahoma	
Tuscarora		Extinct
Unami	10 or fewer	Nearly extinct
Winnebago	1,500 out of 3,500	

SOURCE: Joseph E. Grimes and Barbara F. Grimes, eds., *Ethnologue: Languages of the World*, 12th ed. (Dallas: Summer Institute of Linguistics, 1993).

TABLE 1.2 Pre-Epidemic Population Estimates for Native People of the Northeast

Group	Estimate	Source
New England / E. New York	71,900–156,200	Cook 1970, 84 (71,900); Snow and Lanphear 1988, 24 (156,200)
Mid-Atlantic	31,000–40,000	Feest 1978a, 242; 1978b, 256; 1978c, 272
Huron	30,000	Trigger 1985, 236
Five Nations	30,000	Trigger 1985, 236
Petun and others	8,000	Garrad and Heiden-reich 1978, 395
Nottaway, Meherrin, and Tuscarora	1,700	Boyce 1978, 287–88
Illinois	8,000	Bauxar 1978, 594
Great Lakes	80,000	Tanner 1987, 65
Total	260,600–353,900	

peoples in the Northeast continued to travel widely as soldiers, mariners, or itinerant laborers, and these contacts between communities were significant in keeping a separate native identity intact.

Twentieth-Century Native Population in the Northeast

By the first decades of the twentieth century, Indian communities began to experience the first increase in their populations since the seventeenth century. Indian communities in the Northeast, as in other parts of North America, are steadily growing, with those under 40 making up the largest percentage of each Indian community. Many live in cities such as New York, Boston, and Detroit, although a large percentage still live within a short distance of their ancestral communities. For example, nearly 80 percent of the Eastern Pequot tribe of Connecticut were born within 20 miles of their reservation, and almost 70 percent live in nearby towns today (Bragdon and Simmons 1998). Table 1.3 summarizes recent census information for native people of the Northeast by tribe, and includes nonaffiliated native persons as well.

TABLE 1.3 Contemporary Population Figures for Native People of the Northeast

Connecticut	6,472	Massachusetts	11,857	Ohio	19,859
Delaware	1,982	Michigan	55,131	Pennsylvania	14,210
Illinois	20,970	Minnesota	43,392	Rhode Island	3,987
Iowa	7,217	New Hampshire	2,071	Vermont	1,650
Maine	5,945	New Jersey	14,500	Virginia	14,893
Maryland	12,601	New York	60,855	Wisconsin	38,986

SOURCE: Carl Waldman, *Atlas of the North American Indian* rev. ed., illus. Molly Braun (New York: Facts on File, 2000); *see also* George Aron Broadwell (1995), "1990 Census Figures for Speakers of American Indian Languages," *International Journal of American Linguistics* 61(1) (1995): 145–49.

Reservations

Currently there are several dozen reservations in the Northeast. Of these reservations, some—like those in Connecticut and Virginia, established in the seventeenth century—have remained the focus of native political and social life from colonial times to the present. Even where the reservations were insufficient to support the entire community, they served as the focus of settlement. Map 2 locates present-day Indian reservations in the Northeast.

Indian Tribes and Organizations in the Northeast

Many Indians do not live on reservations, although studies have consistently demonstrated that most native people still reside within a restricted region, with their reservation as a focus (e.g., Mohegan Final Decision; Simmons and Bragdon 1998). Most of these native people are registered members of tribes or organizations. Many of these in the Northeast, and their locations, are listed in part IV, section 1 ("Indian Tribes").

Northeastern Peoples Before Columbus

The native peoples of the Northeast have no written histories that predate the arrival of Europeans, but their rich oral traditions recall a world of tricksters and sacred beings, culture heroes, and creators, whose actions formed the present landscape and who created the human societies that came to live there. A story collected in New England in the seventeenth century, for example, states:

> a great while agon their countrey was drowned, and all the people and other creatures in it, only one powaw (shaman) and his webb (wife) foreseeing the flood fled to the white mountains carrying a hare along with them and so escaped; after a while the powaw sent the hare away, who not returning emboldened thereby they descended, and lived many years after, and had many children, from whome the countrie was filled again with Indians. Some of them tell another story of the beaver, saying that he was their father. [Josselyn 1988, 96–97]

The Northern Iroquois share creation stories that concern the Earth Diver, who carried the mud from the bottom of the primal ocean to the earth's surface, forming the land where people came to dwell. Sacred twins—Tharonhiawagon, "He Who Grasps the Sky," or "Sapling," the good twin, and "Flint," the evil twin—and their mother, Sky Woman, were the first people to live on earth:

> Two birds saw the Sky Woman fall. Just before she reached the waters they caught her on their backs and brought her to the other animals. Determined to help the woman they dove into the water to get mud from the bottom of the seas. One after another the animals tried and failed. Finally, Little Toad tried and when he reappeared his mouth was full of mud. The animals took it and spread it on the back of Big Turtle.

Although some sacred stories suggest a timeless connection between people and their homelands, others, commonly called "migration stories," tell of the arrival of the first people. Persistent tales from Connecticut, for example, suggest the relatively late arrival of the Pequot in that region (Speck 1928). In the seventeenth century the Delaware, too, told stories that suggested a recent movement from a more westerly homeland (Goddard 1978). (In part IV, see section 4, "Spirituality and Worldview.")

However, most of the information concerning life in the Northeast prior to the arrival of Europeans comes from archaeological investigations, which provide details about subsistence, settlement, and technology and hints of social relations, religion, and political organization in the past.

Some archaeologists and anthropologists also use archaeological data to look at broader patterns of cultural process, to show how the native peoples of the Northeast share similarities with other societies in North America and in other parts of the world. This comparative perspective helps to fill in the gaps in the archaeological data and provide a more complete picture of life before the histories of northeastern people were written down.

An Outline of Northeast Prehistory

Archaeologists divide the period before written history in the Northeast into three major periods: the Paleo-Indian period (circa 20,000–7,000 years ago); the Archaic period (circa 7,000–2,000 years ago) and the Woodland period (to 1500 A.D.). A number of Paleo-Indian sites have been excavated in the Northeast, suggesting that (as most scholars agree) after the entry of people of Asiatic origin into the New World from the northwest, their occupation of its territories was rapid and widespread (Fitting 1978; Tuck 1978).[1]

Traditionally understood to focus on migrating big game, the lifeways of Paleo-Indian hunters are still poorly known, and the increasing variety of sites dated to this time period suggest that these hunting people shared many features with more sedentary societies. In particular, the Meadowcroft Rock Shelter in Pennsylvania, for example, contains remains of what appear to be sturdy dwellings, and a wide variety of faunal remains suggesting an intensive usage and knowledge of local game and fish.

Recent controversies over the meaning of some early sites in the Northeast concern the origins of their first inhabitants. Several early sites in the Northeast contain tool assemblages that archaeologist Dennis Stanford describes as "Solutrean," referring to the style characteristic of Paleolithic cultures of southwestern Europe. The Cactus Hill site in Virginia, for example, radiocarbon dated to between 10,000 and 18,000 years ago, contains tools that encourage Stanford and a minority of other archaeologists to suggest that some ancient peoples might have migrated by boat to the New World from Europe 18–24,000 years ago (Parfit 2000, 61). Since this theory proposes that significant numbers of early Europeans were able to make the dangerous Atlantic crossing in primitive boats, is based on stylistic similarities between very distant archaeological assemblages, and contradicts most of the human genetic data now available for Native American populations (who most closely resemble Asiatics in both phenotypical and genotypical profiles), most archaeologists treat this theory as extremely tentative.

By the Archaic period, populations were clearly "settling in" to particular territorial niches, adapting technologies and diets to locally available resources. The Archaic period, however, is also difficult to characterize in a uniform manner, as archaeologists have identified a number of artistically significant "traditions," such as one known as Adena, appearing at the end of the period, which may have signaled the development of socially complex societies with widespread trade and political influence *prior* to the introduction of maize horticulture into the Northeast culture area (Benison 1997; Dimmick 1994).

Archaeological debate also continues over the interrelations between Archaic societies and early Woodland period societies in the Northeast, and in other parts of the New World as well. Newly excavated sites in the Northeast, sometimes seen as something of a "backwater," suggest that certain distinctive "cults" or "complexes" had their origins there, while others show convincing evidence of contact with complex New World societies of the Southeast, the Midwest, and possibly Central America as well. The great Hopewellian culture complex, centered in the Ohio Valley, emerged about 1,800 years ago, and was characterized by large, ceremonial centers, with temple and civic complexes surrounded by farming settlements (Koehler 1997). Archaeological evidence documents trade links to the Rocky Mountains, the Great Lakes, and the Gulf of Mexico. Hopewell society was socially complex, with hereditary rulers, specialized laborers and artisans, and elaborate religious ceremonies. Although the Hopewell hegemony appears to have collapsed by 500 A.D., other complexes, especially the remarkable ceremonial mound-building Mississippian culture and the related Fort Ancient societies (see below), arose to replace them, and flourished for several more centuries (Baker and Pauketat 1992; Earle 1987; Peregrine 1996). The Mississippian culture, most dramatically evident in sites near St. Louis and along the Mississippi itself, also influenced events in the Northeast during the late Woodland period. Archaeology suggests that Mississippian society continued to develop until at least 1500 A.D., and perhaps longer in some localities (Griffin 1993). Dincauze and Hasenstab have recently suggested that the expanding Mississippian sphere induced changes in proto-Iroquoian societies that in turn had an impact on eastern Algonquian-speaking peoples, especially in the Mid-Atlantic and in New England (1987). Farther to the south, the Southeastern Burial Cult and other late Woodland period cultural developments influenced the Algonquian-speaking peoples of the coastal plains and Delmarva peninsula, as well as the Siouan and Iroquoian peoples of the Piedmont and intermontane regions. Another possibly significant but little understood influence is that of the medieval Norse, who journeyed to the New World circa 1000 A.D. and whose colonies in Greenland were an indirect source of trade goods in the Northeast for several centuries thereafter (Ingstad 1969; McGee 1984). (In part IV, section 2 ["Primary Sources and the Northeast"], see "Archaeology, the Adoption of Agriculture, and the Rise of Complex Chiefdoms and Social Inequality in the Northeast.")

Archaeological research is still sorely needed to further investigate these possibilities, which have profound implications for the development of the peoples of the Woodland period in the Northeast, whose histories are the subject of this volume.

SUBSISTENCE

In the early historic period, natives of the Northeast were proficient hunters, fishermen, shellfish collectors, and gardeners. Early European observers frequently remarked on their skills as weavers, basket makers, and carvers, and countless remains of stone tools testify to their abilities as stoneworkers. Except for some cold-hammered copper ornaments, native peoples of the Northeast did not use metal prior to the arrival of Europeans, and they had no large domesticated or draft animals to provide food or power.

Subsistence practices are often the basis for many types of social relationships. For example, animals that typically travel or forage in groups are most effectively exploited by organized hunting parties. The organization of such parties is often in turn dictated by rules established within social groups, rules that are based on kinship, marriage, or experience. The tools that people use, the territories they control, and the knowledge they require to subsist are often subject to rules of inheritance or exchange that also determine or are determined by social relationships. In addition, relationships with the supernatural and the wider principles of cosmic organization are often closely related to the ways in which people make a living. Each region within the Northeast culture area supported peoples with different economic adaptations, but all can be characterized according to two basic orientations: hunting/foraging and a mixed horticulture/foraging/hunting economy. These distinct adaptations were in turn associated with distinct cultural orientations, apparent in the early contact period and in the later historic period as well. (In part IV, section 5 ["Politics and Economy"], see "Economy and Subsistence, Then and Now.")

Hunting/Foraging

Since the earliest period of occupation of the Northeast, the Paleo-Indian period, and especially since the Archaic period, peoples of the Northeastern

Woodlands have been hunters and foragers. The many thousands of archaeological sites that have been excavated in the Northeast testify to this ancient adaptation, which varied according to the availability of local resources and evolved with the changing conditions of the postglacial environment of the region. Game, fowl, fish, plant foods, fruits, nuts, seeds, berries, tubers, and in some areas grains made up the bulk of the diet, according to season. As the glaciers that once covered most of the Northeast receded and the sea level rose, people living in the coastal regions of the Northeast developed a greater dependence on shellfish and other animals and plants that flourished in tidal flats, estuaries, and salt marshes. Similarly, sea mammals came to have a particular significance to the northeasternmost communities (Flannery 1929).

In the late sixteenth and early seventeenth centuries, European explorers and settlers in the northeastern maritime regions, the St. Lawrence River and its drainage, and the interiors of what are now Massachusetts, Vermont, and New Hampshire met groups of people who spent parts of each year in different locations, generally wintering in smaller camps, where they hunted and trapped, and spending the summers fishing, hunting, and foraging. Hunters among the Ojibwa, Abenaki, and Micmac stalked game in the snow using toboggans and snowshoes, while others hunted with dogs. Many groups fished through holes in the ice during the winter, and others snared birds or hunted them with bows and arrows.

Springtime saw many foraging groups relocating to fishing locations, and it was at this time that large gatherings of people were possible (Flannery 1946). Fresh fish was abundant at this season, and what was not eaten was smoked or dried for future use. In those areas where maples grew, sap was collected in the spring for use as a sweetener (Ritzenthaler 1978, 747). In Maine and the maritime regions, people hunted sea mammals and collected shellfish on the coast in the spring of each year (Bourque 1973).

Summer was the time for continued hunting and fishing, as well as foraging, when wild foods became ripe. Some groups moved farther inland in the summer months; others remained by the coast or at fishing stations. Native knowledge of plants and their properties was encyclopedic (Herrick and Snow 1995). Trade was conducted during the summer months as well. Fall was the time for harvesting and processing fruits, nuts, and other foods for use during late winter and early spring. The Menominee and the southwestern Chippewa harvested wild rice by knocking the dried kernels into their canoes (Spindler 1978, 708).

European observers were impressed with the canoes constructed by many northern hunting peoples. The two types—one of birch bark, and the bulkier but somewhat sturdier dugout canoes—had overlapping ranges, but in general, birch-bark canoes were found most often in the Northeast, while the mid-Atlantic and southern groups, to whom birch bark was not available, built large, sometimes oceangoing dugout canoes capable of holding many people.

As many northeastern peoples moved seasonally or otherwise to take advantage of various resources within new territories, or were required to shift village location as new planting fields were required, the housing of most foraging people was designed for easy setup and removal. The wigwam so common to the Northeast came in several different varieties, but most were constructed of a sapling frame bent to form arched ovals, some as long as forty or sixty feet, but most about fifteen to twenty feet in length. These frames were covered with woven mats, skins, or sheets of bark that were generally easy to install, remove, or replace. These houses had openings at either end and a central hole covered by a moveable flap, allowing the smoke from the fires kept constantly lit indoors to escape. Smaller or more temporary brush- and skin-covered shelters were also used by hunting parties.

Foraging peoples of the Northeast wore tailored clothing of skin and fur, generally a breechclout, leggings, and moccasins for men, and a skirt and leggings for women. Fur-lined cloaks worn over one shoulder were common in many groups, and women in some areas also wore longer shirts or shifts over their skirts and leggings in cold weather (e.g., Speck 1940). In temperate seasons, children often went naked, although girls in several groups wore strings on their legs and around their waists.

Hair and skin were often dressed with grease, both for protection against cold, heat, and insects and because it was believed beautiful. Many foraging people were tattooed or painted, and wore ornaments of all kinds in their hair and as jewelry. Marriageable girls or new brides sometimes wore special head coverings or dressed their hair over their eyes, a widespread practice in native North America probably associated with a recognition of women's powerful fertility and its danger if improperly unleashed.

Political organization among foraging people seems to have been of the "band" type, with leaders, generally men, deriving all authority from consensus (e.g., Leacock 1954). In the early seventeenth century, some local leaders in coastal foraging communities, including the Abenaki and Micmac, became powerful brokers between fur trappers in the interiors and European traders and explorers, and used their positions to enhance their authority and that of their families. These "big men" were often successful in forging alliances among several smaller groups, but the coalitions they created seldom survived their deaths.

Archaeologists and anthropologists have, in recent years, asked a number of interesting questions about the social correlates of the hunting/foraging way of life. What, for example, would the rules be for determining the boundaries between the territories of different groups? In one instance, Dena Dincauze argues that, during the Woodland period in what is now New England, "hinterlands" between principle communities were left largely unoccupied (personal communication 1998). Lewis Binford's study of subarctic hunting peoples (1980) suggests that the boundaries between territories were well known and respected by members of contiguous groups. Resource sharing—for example, the use of shellfish locations or productive fishing spots— would have required negotiation between groups, but many such groups worldwide also have rights to various resource locations through marriage ties.

A foraging way of life also impacts social relationships within communities, with men and women often occupying separate "spheres" (Rosaldo 1974). At the same time, scholars such as Eleanor Burke Leacock suggest that relationships between the sexes were essentially egalitarian (1978). Interesting research on the psychological "profile" of the subarctic hunters by E. Irving Hallowell in the 1940s also points to the possibility that a life dependent on unpredictable resources can well shape the worldview and emotional experiences of hunting peoples (Hallowell 1960), leading to a fatalistic outlook and a reserved demeanor.

Horticulture/Foraging

The cultivation of domesticated crops came relatively late to the Northeast, but ongoing archaeological investigations in the region suggest that no sharp lines can be drawn between horticultural practices and the "encouragement" of naturally occurring resources in many areas. The seasonal collection of plants such as amaranth, the various chenopods, and tobacco, as well as the systematic cultivation of nut and fruit tree groves, may have preceded the adoption of maize/bean/squash horticulture by several centuries.

Farmers in the Northeast also shared in the foraging practices of their neighbors, and many communities continued to depend on game, fish, shellfish, and seasonally available wild plants. In the winter months, even committed farmers often moved inland to more protected locations to hunt and trap. Spring likewise signaled a move to fishing locations inland and on the coast (Bennett 1955). Summer activities varied by region. Some groups moved inland after game and freshwater fish; others remained at the coast for shellfishing and offshore fishing with nets, weirs, and harpoons. John White's famous illustrations of the native people of Secoton (on the south shore of the modern-day Pamlico River) show them using a variety of traps, nets, weirs, and fishing implements, and give some notion of the wide range of fish, crabs, and other shellfish available. The fall was harvest time, an important period in the ritual calendar of farming peoples.

Farming people in the Northeast lived in housing similar to that of the foragers, although some, like the Iroquois, built larger dwellings known as longhouses, where several married couples and their children might live. The people known as the Powhatan, members of the paramount chiefdom of the same name, also built "temples" of mat-covered frames elevated above the ground, which contained both sacred sculpted images and the mummified remains of former chiefs. Storage houses and semisubterranean "barns" were also common in farming communities.

Northeastern farmers also built temporary structures for important ceremonies, for mourning, and for seasonal rituals such as green corn celebrations. These constructions were generally described as "arbors," and were often hung with greenery and objects of sacred significance.

The clothing of farming people was also similar to that of their foraging neighbors, although some early descriptions suggest that it was occasionally more elaborate. Feather cloaks and headgear were worn by members of elite families and by elderly men and women among coastal societies in New England and Virginia. The paramount sachem Powhatan of Virginia had a cloak elaborately decorated with shells, and many people wore clothing decorated with paint, beads, and quills.

Most farmers were active traders, and traveled many miles on foot or by canoe in pursuit of trade. The heavy dugout canoes of the southern Algonquian people could hold as many as fifty people. Dugouts were suitable for ocean travel, and were used for deep-sea fishing as well.

The differences between the social organization and the political activities of farming and foraging people have long fascinated anthropologists. Northeastern farmers were probably members of societies that were more stratified, and often had hereditary leaders from high-ranking families (see also part II). These differences were especially marked among Algonquian-speaking communities. Northern Iroquoians were organized into family units known as matrilineages, and clans and representatives from each lineage participated in community and intercommunity decision making. The Northern Iroquoians, founders of the much-admired League of the Iroquois, created this remarkably democratic form of government early in the colonial period (see also "Peoples and Cultures of the Northeast: An Overview," the third main section of this chapter), according to principles probably established centuries earlier. (In part IV, section 5 ["Politics and Economy"], see "Iroquois Politics, the League, and the Origins of the Constitution.")

Contact with Europeans had significant and early repercussions among the farming people of the Northeast. The diseases inadvertently introduced into Indian communities by traders and explorers had devastating effects on these sedentary and populous peoples, and their cleared fields and parklands were often too tempting a prize for land-hungry settlers. Coastal farming peoples became middlemen in the early fur trade, and some, such as the Pequot of coastal Connecticut, were "minters" of the wampum that served as currency in the early decades of trade in the Northeast. New kinds of wealth introduced by the fur trade disrupted social, economic, and political relations within Indian communities. On the other hand, it is possible that the arrival of Europeans and their goods accelerated trends toward political centralization, and increased the likelihood of warfare among Indian peoples themselves (e.g., Carneiro 1970). Some scholars believe that the Powhatan chiefdom of Virginia, for example (fig. 2), was consolidated in the early years of the contact period.

Indian Economy in the Early Colonial Period

The most complete descriptions of Indian life in the Northeast during the colonial period were written after many changes had already taken place in native communities, and after many native people had became involved in the colonial economy. Indian men became traders, wampum manufacturers, interpreters, producers of skins and furs, agricultural laborers, soldiers, sailors, and whalers (Strong 1989). Native women processed skins, wove wampum belts, and sold or traded their pottery and baskets and the plants they gathered and processed. Others became slaves or indentured servants in English, French, and Dutch colonial households. Some Indian people occupied what historian Richard White has called the "middle ground," sharing territories with European colonists who came to depend on Indian labor and resources (1991). Natives in the Northeast thus lived in a range of conditions, from the isolation of hunting camps in the interior, as did the historic Micmac and Ojibwa, to circumscribed "praying towns" of Indian converts in southern New England, to powerful communities with separate nation status, as among the Iroquois. The specific changes undergone in in each subregion of the Northeast are discussed in chapters 2 and 3 of part I. (In part IV, section 5 ["Politics and Economy"], see "Economy and Subsistence, Then and Now.")

RELIGION AND WORLDVIEW

Since the ways in which people make a living help to define the kinds of social ties they create, the economies of the peoples of the Northeast often served as "models" for their relations with the supernatural as well. Many people conceived of their relationship with "beings other than human" as being one of deferential reciprocity (Bragdon 1996). The peoples of the Northeast generally shared a belief in a pervasive supernatural force, called *manitou* among the Algonquian-speaking peoples of New England. *Manitou* might inhabit plants, animals, or inanimate objects, and could be manifest in phenomena such as thunder or earthquakes. Some peoples recognized *manitous* associated with directions, social groups, or animals, and sought their help with the intervention of religious specialists, who were called *powwaws* or shamans among the southern New England Algonquians (Simmons 1976). The Narragansett told Roger Williams of thirty-nine different "gods," including "the women's god" and the "children's god" (Williams 1936).

People sought access to supernatural beings and their power over human affairs through prayers, fasting, gambling, and "sacrifice" of wealth (Tooker 1979) to gain their help in hunting, love, or curing the sick. Religious specialists, the shamans in many communities, were especially adept at achieving the trancelike state required for communicating with supernatural beings and harnessing their powers. Many northeastern people shared a belief in the dual soul, in dream travel, and in the existence of shape-changers.

The complex interrelationship of ideas about health, well-being, and cosmology in the Northeast was difficult for many Europeans to grasp, although, as historian Karen Kupperman points out, the links between folk medicine and religion had deep roots in many parts of rural England and France in the early modern period (Kupperman 2000). Curers in native societies were adepts whose knowledge of medicines and treatments was enlightened by their unique relationships with supernatural forces or beings, and whose own actions might affect the health of individuals or groups (Carpenter 1999). Medical theory in many societies in the Northeast also posited a relationship between morality and wellness, and attributed ill health to witchcraft or sorcery. Native curers thus used their special relationship to the supernatural to seek out all the causes of illness. If it was determined, for example, that an individual had been made ill through witchcraft, the curer might "suck" the illness out, as English observers on Martha's Vineyard observed a shaman there do. Other curers were able to plead the cause of their patient to their spirit guardians, and thus secure health. Dreams were also regarded as important diagnostic tools. The Huron, for example, believed that unfulfilled dreams caused people to sicken, and elaborate measures were often taken to ensure that those afflicted by illness were accommodated in all the "dreams and wishes" of their souls (Wallace 1958).

Community Health

Anthony Wallace also suggests that the health of the individual was often understood to be a mirror of community well-being, and that it was necessary for those whose behavior caused disharmony to be brought to a sense of their wrongdoing through the efforts of shamans and curers. The identification of the individual's health with that of the group is an important theme in northeastern spirituality, marked in a number of ceremonies and rituals that appear to have been enacted to promote both group solidarity and prosperity. In southern New England, for example, community-minded individuals sponsored feasts or dances during which large quantities of food and other wealth were given away. The redistribution of resources such feasts afforded protected all community members; the "sacrifice" of goods was believed to ensure future prosperity and health for the entire community as well.

Europeans were often misled by the absence of an established priesthood or permanent structures for worship among the native people of the Northeast. Edward Winslow wrote in an early letter that the people of southern Massachusetts Bay "had no religion." Those more familiar with native cultures found instead that sacred beliefs and tales abounded. Micmac and other peoples of the Northeast have many sacred stories concerning a creator whose actions formed the world and its denizens. Shawnee "witnessed" their creator, "Our Grandmother," and her grandson "Cloudy Boy" through intermediaries such as smoke, tobacco, water, and fire. Many people also tell of culture heroes, often giants, such as Gluskap, a warrior whose footprints became lakes and whose smoke rises still from the tops of sacred mountains. Tricksters, such as Raven, Rabbit, and Raccoon, figured in stories concerning the origins of social conventions or teaching moral lessons. For the Ojibwa and other Great Lakes communities, the cosmos is divided into tiers or levels, each occupied by or under the control of certain supernatural beings. Northern Iroquoian peoples looked to their creator, Sky Woman, who, falling from the heavens, came to rest on the soils that covered Turtle's back. One of her twin grandsons, Tharonhiawagon, "He Who Grasps the Sky," created the world known today.

A number of widespread cosmological themes link the native people of the Northeast to one another, and to peoples of other regions as well. Among these are beliefs in the dual soul, shamanic powers of shape-changing, soul and dream travel, animal guardians or helpers, and a pervasive sense of the spiritual nature of everyday experience. As in many parts of North America, shamanic practices included trance induced by deprivation or the use of hallucinogenic substances. Tobacco and pipe smoking had shamanic associations in most of the region.

The endless cycle of birth, growth, and death was commemorated in many ceremonies, rituals (Witthoft 1949; Tooker 1970), and stories, and linked to such diverse practices as the torture and sacrifice of prisoners (especially ritualized among the Northern Iroquoians), gambling games (found in nearly all parts of the Northeast), and the mummification of high-status individuals after death, as was described for the Powhatan in the early seventeenth century.

Avoidances—of the dead and of newly pubescent or menstruating women—were common among the peoples of the Northeast as well. In other parts of North America, women were required to remain in seclusion in special "menstrual huts," and, upon reaching the age of childbearing, were often required to cover their faces and heads for a period, sometimes in avoidance of sunlight or the heat and light from the fire.

Seasonal rituals, such as the Iroquoian Mid-Winter Ceremony and the widespread Green Corn Ceremonials of the Northeast, marked the annual cycle of death and renewal, and were often commemorated with feasts, dancing, gambling, and prayer. In many societies, religious specialists presided over these rituals along with community leaders, underlining the connections between spiritual well-being and secular authority.

Each community had its own sacred traditions and practices as well. The Narragansett, for example, were well known in the seventeenth century as "experts at ritual," which appeared to explain to their contemporaries their avoidance of the terrible epidemics that struck many other communities in the region. The Huron staged elaborate Feasts of the Dead, in which all the bodies of those who had died within a given period of time (about every eight years) were disinterred and reburied in large ossuaries along with rich offerings (Heidenreich 1978, 374). Among the North Carolinian Algonquians at Pamlico, John White observed a dance ground decorated with wooden posts onto which humanlike faces had been carved.

While many of the details of northeastern spirituality are undisclosed or unknown, it is clear that the native peoples of the Northeast understood themselves to be surrounded by and endowed with sacred power. Supernatural forces inhabited the world, and might be tapped by human beings. (In part IV, see section 4, "Spirituality and Worldview.")

Peoples and Cultures of the Northeast: An Overview

St. Lawrence Iroquoians

The people whom Champlain and other French explorers encountered on the St. Lawrence River in the mid-sixteenth century were speakers of Iroquoian languages who made up at least two distinct groups in the region, and who were evidently unaffiliated with any of the more numerous and powerful Iroquoian groups, such as the Huron or the Five Nations (Trigger and Pendergast 1978, 357). These groups lived in two principal villages: Stadacona (near modern Quebec) and Hochelaga (near modern Montreal). Both groups were farmers, though the Stadacona were more dependent on fishing and appear to have shared fewer of the traits that characterized the sedentary farming way of life thought typical of other Iroquoian people (Trigger 1978c).

By the early seventeenth century, most of the St. Lawrence Iroquoians had disappeared, possibly the victims of attacks by other Indian groups anxious to secure a more advantageous position in the developing fur trade with Europeans.

Huron, Petun, Erie, and Others

The most populous and best-known of the Iroquoian peoples in the sixteenth and early seventeenth centuries were the Huron, who lived below and to the west of the large, swampy territories that mark the southern Canadian Shield (Tooker 1991). This land was rich agricultural territory, and the Huron were committed farmers well before the arrival of Europeans. Prior to the epidemics of the 1630s, the Huron numbered about 20,000 people, living in several densely settled communities (Heidenreich 1978, 369).

Because French missionaries lived among them for many years, the Huron's customs and beliefs are well described. The Huron were matrilineal and matrilocal, and the maternal lineage was the principal property-owning and domestic group. The Huron had eight clans; each person belonged to one of those eight. The historic Wyandot peoples had a similar structure. Each clan or clan segment had a war chief and a civil chief, so several of each type might reside in a single community where more than one clan was represented. Decisions were made by a council, and wider intervillage councils met yearly. The Huron lived in longhouses of arched saplings covered with mats, each dwelling housing a single extended family. Villages were comprised of up to one hundred of these longhouses, always clustered in defensible positions near arable land.

All observers agree that the staple of the Huron diet was corn, which was served boiled, parched, baked into cakes, or roasted fresh, depending on the season of the year. Beans, squash, other wild plant foods, nuts, and tubers were important foods as well. Meat was rarely served, but fish was a common dish (along with turtles and shellfish), served roasted or dried or used as a flavoring for corn-based soups.

The Huron followed a seasonal settlement pattern, with men leaving the village in early spring to hunt and fish while women remained behind to prepare the fields for planting. During the planting season, men were frequently absent, trading or at war. Summers were spent tending the crops and gathering flags and other wild fruits. Corn harvest in early fall coincided with the return of most adult men, who then prepared for autumn deer hunts. The entire village cooperated during fall fish-spawning runs, drying most of the catch for winter use. An interesting economic alliance existed between the Huron and certain Algonquian hunting people, especially the Nipissing and some Ottawa Valley people. These groups traded with the Huron for meat and fur, and lived near Huron villages during the winter months.

The Huron were religious people, revering spirit beings called *oki*, but recognizing a pervasive supernatural force that inhabited animals and other natural phenomena. Huron were also skilled at dream interpretation, and used dreams and their meanings to cure those who were ill or unhappy. Feasts where gifts were exchanged were common, as were formal dances and gambling or gaming. All had both social and religious significance.

Active traders and brave in war, the Huron traveled great distances for both. War captains determined the fate of prisoners, who might be adopted into the community, kept as slaves, or tortured in an elaborate ritual that had important religious significance and allowed for group catharsis (Trigger 1976).

The disastrous epidemics of the 1630s caused population losses of nearly 60 percent in the space of five years, including many of the leaders. At the same time, other Iroquois groups were raiding northward to destroy whole villages, and to block the trade route down the St. Lawrence (Trigger 1985). By 1649, the Huron had abandoned their homeland, joining the Petun, Erie, and Neutral. Another group moved to Quebec, where they became known as the Huron of Lorette (Morissonneau 1978, 389). Others intermarried with the Ottawa or were adopted into other Northern Iroquois groups.

Petun (Khionontateronon), Wyandot, and Other Great Lakes Iroquoians

Jesuit missionaries living among the Petun by 1639 found them divided into two "nations," each with several villages (Garrad and Heidenreich 1987; Trigger 1991). Very similar in culture to the Huron, the Petun practiced the same seasonal round, spoke a similar language, and also conducted a number of important rituals, especially the ossuary burial known as the Feast of the Dead. The Petun also cultivated tobacco and traded it to other tribes in the region. The Petun were allied with the Neutral to the west, and also had an important relationship with the Algonquian-speaking Ottawa.

The Wyandot, who lived west of Huronia in the upper Great Lakes in the seventeenth century, were called Tionontati by the French, and, after 1650, included in their communities Huron people who had been displaced by the Iroquois. Wyandots were very active in the fur trade, and many of their subsequent relocations were due to their continued interest in the trade (Tooker 1978, 398). Also allied with the Ottawa in the mid-seventeenth century, they lived first near Michilimackinac, and later at the western tip of Lake Superior. Threatened by Iroquois from the east, some allied themselves with the French, while others entertained English overtures. The Wyandot eventually relocated to the new French settlement at Detroit, where they continued to be embroiled in French-English-Iroquois conflict throughout the eighteenth century. The Wyandots joined Pontiac's Rebellion in 1763. Extensive land cessions negotiated at the Treaty of Greenville and Fort Industry (Toledo) and finally at Detroit, and similar negotiations with the French, left many Wyandot eventually on two major reserves in Ontario. Those who remained in Ohio later ceded their territories there, taking in exchange lands in Kansas and, later, in Oklahoma, where many eventually settled on the Oklahoma Seneca reservation.

The Neutral and Wenro—other Iroquoian speakers who lived between Huronia and the territories of the Five Nations—were not well known to the Jesuits in the seventeenth century, but were thought to share many of their ways of life. Unfortunately situated between the warring factions of the Huron and Seneca, the Neutral and Wenro found themselves harried and dispersed prior to 1656, as were the Erie, who lived south of the lake of that name in what is now western New York, Pennsylvania, and Ohio. In 1654, a large party of Onondaga and Mohawk laid waste to Erie country, dispersing the inhabitants as far south as Virginia. Some settled near Quebec and others merged with the Five Nations, especially the Seneca (White 1978, 416).

The Northern Algonquians and Others: Beothuk, Micmac, Maliseet-Passamaquoddy, and Abenaki

BEOTHUK

Traditionally included in the Northeast culture area, the Beothuk peoples of Newfoundland remain a mystery. Although four word lists in their language were collected during the period of exploration and settlement of Newfoundland, linguists are unable to determine whether it most closely resembles other Algonquian languages of the Northeast or represents a separate linguistic family (Reynolds 1978, 101). Trading and possibly marriage ties between the Beothuk and the Montagnais of Labrador, as well as trading relationships with the Micmac and Abenaki, linked them to the mainland.

By virtue of their location, the Beothuk had frequent contact with Scandinavians and Europeans, possibly as early as 1000 A.D. Trade for fur increased enmity between Indian groups in the sixteenth and seventeenth centuries, and also led to hostilities between the Beothuk and French traders in the region. The French reputedly began to pay the Micmac for Beothuk heads (Reynolds 1978, 101). In the ensuing war between the Micmac and the Beothuk, the latter were driven toward the interior of their territories. Unsafe even there, the last Beothuk peoples abandoned Newfoundland in the early nineteenth century, possibly joining Montagnais relatives and trading partners in Labrador.

Like many peoples of the far Northeast, the Beothuk were skilled watermen, and constructed distinctive birch-bark canoes with peaked gunwales and sharply pitched prow and stern. They used snowshoes and sleds in snow to transport game. Their houses were conical pole-framed dwellings, covered with sheets of birch bark or caribou skins. Perhaps the Beothuk were best known for their prodigious use of red ochre as body decoration, for ritual purposes, and in the decoration of tools, clothing, and other objects. They were the first to acquire the epithet "Red Indians"; their use of this pigment suggests ancient connections to the so-called "Red Paint" cultures of the Archaic and Woodland periods in the Maritimes and northern New England.

The Beothuk also shared with their Algonquian neighbors some elements of the widespread shamanic complex, and used traditional sweatbaths for curing.

MICMAC

The Algonquian-speaking Micmac occupied territories that once extended from the Gulf of St. Lawrence inland along the Gaspé Peninsula, and included what is now the eastern Maritime Provinces and the island of Nova Scotia. French missionaries described Micmac culture in great detail, and many historic writings in their language survive, composed in the remarkable Roman alphabet-based writing system of their own invention, later modified for print by the Jesuit Father Pacifique (Bock 1978, 109). Micmac spent part of each year at the coast, seal hunting, then moving inland to chase large game. Spring brought them to fishing spots, and back to the coast for sturgeon, salmon, and eggs. In the summer, fish and shellfish formed much of their diet, and later eels. Fall was also a hunting season. Pairs of related men might hunt and trap together in winter, while their wives were expected to process skins and haul the carcasses. Micmac traditionally practiced the kind of bride service in which a prospective son-in-law hunted with his father-in-law-to-be for two or more years before marriage as well. Summer fishing camps allowed more compact settlements, when the more complex aspects of Micmac social organization were operative. Like the Beothuk, the Micmac constructed conical wigwams covered in overlapping sheets of birch bark, skin, and later trade cloth and paper (Bock 1978, 113). After the French colonized their territories, Micmac began to congregate for longer periods near the mission churches, but many continued to move seasonally until the end of the nineteenth century.

The arrival of the French brought many changes to Micmac life, and some of the most beautiful of their arts reflect French influences. Their quillwork boxes, for example, may have been inspired by converts of the Ursuline nuns at Quebec. In the nineteenth century, Micmac men and women wore gorgeously decorated jackets with beaded cuffs, armbands, and collars. Women wore conical caps, beaded in colorful floral or geometric designs and decorated with bands of appliquéd ribbon (McGee 1974).

Later disruptions caused by disease, the Micmac's uneasy position in the Anglo-French rivalry, and the effects of alcoholism caused Micmac populations to decline in the seventeenth and eighteenth centuries, but their population has now surpassed its estimated precontact numbers.

The Micmac were led by men called *sagamores* (from the proto-eastern Algonquian *sakimawa*), whose powers were generally dependent on consensus. But in the eighteenth century some controlled the allocation of hunting territories within their homelands, giving them authority within their own communities and a certain standing with the French.

Thanks to early missionary writings, much of Micmac cosmology has been preserved. In addition to their culture hero Gluskap, the Micmac told stories of powerful pranksters known as "strong men," who also performed feats of incredible strength. The Micmac spoke also of shamans or witches who could predict the future and, in some cases, walk on water (Bock 1978, 116). Supernatural beings also inhabited the Micmac world, and the pervasive power known in other Algonquian regions as *manitou* was evident in all manner of phenomena and events.

MALISEET-PASSAMAQUODDY

Contacts between Maliseet-Passamaquoddy speakers and Basque, Breton, Norman, and Portuguese fishermen preceded their recorded contacts with Champlain and other French explorers in the seventeenth century (Erickson 1978, 123; see also Bakker 1985). These seasonal visitors also brought change in the form of new trade items (Kaplan 1985).

These people lived in the territories of the St. John and St. Croix River valleys, and may have been the "Etechemins" identified by Champlain. Since 1842, the Maliseet have lived mainly within the borders of Canada, while the Passamaquoddy came to occupy two reservations in northeastern-most Maine. In historic times, the inland peoples of this language group were caribou hunters, while those on the coast concentrated on sea mammals.

As did many of their neighbors, the Maliseet and Passamaquoddy lived in dispersed winter camps and concentrated summer settlements. They built both small, single-family dwellings and large rectangular "lodges" sometimes used for council meetings or feasts. In the eighteenth century, the Maliseet and Passamaquoddy removed to several different principal villages, including Meductic on the lower St. John and Aukpaque near Fredericton, New Brunswick. By the end of the century, many Passamaquoddy were living at St. Andrews, on the eastern shore of Passamaquoddy Bay.

During what Teeter calls the "loyalist" period of their history, the Passamaquoddy and Maliseet came under the influence of the British government, and many settled on reserves within the present-day province of New Brunswick (Teeter 1978, 125). By the beginning of the twentieth century, their populations were concentrated in a smaller number of communities.

Like the Micmac, the Maliseet-Passamaquoddy are hunters and fishermen and follow a seasonal round, with access to family-owned hunting territories probably first established in the eighteenth century. They were accomplished woodworkers and canoe builders, and still practice these crafts today (Bragdon 1990). Women and men make splint and sweet grass baskets, and many still hunt and trap. Like other Northern Algonquian peoples, the Passamaquoddy and Maliseet are organized into bilateral families, with dual political bodies made up of members of different family lines.

In the twentieth century, Passamaquoddy men were often employed as guides to visiting sportsmen, including Teddy and Franklin Roosevelt, the latter summering on nearby Campobello Island. Baskets and etched birch-bark boxes created by Passamaquoddy men and women were much prized by tourists, and many beautiful examples of sweet grass baskets are still created by Passamaquoddy and Maliseet artists. The Passamaquoddy joined with the Houlton band of Micmac and the Penobscot in one of the earliest successful land claims suits against the state of Maine (1980). They are also the creators of a well-conceived language preservation program, in cooperation with linguists and educators.

EASTERN ABENAKI (PENOBSCOT)

A populous group of communities and bands occupying the drainages of several of central Maine's principal rivers, the Eastern Abenaki are now represented by the Penobscot of the reservation at Old Town (near Orono), Maine (Morrison 1976). The Eastern Abenaki were heavily involved in the fur trade in the late sixteenth and seventeenth centuries, and were frequent victims of the Anglo-French contest over their territories. Farming was only intermittently possible in their territories, particularly during the "Little Ice Age" (1550–1800?), and most Abenaki people were seasonal collectors, hunters, and fishermen. Their commonalities with other Algonquian speakers in the area included torch fishing, the use of snowshoes and toboggans, hunting magic, and the use of stalking disguises (Speck 1940).

The Eastern Abenaki were avid players of various counting games, on which they gambled; they also played a ball and stick game and the snow snake game. Their cosmology included tricksters such as Hare and Raccoon, and giant culture heroes.

Many famous Penobscot shamans still practiced in historic times. The best known, John Neptune, claimed to control seven spirit helpers, and he also claimed to take on their shapes. The well-known nineteenth-century Indian "doctress" and traveling midwife, Molly Ockett, was also an Eastern Abenaki (McBride and Prins 1996).

Their political organization was also based on dual bodies, which anthropologist Frank Speck suggested were descended from an older clan/moiety organization. Members of the so-called Wabanaki league in the eighteenth century, the Abenaki conducted diplomacy through the exchange of wampum belts (Speck 1940).

WESTERN ABENAKI

Slipping in and out of documented history, the Western Abenaki occupied territories west of the Saco and north of the Merrimack Rivers (Day 1978a). Jesuits and Recollets met them and recorded some of their language, but they remain the least known of the New England peoples. With close connections to the Pawtucket to the south, the Abenaki were among those people who practiced an ancient foraging subsistence pattern best suited to a bilateral band structure and seasonal mobility. Their involvement in the border wars between the French and English and their vulnerability to attacks from the ferocious Mohawks, encouraged by New York's Governor Andros to raid eastward into the Massachusetts Bay colony, caused the Abenaki to withdraw from much of their traditional land base toward the north in the seventeenth and early eighteenth centuries (Calloway 1990).

The Algonquians of Southern New England

In the first decade of the seventeenth century Samuel de Champlain and John Smith recorded meeting with a group known as the "Almouchiquois," living in the coastal regions of Massachusetts Bay, and a group or alliance of "Chowum" near what is now Cape Cod. These people probably included the group known historically as the Pennacook (Stewart-Smith 1999), as well as the better-known southern New England groups. Dutch explorers on the Connecticut River and on Long Island Sound wrote of a number of groups whose names—the Horikans and the Sickananes—are no longer familiar. Between 1620 and 1640, however, the six "nations" of southern New England—Pawtucket, Massachusett, Pokanoket, Narragansett, Pequot, and Nipmuck—were active players in the fur trade and colonial power politics that characterized the region (Salwen 1978). The Pawtucket, like their Aben-aki allies, soon moved north and west, especially after King Philip's War. The Massachusett, who lived, according to Smith, in "the paradise of these parts," were sent reeling by diseases probably introduced by French traders between the years 1616 and 1619. The survivors were able to play only a limited, if active role as negotiators between other native polities and the colonists of Massachusetts Bay. (The Massachusett and their Nipmuck allies were among John Eliot's first converts, and it was the Massachusett language that formed the basis for Eliot's vernacular literacy program [see below]).

The Pokanoket (whose descendants are known as Wampanoag), led by the paramount sachem Massasoit, became allies of the early Plymouth set-tlers, and were thus themselves protected from their enemies, the Narragan-sett, who lived on the western shore of the Narragansett Bay. The natives of Martha's Vineyard and Nantucket were also related to the Pokanoket, and tributary to Massasoit and, later, to his son Philip. The populations of these islands also accepted Christianity, and members of the prominent English Mayhew and Folger families worked as missionaries on these islands throughout the seventeenth and eighteenth centuries. Most of the Nan-tucket Indians succumbed to a yellow fever epidemic in the late eighteenth century, but the native population of Martha's Vineyard remained very stable throughout the colonial period.

The Narragansett—ceremonious and, of the southern New England peo-ples, the most devoted to ritual—developed a powerful and long-lasting re-lationship with exiled English colonist Roger Williams, who successfully negotiated many truces with them, most of great benefit to the English. The Narragansett remained a powerful force in the region until the end of the seventeenth century and their defeat in King Philip's War (Simmons 1978).

The most powerful group in the region before the 1630s was the Pequot, who controlled production of wampum, the currency of the fur trade. The colonies of Connecticut, Rhode Island, and Massachusetts and their Indian allies attacked the Pequot fort at Mystic in 1636, ruthlessly slaughtering several hundred; with that single blow, Pequot hegemony in the region was destroyed. The scattered survivors were eventually resettled on two reserva-tions in eastern Connecticut, where their descendants remain today.

Early descriptions of the coastal people of New England give many details of their political organization that suggest some of these groups were chief-doms with hereditary leaders, social stratification, and two-tiered religious leadership. Their cosmology centered on a belief in *manitou*, which could inhabit inanimate objects, animals, and natural phenomena. Shamans called *powwaws* were curers and seers, with special ties to the supernatural. Seasonal rituals, and dances called *Nickommo*, were occasions for the display and conspicuous disposal of wealth. Sacrifices of this kind were thought to ensure health and power for family and community. Sachems had elite advisors and military guards, and collected tribute from their followers. Their houses and clothing were more elaborate, and they often had several wives, the first generally of the highest status. The Narragansett had a dual sachemship.

The Nipmuck, the general name for a group of loosely linked bands who lived much like their Abenaki and Pawcatuck neighbors to the north and east, also lived in a few large village communities on the upper Connecticut River, especially at Pocumtuck. Without the coastal resources of the Mohegan and Narragansett, their position became more tenuous as settlement moved farther west and more and more of their lands were acquired or purchased by newcomers. Many Nipmuck peoples also moved north and west, but a few remained on tiny reserves at Hassanimisco (Grafton) and Dudley, Massachusetts.

People of the Connecticut River, including the Quiripi speakers (also called Wapanoo), Podunks, Wagunks, and Tunxis, left little for the historic record, but a number of these people settled together in communities at Paugusset, including their reservation at Golden Hill. Some Paugusset joined the Schaghticoke and the mixed Indian community at Stockbridge, and later followed Samson Occom to Oneida and Brotherton, Wisconsin.

The Unquachog of eastern Long Island, speakers of a language closely related to Quiripi, were tributary to the Narragansett and Pequot, and later to the Mohegan. Sachems of the island took care to steer a middle course away from outright rejection of Indian overtures, yet maintaining neutrality in disputes with the English. Their communities were gradually restricted to the eastern end of the island, at Montauk and Shinnecock.

Eastern New York, Mid-Atlantic, Virginia, and North Carolina

The Mahican peoples and the Delaware of eastern New York, western Long Island, and coastal New Jersey were also Algonquian speakers with a matrilineal organization, as well as a social organization that shared much with Iroquois peoples to the west (see below). To their south, the Algonquian-speaking Nanticoke and the Virginia and North Carolina Algonquians resembled the coastal chiefdoms of New England.

The most unique of these was Powhatan, Virginia's paramount chiefdom, which flourished in the early years of the seventeenth century (Rountree 1989). Powhatan controlled close to thirty separate polities, who owed him tribute and were required to contribute warriors to Powhatan's expansionist efforts. Religious worship was conducted by specialists, and while shamans still operated in these societies, the overseers of worship were responsible for tending the temples where community wealth was stored and the desiccated bodies of dead chiefs were maintained. Powhatan himself was said to have close to one hundred wives, and his recorded actions suggest that he served as a symbol of fertility for the polity as a whole. Warriors were highly regarded in Powhatan society (Gleach 1997), which was also matrilineal (fig. 3).

Powhatan's brother, Opechancanough, led the first successful uprising against the English in 1622, although the English recovered sufficiently to continue their expansion westward into Powhatan's territories. In 1644, another uprising affected all English communities, but the power of the Powhatan confederacy was broken, and most native people were pushed westward (Axtell 1995). By the end of the seventeenth century, the remaining Virginia Indians were confined to reserves in King William County. By the nineteenth and early twentieth centuries, Virginia's Algonquian people were very isolated, due to the racist policies of the state government. However, many cultural practices recorded in the seventeenth century still survived.

Northern Iroquois

Perhaps the most influential of all Eastern Woodland people, the Five Nations—made up of the Mohawk, Oneida, Onondaga, Cayuga, and Seneca peoples—formed the powerful League of the Iroquois so crucial in the contest for the continent that was waged between the French and the English in the seventeenth and eighteenth centuries. By at least 1630, and the Iroquois say much earlier, the Five Nations joined together for mutual defense and trade with the western Seneca, "Keepers of the Western Door," and the Mohawks of the Eastern Door (Bonvillain 1995; Graymont 1991). The Onondaga, in the center, became "firekeepers" of the League (fig. 4). The Five Nations effectively controlled territories from Albany, New York as far as Lake Erie, and south to central Pennsylvania and New Jersey. The three great rivers of their territories, the Susquehanna, Delaware, and Ohio, were ideally suited for access to western and southern hunting territories, and via Lake Ontario, to the north, members of the Five Nations could travel far to the northeast along the St. Lawrence.

League diplomacy was conducted through council meetings, where important decisions were commemorated with specially woven, mnemonic wampum belts, which became common in the seventeenth century (Tooker 1978b). Wampum, made from shells originating on the southern New England coast, was what Lynn Ceci called a "peripheral resource" in the centuries-long fur trade (1980), serving both ritual and economic functions among the Iroquois and their allies (Foster et al. 1984).

The "Three Sisters"—corn, beans, and squash—as well as fish, game, and other foraged foods, made up the bulk of the Iroquois diet. Largely sedentary, the people lived in towns, surrounded by hunting territories and near ample supplies of wood. Fenton reports that wild greens, the groundnut, and a variety of berries and nuts were important foods, especially in times of scarcity (1978, 299). Their year, divided into cross-cutting "ecological" cycles, was determined both by the seasonal availability of game and wild foods and by the demands of planting, tending, and harvesting crops (300).

Skilled woodcarvers, now best known for the so-called "False Face" masks, the Iroquois also made and make baskets, woven bags, and lacrosse sticks. Many fishing tools and nets were manufactured by men and women, and women also embroidered clothing and footgear with moose hair and porcupine quillwork.

The matrilineal Iroquois were divided into lineages, clans, and moieties, understood in terms of symbolic and structural oppositions between men and women. Men held office by virtue of their relationship to women in each lineage, and women's authority was recognized within each lineage. The Iroquois typically organized larger political bodies by analogy with the "fireside" families of the longhouse. The lineage and clan structure also determined marriage partners, the allocation of ritual responsibilities, and ultimately, diplomatic relations with other tribes (Fenton 1978, 313).

The Iroquois speak of the "first times," when the basic structures of their society were created. Their widely shared belief in the supernatural powers animating the cosmos is commonly linked to faith in the communicative power of dreams and "other-world" journeying (319).

THE LONGHOUSE RELIGION

Handsome Lake, a member of the Allegheny band of Seneca, shared with his people the disheartening events of the late eighteenth century. After their losses in Pontiac's Rebellion, and especially after the defeat of the English and their Iroquois allies in the Revolutionary War, their League was destroyed, their territories were breached, and their autonomy was compromised.

Plagued by alcoholism and confined to small reservations within their formerly vast territories, the Seneca, under the leadership of Cornplanter, lived on a reserve near Pittsburgh. Quaker missionaries shared the community, where Handsome Lake, Cornplanter's brother, also lived. Handsome Lake had a series of visions, similar to the soul journeyings of traditional religion, which told him that he and his people must give up alcohol, wife-beating, witchcraft, promiscuity, and gambling, and return to their traditional ceremonials, especially the Mid-Winter ritual. These visions, later recorded as the Code of Handsome Lake, became the basis for the Longhouse religion, which united and sustained most Iroquois people in the succeeding centuries.

Other Iroquoian Groups: Susquehannock, Tuscarora, Meherrin, and Nottoway

Sometime before 1570, the Susquehannock, Iroquoian speakers whose homeland has been pinpointed to the north branch of the Susquehanna River, settled into a single, large community in what is now Lancaster County, Pennsylvania (Jennings 1978, 362). Formerly known as the Dandastogué or Andaste by other Iroquois, they may also have been known as "Minquas" in other early records. Devastated by epidemics in the seventeenth century, some Susquehannock may also have merged with the Five Nations. They, like the Northern Iroquois, were farmers with a heavy dependence on maize.

Because they controlled the upper Susquehanna River, their position in the early fur trade was crucial. Visited by English, Dutch, and French emissaries and traders in the early seventeenth century, the Susquehannock found themselves enmeshed in the so-called "Beaver Wars" between the colonies of Maryland and New York, and later Virginia. Governor Andros of New York persuaded his Five Nations allies to invite the surviving Susquehannock to join them, while others merged with the Delaware. At their urging, the Five Nations raided the former enemies of the Susquehannock in Virginia and Maryland. A century of warfare and disruption ended for the Susquehannock when many of them returned to their original homelands in the early eighteenth century, where they were joined by a number of people of different ethnic identities, including the Delaware, Nanticoke, Tuscarora, and Tutelo (366). Ever-increasing English settlement, however, eventually forced most Susquehannock west into the Ohio region, and the few remaining were attacked and slaughtered by the notorious Paxton Boys in 1763.

Living in the Piedmont territories of what is now Virginia and North Carolina, the Tuscarora, Nottaway, and their allies, the Meherrin, were dispersed peoples with a mixed farming/foraging economy, suited to the varied resources of their territories. Among important rituals observed among them in the eighteenth century was the huskanaw, a ritual marking the onset of puberty. In this ritual, candidates were isolated while they underwent fasting and other ordeals, seeking visions.

Ohio Valley, Illinois, and the Great Lakes

FOX, SAUK, MIAMI, ILLINOIS, AND POTAWATOMI

Although Algonquian speakers, and apparently sharing in the widespread Algonquian farming/foraging patterns from earlier in their history, the Fox, Sauk, and Illinois increasingly came to share in the prairie adaptations more similar to their Siouan neighbors (Callender 1978, 637). In summer, rectangular framed houses with bark coverings were arranged around a central dance ground, also used for horse races and ballgames. In winter, the Fox lived in smaller wigwamlike dwellings. Spending part of their year hunting buffalo, the Fox farmed as well.

Fox men generally came to live with their wives' parents, in matrilocal extended families. Men and women worked at different activities, and brothers-in-law formed hunting parties. Fox communities had war and peace chiefs, and in the nineteenth century were constantly at odds with other buffalo-hunting peoples, especially the Dakota to their west (Callender 1978c).

The Fox cosmos was divided into levels, each controlled by deities, which also controlled the four directions. Vision quests were undertaken to acquire power through contact with the supernatural.

The Sauk, although linked by fiat with the Fox by the U.S. government, were a separate people who nevertheless shared many characteristics with their Fox, Kickapoo, Mascouten, and Potawatomi neighbors (Clifton 1978; Callender et al. 1978). Moving seasonally between large summer dwellings and smaller winter lodges, the Sauk were divided into named clans jointly governed by a paramount chief from the Sturgeon clan. The clans had primarily ritual functions, and each had a sacred "pack" under its special care.

The Illinois, who historically lived between the Mississippi and Ohio rivers in what is now Arkansas and Missouri, were once a large alliance of at least twelve tribes. Sharing a similar language with the Miami, the Illinois also had much in common with the prairie Siouan (Bauxar 1978).

The Illinois believed in a creator, a "Master of Life" sought by vision, especially during puberty rites. They had shamans who were skilled prestidigitators and healers. As among the Siouans, the calumet ceremony, combining references to birds, tobacco, smoke, and the supernatural, was of central importance to Illinois life, and particularly to their cementing of political alliances.

WINNEBAGO

The Siouan-speaking Winnebago of Wisconsin were, like many peoples of the northern Great Lakes, heavily influenced by the fur trade in the seventeenth through the nineteenth centuries. Organized into clans and moieties, the Winnebago were governed by war and peace chiefs, and suffered great losses in their many conflicts with the Algonquians and Iroquoians prior to the Revolutionary War (Radin 1923; Lurie 1978).

Of greatest interest to anthropologists has been the Winnebago cosmological system, which included a multilevel universe peopled by numerous supernatural beings and multiple souls. The Winnebago also believe in reincarnation, and the interference in human affairs of such beings as Trickster and Hare.

MENOMINEE

Menominee, speakers of the language subject to Bloomfield's masterful analysis of Algonquian grammatical structure, lived on the western shores of Lake Michigan. They, too, were greatly influenced by the fur trade, and were in early contact with French missionaries as well.

A group well known to anthropologists since the late nineteenth century, the Menominee spoke with them about their beliefs, which centered around the effort to acquire power through contact with the supernatural (Keesing 1939). Dreaming, fasting, and other ordeals typified Menominee religious worship, with the ultimate goal of acquiring a guardian spirit. Traditionally, guardian spirits gave guidance, and taught songs to those they especially favored.

CHIPPEWA, OJIBWA, OTTAWA, AND NIPISSING

Rice cultivation distinguishes the Chippewa and Ojibwa from their Algonquian-speaking neighbors. The forested regions of Wisconsin and

Minnesota provided a broad range of materials for carving, weaving, and basket making. Seasonal moves were made from a summer base to fall rice harvests, and then to hunting camps in winter; the camps were made up of bark- or mat-covered wigwams, or A-frame lodges used as temporary shelters (Hickerson 1970; Rogers 1978; Day 1978b).

The Ottawa, who were lake dwellers, were also great fishermen, and the women planted crops of corn, beans, and squash. Although the Ottawa once used the barrel-shaped lodges similar to those of other Iroquoian and Algonquian people, in the eighteenth century their dwellings came to look more like the tipis of the prairie dwellers to their west (Feest and Feest 1978).

The Nipissing people, whose language was similar to Ojibwa, were in early contact with Jesuit missionaries. Their territories were in the region between Lake Nipissing and Georgian Bay on Lake Huron. By the early eighteenth century most Nipissing were settled in Catholic missions at Oka, near Montreal. Later in the nineteenth century, most had moved to Maniwaki and the Ottawa Valley (Trigger and Day 1994).

Note

1. This controversial subject deserves a separate and book-length treatment. Archaeological consensus suggests that the first peoples arrived from Asia via the Bering land bridges during one of the last two interglacial periods, when the land bridge was exposed. Sites dating to prior to 15,000 BP (before present) have been located in several parts of North, Central, and South America, although many of the earliest sites are the subjects of controversy among scholars. Native people themselves question the validity of archaeological data, which appears to many of them to contradict their own sacred traditions. Recently, certain archaeologists have also questioned the Asian origin of America's first peoples, suggesting that certain groups may have migrated east from Europe. These claims, derided by most reputable scholars, have added to the controversy over the rights of native communities to have archaeological remains repatriated to them under NAGPRA legislation.

2 The Northeast During the Period of European Exploration and Colonization

Chapter 2 treats both the history of the Northeast during the first century of contact between indigenous peoples and Europeans and some of the general themes of the early contact period as they are understood by ethnohistorians, archaeologists, and anthropologists.

Ted Brasser's label for the people of the Northeast—"people of the first frontier" (1971, 64)—is an apt characterization. Although Spanish and French explorations and outposts in the Southeast and Southwest greatly impacted Indian lives in those regions, the natives of the Northeast were the first to endure the sustained multiple shocks of disease, colonization, and military defeat that native peoples of North America elsewhere experienced only much later (Wolf 1982). Because of this long period of sustained interaction between Indians and non-Indians, the Northeast has developed a distinctive character. At the same time, policies and patterns of interaction initiated in the Northeast preceded and often served as models for federal Indian policy, which can often be best understood as the outcome of experimental efforts in the Northeast. Finally, many significant events in Northeast native history had ramifications elsewhere in North America.

Initial Contact, Exploration, and Trade

The drama of contact between peoples previously unknown to one another is a dominant theme in early exploration literature, and in the histories subsequently written about these events. George Percy famously described his first sight of a Powhatan werowance in 1607 as follows:

The Werowance comming before them playing a Flute made of a reed, with a Crown of Deares hair colloured red, in fashion of a Rose fastened about his knot of haire, and a great Plate of Copper on the other side of his head, with two long Feathers in fashion of a paire of hornes placed in the midst of his Crown. His body was painted all with Crimson, with a chaine of Beads about his necke, his face painted blew, besprinkled with silver Ore as wee thought, his eares all behung with fine Copper or Gold, he entertained us in so modest a proud fashion, as though he had beene a Prince of Civil government, holding his countenance without laughter or any such ill behavior.

Himself a nobleman, as historian Karen Kupperman points out, Percy likened this native leader to noblemen in his own land (Kupperman 2000, 63), even as he dismissed his political importance.

Indian testimony about first contact, even recorded secondhand, is also revealing about the preconceptions of Native Americans and their attitudes toward the newcomers. William Wood, a settler in the infant colony at Naumkeag, near modern Salem, Massachusetts, wrote in 1634:

These Indians being strangers to arts and sciences, and being unacquainted with the inventions that are common to a civilized people, are ravished with admiration at the first view of any such sight. They took the first ship they saw for a walking island, the mast to be a tree, the sail white clouds, and the discharging of ordnance for lightning and thunder, which did much trouble them, but this thunder being over and this moving-island steaded with an anchor, they manned out their canoes to go and pick strawberries there. But being saluted by the way with a broadside, they cried out, "What much hoggery, so big walk, and so big speak, and by and by kill", which caused them to turn back, not daring to approach till they were sent for [1977, 95–96].

Both of these passages, typical of much of the "contact literature" of the Northeast, are illustrative of several truths about the contact period. First, Indian peoples and Europeans were not unaware of each other's existence at the time of even the earliest of the contact narratives. Aside from the Norsemen, whose presence in North America by at least 1000 A.D. is proven by archaeological evidence at the L'anse aux Meadows site in Labrador (Fitzhugh 1985), Basque, French, and Portuguese fishermen were likely to have made significant contacts and established trading relationships with native people of the Northeast at least a century prior to the earliest permanent European settlements in the region.

"Deconstruction" of these narratives provides more clues to the nature of this unrecorded period in contact history. Percy's description, for example, written in 1606, speaks of the copper plate worn on the werowance's head, a plate likely to have been fashioned from a copper kettle or other metal container brought by some unrecorded visitor and acquired from Indian trading partners or as a direct gift from Europeans. It could also have derived from the earlier and disastrously unsuccessful English settlement at Roanoke, or from the short-lived 1585 Spanish mission on the York River. Many early contact narratives describe such metal ornaments, and archaeological data show that metal derived from European sources begins to appear with some regularity by the early sixteenth century (e.g., Bradley 1987).

Linguistic evidence for the very earliest contact period consists of Indian words found in fifteenth-century European records, and European loanwords in native languages. Sailors throughout the port cities of Europe exchanged information about the New World and its people well before any colonies were established there (Greenblatt 1976). Historian David Quinn provides numerous other references to encounters between Europeans and Indians in the period between the Norse voyages and 1612 (1975). William Wood's description of the "Aberginians" of his area, cited above, contains the English phrase "What, much hoggery, so big walk, so big speak, and by and by kill." According to linguist Ives Goddard (1968), the speech recorded here includes evidence for both an English- and an Algonquian-based pidgin, presumably well established in coastal regions prior to English settlement in New England. Goddard also finds evidence for pidgins based on or including terms from Basque, French, and Portuguese (2000, 63). A Delaware-based pidgin was used by the Dutch in New Netherlands and by the Swedes in Pennsylvania throughout the seventeenth century (64).

Percy's and Wood's descriptions also raise interesting questions about the protocol of early encounters. It is evident that traders and explorers employed popular European folk customs and "revels" as a context and inducement for trade (Dempsey 1999, 131). When Captain John Davis encountered native people in Newfoundland, for example, he ordered the English sailors to "play, ourselves dancing and making signs of friendship." Sir Humphry Gilbert, sponsor of the English colonies of Maine, brought along with him "Morris-dancers, hobby-horse, and May-like conceits, to delight the savage people" (Quinn 1975 II, 385). Martin Pring, who visited coastal southern New England in 1603, entertained the natives with whom he traded with dancing accompanied by music played on the "gitterne." Likewise, Champlain instituted the *Ordre de bon Temps*, the custom of sharing food throughout the winter (Champlain 1604–7: 1907, 110).

The description of the bedecked, dancing werowance of Virginia therefore suggests that native people had adapted their protocol to conform to what seemed to them to be English expectations. Jack Dempsey argues, too, that these early "revels" were evidence of the initial cordiality of trade relations between Indians and Europeans, which was obscured by later hostilities and the repressiveness of the Puritans and other religiously motivated colonists who came later (1999, 196). As ethnohistorian Gordon Day remarked in an early programmatic statement about the needs and opportunities for ethnohistorical research in the Northeast:

> An awareness of the sixteenth century prevents us from assuming that a particular trait was a Native trait merely because it was observed by an explorer in the early seventeenth century. [Day 1998, 66]

The craft of ethnohistory requires that scholars seek out all data that might shed light on this complex and poorly documented period preceding the establishment of permanent European colonies in the Northeast.

Another feature of the early contact period was the florescence of native decorative arts and sculpture in many parts of the Northeast. Beautiful objects crafted in brass, copper, and other metals derived from kettles and other objects appear in native graves and as trade objects by the early seventeenth century. Pendants, necklaces, earrings, and other jewelry were also made of imported metals, and further enhanced with glass trade beads and native wampum, as well as feathers, deer and moose hair, bone, minerals, and shells. The remarkable metal combs, fashioned after the bone models that appear on many Iroquoian sites, are clever and distinctive adaptations of new materials. Sculpture, a feature of prehistoric pipe manufacture in the Northeast as well as of certain artistic traditions on the fringes of the southeastern culture area, also expanded to include freestanding figurines, whose meaning is still obscure.

Clothing in many parts of the Northeast underwent many interesting transformations as Indians gained increased access to European textiles, leather goods, and decorative objects such as buttons, bells, brooches, and medallions. Huron and other Iroquoian women instructed in Catholic missions in New France learned new embroidery techniques and decorative styles, and began to combine beading and ribbon embroidery with the more traditional clothing decoration of paint, and quills, moose, and deer hair embroidery.

Native dress soon came to display a distinctive mix of European and indigenous features: typically, leather leggings and moccasins with woolen or cloth cloaks, jackets, waistcoats, and shirts. Women in the maritime Northeast adopted the famous "peaked" caps of embroidered wool, along with other features of French costume. With their body paint, varied and elaborate hair styles, and eclectic wardrobe, native people created a distinctive costume that seemed to celebrate both new and old.

Native domestic surroundings (Bragdon 1988) and settlement patterns underwent several changes in the early contact period. Archaeological evidence suggests that in several parts of the Northeast people began moving from scattered settlements and unprotected villages to centralized, and sometimes fortified, locations. The Pequot fort at Mystic, Connecticut, totally destroyed by combined Mohegan, Narragansett, and English forces in 1637, was an example, and its vulnerability to concerted attack perhaps explains why these fortified settlements were in turn replaced by more dispersed patterns (Grumet 1995, 65).

The symbolic content of European goods adopted by native peoples of the Northeast has only recently received scholarly attention. Previous formulations of culture change, often grouped under the heading of acculturation theory, suggested that the adoption of European goods was largely functional, and that the quantity of such goods in an otherwise native setting suggested a greater degree of acculturation (e.g., Quimby 1960). George Hammel, on the other hand, argues that the European goods that found their way into native graves were deeply symbolic, embodying native concepts of sacred directions, colors, and associations with the supernatural. Only those goods, he argues, that resonated with native categories of the sacred acquired an important place in contact-period native societies; otherwise, the substitution of metal for wood or bone, or cloth for leather, was insignificant. Hammel's thesis applies equally to materials recovered from the interments of Iroquoian- as well as Algonquian-speaking peoples of the Northeast (1987).

Diseases originating in Europe ravaged much of the Northeast, and scholars are undecided about whether such diseases predated the early years of the seventeenth century. The leader of the Powhatan, also known as Wahunsonacock, told John Smith in 1607 that:

I have seen two generations of my people die. Not a man of the two generations is alive now but myself. [Smith 1614]

The Delaware told early settlers similar stories, as did the native people of southern New England, who suffered well-documented epidemics in the early seventeenth century as well. Some scholars believe that European-introduced epidemics were responsible for population losses that led to the decline of chiefdoms far into the interior.

While the demographic effects of such devastating losses are clear (e.g., Robinson et al. 1985), the social and ideological effects of massive population decline are harder to evaluate. William Starna points out that, in other parts of the world, responses to epidemics typically include an increased intensity in ritual (1992), and others have suggested that the role of religious leaders was altered in reaction to such widespread disease, illnesses that traditional shamanic healing practices were unable to stem (Salisbury 1975; Axtell 1985; Nassaney 1989). Raiding increased during the contact period, at least in part to replace community members lost to disease (Richter 1983). Examination of native cemeteries and interments from the early contact period demonstrate a number of features that distinguish them from their precontact predecessors: they are increasingly accompanied by a rich and varied set of grave goods, many of European origin; the quality and quantity of grave goods is variable among individuals, suggesting social differences existing in the living community; communal or concentrated burial grounds became more common through time. Nassaney argues that, in particular, the role of the ritual official who oversaw burial rites became central in those years when deaths from disease were frequent (1989), and that his or her social standing might have thus increased.

Alternatively, scholars such as Calvin Martin (1976; but see Krech 1978) have suggested that the decline in confidence in religious specialists and in the traditional ideologies that supported native theories of disease, caused by their religious specialists' patent inability to stem the tide of disease, led to *anomie* among native peoples, or a willingness to seek alternative theories, provided most readily in the Christian doctrines of Catholic and Protestant missionaries, who followed explorers and settlers to live among Indian communities in the Northeast.

Certainly the need to replace lost community members in native polities based so solidly on kin relations led to an increased occurrence of what have been termed the "mourning wars," raids designed to acquire women and children to rebuild shattered communities. Raiding disrupted native social relations within and between native communities and polities, as amply testified to by the devastation of the northern Massachusetts Bay by "Tarrantine" (Micmac) raids in the early seventeenth century (Smith 1614; Wood 1634).

The biological effects of contact were not confined to the impact of disease. Historian Albert Crosby (1986) reminds us that the long-term impact of pandemics includes distorted demographic profiles, disrupted fertility and fecundity, and lingering ill health due to the conditions of poverty and despair that often follow in the wake of disaster.

Perhaps less well understood are the more subtle biological effects of contact. Historic period native cemeteries excavated in New England and New York, for example, demonstrate that dietary changes, most notably the introduction or drastic increase in the use of sugars, led to high rates of dental caries and other diseases of the mouth. Skeletal remains reflect increased traumas due to tuberculosis, rickets, and venereal disease. Women may have been more malnourished relative to males in the contact period, perhaps a reflection of native women's falling status after the arrival of Europeans. Finally, the evidence of increased frequency of traumas resulting from injury, probably inflicted by weapons, suggests that warfare was a significant health risk in the early contact period.

The animals early settlers brought with them, the crops they planted, and the new ways in which Europeans used the natives' former territories had biological and ecological effects as well. Alfred Crosby writes of the "Columbian Exchange," during which new species of animals and plants brought to the New World had profound effects on the ecology of both continents. The animals brought by settlers disrupted native shellfishing locations, trampled and devoured native gardens, and competed for food sources required by indigenous game. The requirements of the English and European dairy/grain economy were incompatible with native land use practices, and soon came to dominate in the regions heavily settled by the English and Dutch (Crosby 1980; Cronon 1982).

The fur trade, satisfying the desire in Europe and England for furs and products made from furs (such as felt for hats), also had a singularly profound effect on Indian lives and communities well before the first colonies were established. The impact of the fur trade has been examined from a number of different angles, from the ecological effect of overhunting (Martin 1975) to the social effects of a shift in seasonal subsistence activities, the disruption of traditional work patterns, and the shift in emphasis from balanced self-sufficiency to "debt peonage," engendered by the credit system established by the early fur-trading companies.

In southern New England, three species of shellfish—*busycon canaliculatum* and *busycon carica* (channeled whelks), as well as the common quahog—became the materials from which wampum was made. Wampum, sacred to the Iroquois and essential to their political structure and relations, became the currency of choice in the early fur trade, making it, in Lynn

Ceci's words, "a peripheral resource in the Seventeenth Century World System" (1990). The most abundant sources of these shellfish were located along the coastal regions of what are now Connecticut and Rhode Island, including eastern Long Island and Block Island. These centers of wampum manufacture were crucial to the early trading efforts of the Dutch and English in New England and New Netherlands, and their chance occurrence there had important implications for the development of social hierarchies in native polities of the region (Ceci 1990, Salisbury 1982).

Also, as Kevin McBride has demonstrated, the correlation between early Dutch trading posts and fortified Pequot and Narragansett wampum "factories" was not a random one, suggesting that European presence in the region had a significant impact on precolonial native settlement and political interrelations (McBride 1993).

Common themes in the early history of Indian-white relations in the Northeast also include the possibility that certain polities were strengthened and enlarged in response to threats from without. The so-called "Wabanaki Federation" in coastal Maine, the Powhatan paramount chiefdom, and perhaps even the League of the Iroquois may represent the kind of patterned response to warfare and threat known to anthropologists as "segmentary opposition" (Evans-Pritchard 1982). While all these confederations had roots in the developing complexities of coastal societies and interior societies that predated the arrival of Europeans, there is no doubt that chiefs and their families became increasingly influential as redistributors of goods, arbiters of trade, and organizers of warfare (Carneiro 1970; Custer 1986; Potter 1993; Upham 1990). The growth in popularity of wampum as means of exchange brought new vigor to chiefly societies in New England (Ceci 1990), while the Northern Iroquoians waged a highly effective, and coordinated, war against their rivals in the fur trade along the St. Lawrence, as far west as the Ohio Valley and the Great Lakes and as far south as western Virginia.

Another feature of the early contact period is the virtual disappearance of many groups who escaped the attention of early explorers and chroniclers and are, hence, nearly invisible in the historical record. The most dramatic example of such tragic disappearances are the Beothuk, who, although surviving in small settlements in the interior of Labrador until the nineteenth century, were never accurately or fully described, and much of their language and culture remain a mystery today. The interior of New England is another region where many peoples lived in the late Woodland period, but, by the earliest period of settlement, they had moved north or west, leaving their former homelands only sparsely settled. Through a combination of

archaeological, historical, and linguistic sources, Gordon Day has identified
many of these people as Western Abenaki, the descendants of whom settled
in mixed Indian communities along the St. Lawrence, particularly the Indian community of St. Francis or Odanak (Foster and Cowan, 1998). Likewise, the Shawnee, Algonquian speakers of the Susquehanna region of interior New York and Pennsylvania, were displaced so early in the historic
period that their original territories cannot now be determined with confidence. The Siouan and Iroquoian speakers of what is now the Blue Ridge
region of Virginia likewise elude historians, who know little about their
language or ultimate fate.

The importance of missionary efforts in the early years of contact and
settlement of the Northeast cannot be discounted. The short-lived Spanish
Jesuit mission on the York River in 1585 mirrored equally early missions
established along the St. Lawrence by Jesuits and Recollets who followed
Cartier and Champlain. The Jesuit mission to the Huron and their neighbors provided the vast collection of descriptions known today as the *Jesuit
Relations*, which form the basis for the ethnographic reconstruction of Huron culture (Thwaites 1896–1901). At the same time, Protestant missionaries, under the auspices of the Society for the Propagation of the Gospel,
established missions in southern New England and later among the Mohawks. Moravians established mission towns among the Delaware, while
another Jesuit mission was established in Catholic Maryland. Missionaries
founded most of the early native schools (Szasz 1988). Among many other
impacts, missionaries working in all areas of the Northeast were responsible
for most of the translations and linguistic descriptions of northeastern native
languages (fig. 6). Some, like the complete edition of the Bible translated
into the Massachusett language (Bragdon 1991, 1991a), were printed and
distributed to Indian converts. Others, like the *Mots Loups* of Father Mathevet, remained in manuscript form, primarily for the use of missionaries
themselves (Day 1975). Northeastern languages captured in religious translations include the following:

Algonquian: Montagnais (1632 Massé); Massachusett (Eliot, various);
Pokanoket (Mayhew, various); Quiripi (Pierson); Algonkian (Nicolas);
Ottawa (Andre); Illinois (Campanius); Abenaki (Aubery; Mathevet);
Delaware (Zeisberger); Mahican (Edwards); and Ottawa (Dejean).

Iroquoian: Huron (Lalemont); Petun, Neutral, Oneida (Milet, *Jesuit
Relations*); Mohawk (Cuoq, *Jesuit Relations*); Ondondaga (Beau-

champ, *Jesuit Relations*); Cayuga, Seneca, Wyandot (Barbeau); Wenro, Erie (*Jesuit Relations*); and Susquehannock (*Jesuit Relations*).

In addition to the linguistic contributions of early missionaries (Minor 1975; Hanzeli 1969), these men and women had an extraordinary influence on the lives of Indian people. Mission schools taught new crafts and skills, instructed native people in reading and writing, and encouraged the abandonment of Indian lifeways and values in favor of those closer to European norms (Greenfield 1999, 189; Szasz 1988). Missionaries in southern New England were particularly successful in attracting native people to a radically different way of life (Salisbury 1982; Axtell 1985; Von Lunkhuyzen 1990).

These common themes or experiences of native people during the early years of the period of European exploration and settlement were later reenacted in the interior and western parts of North America, as settlement advanced. As elsewhere, each subregion of the Northeast was also the setting for numerous distinctive histories, each dependent on the character of the native peoples, their European antagonists or allies, the specific economic and environmental settings, and the imponderables of "contingent events" (Sahlins 1985). The outlines of subregional histories are summarized in the following sections.

The Early Colonial History of the Northeastern Maritime Region

The northeastern maritime region, comprising the territories now part of Canada's Maritime Provinces and the modern state of Maine and including Labrador, Newfoundland, and Nova Scotia, was the point of entry for Europeans of many nationalities into the New World. Population densities in the region were, due to the sometime harsh climatic conditions, lower than in southern New England, averaging about 3 persons per 100 square kilometers (Brasser 1978, 78).

Between 1500 and 1520, peoples of Newfoundland, Nova Scotia, and Labrador came into increasing contact with European explorers and fishermen. John Cabot of England claimed Newfoundland for England in 1497, and explored the coasts of Labrador and Nova Scotia in 1498. The Portuguese Gaspar Côrte-Real sailed along the Newfoundland coast in 1500 and 1501. Côrte-Real captured more than fifty Indians, some already possessing goods of European manufacture, and established a long tradition of kidnappings perpetrated against Native Americans during the period of exploration and settlement.

Fishermen, including English, Bretons, Normans, Basques, and Portuguese, sought out the rich fishing ground off Newfoundland, Labrador, and Nova Scotia by at least 1500. Although they left no written records of these annual voyages, cartographic evidence suggests that the coastal regions of the Maritimes were well known by the mid-sixteenth century. The geographer Carl Sauer counted 50 English, 150 French, and 100 Spanish ships in the maritime regions on an annual basis by 1578 (1971, 240). Fishing camps, where catches were dried, became common in many coastal areas of Labrador, and the Montagnais and other native peoples themselves were sometimes employed by European fishing parties (Brasser 1978, 79; Calloway 1991).

Hostilities between these frequent but casual visitors and the native inhabitants of the maritime regions were perhaps inevitable. Hunting was disrupted, competition for trade goods led to inter-Indian rivalries, and the capture and otherwise brutal treatment often meted out to native people by European visitors led to the outbreak of a number of skirmishes. The Beothuk of Newfoundland, in particular, were driven farther and farther inland, and their communities constantly harassed.

Relations between Europeans and Indians intensified with the inauguration of the trade in furs, sometime after 1520. Explorers such as Cartier were met by Indians already prepared to trade in furs by 1524. Native people were also ready to travel far up the St. Lawrence in pursuit of the trade in 1540 (Hoffman 1967, 23). Giovanni da Verrazano's visit to coastal Maine, the earliest visit by a European to that region to be described in a surviving report, demonstrated a contrast between the natives of that region and those of the more southern territories of New England. Verrazzano found the Indians of coastal Maine to be rude and dismissive, signaling perhaps their disillusionment with Europeans even at that early date. Natives of Maine became active in the fur trade, raiding down into southern New England (Bourque and Whitehead 1985). The fur trade also came to dominate relations between rival European powers, particularly the 150-year conflict between France and England for the fur-producing territories of the Northeast. Subsequent visits by Martin Pring (1603) and John Smith (1614), as well as continued contacts with the French, enmeshed the Abenaki in inter-colonial conflict and made them vulnerable to the epidemic diseases that ultimately halved their population by the mid-seventeenth century. After 1624, Eastern Abenaki were visited regularly by Pilgrim traders from Plymouth colony.

Although several unsuccessful attempts at colonization in the southern reaches of the Northeast culture area were initiated by the Spanish, in what are now Virginia and North Carolina, the first long-standing European settlements were to be found in the northern Maritimes: the founding of the French settlement at Sable Island in 1598; Tadoussac in 1601; and the St. Croix River settlement established in 1604. The earliest English settlement in the region, on the Kennebec River, was founded by Captain George Waymouth in 1607, although hostilities with Indians already apparently loyal to the French caused the settlers to return to England in 1608.

Several of the locations where early interactions occurred between native people and French and English explorers, traders, and settlers have been investigated archaeologically. For example, excavations at Fort Petagoet, located near the mouth of the Penobscot River, near Castine, Maine, reveal architectural remains and artifacts dating to the period 1635–74. Many objects of French manufacture are found at the site, including glass, white-clay smoking pipes, tin-glazed earthenware vessels, and gun parts. Of particular interest is the related site, known as the Saint-Castin Habitation, where Jean Vincent Abaddie de Saint-Castin, renowned interpreter, and his wife, the daughter of a local native ruler, lived along with a number of French soldiers and their wives and more than thirty Indian families (Falkner 1991; Falkner and Falkner, 1987). The Habitation provides fascinating evidence of the close interrelations between French explorers and the native people of the region, joined together for trade and protection.

Indians of the region became increasingly involved in intertribal rivalries, while traditional subsistence activities were subverted by the increasing investment in hunting and processing furs for trade. Agriculture, only possible south of the Penobscot River, was abandoned by the Eastern Abenaki, who, along with their "Tarrantine" (Micmac) neighbors, took up the practice of raiding southward into Massachusetts Bay, terrorizing local native populations there. Charismatic and daring local leaders rose to prominence, such as the Eastern Abenaki leader, Bashebes, who created a confederation of communities that claimed controlling rights to the fur trade in their territories (Snow 1978, 137).

At the same time, Jesuit and Capuchin missionaries were making inroads into many native societies. The Jesuit mission at Port Royal in Nova Scotia began its activities in 1611. These missionaries helped secure the allegiance of many of the native people of the Maritime Provinces for the French, who continued to support missionary efforts among them throughout the colonial period.

Events outside the maritime regions, particularly King Philip's War of

1675–76, still had repercussions there. Indians had become involved at the fringes of that conflict, and in the constant raiding that characterized French–English colonial relations throughout the first half of the eighteenth century. The continuing trade and diplomatic importance of the Abenaki and Micmac allowed them a certain autonomy, however, and the well-known "Wabanaki Confederacy," an alliance of Micmac, Maliseet, Penobscot, and Passamaquoddy communities, served to provide a measure of protection to polities in the region after 1800 (Bock 1978, 109).

Southern New England in the Colonial Period

Giovanni da Verrazano's visit to what is now called Narragansett Bay in 1524 marks the beginning of documented history in southern New England, but undoubtedly previous sporadic contacts with Europeans had taken place prior to and following that encounter. The English and French were regular visitors by the early years of the seventeenth century, and even the Spanish had made an appearance. William Wood, whose 1634 *New England's Prospect* included one of the earliest descriptions of the native people of southern New England, noted that the Indians there were familiar with all manner of Europeans:

> The Spanish they say is all one aramous (viz., all one as a dog); the Frenchman hath a good tongue but a false heart; the Englishman all one speak, all one heart. [Wood 1977 (1634), 92].

The native people of southern New England had much to regret in their involuntary involvement with Europeans. Several expeditions to their territories, especially those of Captain Edward Harlow in 1611 and Thomas Hunt in 1614, took unwilling captives back to England or sold them into slavery, including Epanow of Martha's Vineyard and Squanto of Patuxet, the future location of Plymouth Plantation. Most significantly, diseases introduced in the area between 1614 and 1619 caused cataclysmic losses in most coastal communities; some, like Patuxet, were entirely wiped out, others so devastated by disease that the survivors could not bury the numerous dead (Morton 1947). Snow and Lanphear estimate 90 percent losses in some coastal and interior regions (1988, 23).

The abandonment of Indian villages and farming lands and the social devastation caused by these epidemics seemed evidence of divine providence to the first English settlers at Plymouth, and to those who followed them in establishing settlements at Salem and Boston. By 1640, the "Great Migration" of English colonists had brought nearly 18,000 new settlers to southern New England, causing them to outnumber the indigenous population in many parts of the region (Bailyn 1986). Soon, expanding settlement along the Connecticut River and in coastal Rhode Island and Connecticut put further pressure on native communities, who could no longer pursue their traditional seasonal round of gathering, hunting, and farming (Thomas 1979; Cronon 1982). The furious determination of the English to dominate Indian-English affairs (G. E. Thomas 1975) resulted in the Pequot War of 1636, when, after the destruction of the Pequot fort at Mystic with its 400 men, women, and children, Pequot hegemony was forever destroyed. The aftermath of the Pequot War saw Indian communities that chose to remain in the region gradually surrounded and restricted, with only the Narragansett and Mohegan retaining any measure of autonomy in the later seventeenth century.

In spite of their many misfortunes, Indian people of the region continued to play a significant role in colonial history. Indians were active participants in the fur trade, particularly as producers of wampum for exchange with the Iroquoian peoples to the north and west, and were also consumers of English goods in the period between 1640 and 1660, when the New England colonies were isolated from England during the reign of Cromwell (Salisbury 1990). Indian men and women provided labor in the maritime trades and contributed their expertise to the growing whaling industry. Frontier settlements served as a buffer between the English and hostile Indians, especially Mohawks to the west who, encouraged to raid east in aid of the colonial ambitions of New Netherlands and New York, wreaked havoc on the New England frontier in the seventeenth century.

Philip, or Wamsutta, son of Osamequin (Massasoit), the longtime ally of the Plymouth colony, was frustrated by the ceaseless incursions onto his remaining lands and the increasing arrogance of colonial officials. He took the fateful course of organizing and leading a fearsome rebellion, known as King Philip's War of 1676, during which most outlying English settlements in southern New England were put to the flames and their inhabitants killed or captured (Leach 1958). The failure of many Indian groups to support him against the English and the determined vengeance of the English themselves were among the factors that led to Philip's defeat and execution (Ranlet 1988; Bourne 1990; Drake 1995), along with most of his family. The Narragansett who supported Philip were likewise devastated, particularly after the cruel slaughter of several hundred warriors and noncombatants at the "Great Swamp Fight" near Charlestown, Rhode Island in December of 1675. Only the Mohegan, led by Uncas—who remained staunch English allies throughout the conflict—survived intact in the early eighteenth century.

Those native people who remained in southern New England gradually worked out several survival strategies. Many adopted Christianity and became members of settled communities sometimes called "praying towns." Although only two of the original seven established by John Eliot survived the upheaval of King Philip's War, many permanent native Christian communities were established in Massachusetts Bay and the Plymouth colonies by the beginning of the eighteenth century. In these communities, which were largely self-sufficient and self-governing, native people supported churches and schools (Hankins 1993, Von Lunkhuysen 1990). Literacy in the local native languages was common (Bragdon 1991, 1991a), and native people led lives that combined many elements of both traditional culture and innovations introduced by European colonists. Because many spoke only their native tongue, these communities remained distinct from their non-Indian neighbors.

Elsewhere in southern New England, people such as the Pequot and Mohegan of Connecticut were granted reserves within their former territories, where they were relatively isolated from English interference until the mid-eighteenth century. The Pequot, in particular, vanquished in the Pequot War, reestablished communities in territories surrounding the Thames River, and were eventually granted two reservations, one at Lantern Hill (Eastern or Stonington Pequot) and one at Ledyard, under Robin Cassacinnamon (Western or Mashantucket Pequot). Native people sold baskets (McMullen 1991), berries, and shellfish, or became laborers in white households or in white-owned enterprises (Porter 1987).

Finally, some native peoples, and even entire communities, moved north and west, joining allies among the Abenaki and even the Iroquoian-speaking peoples in French-controlled territories (but see Ghere 1988, 1993, 1997). Pocumtuck, Pigwacket, Pennacook, and Sokoki were among those communities of Nipmuck or Western Abenaki origin who chose this strategy (e.g., Day in Foster and Cowan 1998, 89). The Christian converts of Mohegan Samson Occom, determined to remove themselves from the pernicious influences of paganism, alcoholism, and despair, followed Occom first to the Christian community at Brothertown in Oneida, New York in 1775, and later to Brothertown, Wisconsin (Love 1899).

On the western frontier of New England stood the Mahican, Algonquian

speakers with strong affinities with their Iroquois neighbors. In contact with
the Dutch as early as 1609, the Mahican permitted the establishment of a
trading post within their territories, acting as middlemen in the fur trade
with the Mohawk. The increasingly jealous Mohawk attacked the Mahican
in 1624, dispersing the western Mahican settlements during the next three
years. Subsequently concentrated east of the Hudson, the Mahican continued to plant and hunt as they had previously, and participated actively in
the fur trade with the Dutch, French, and English. Controlling the wampum
trade after 1640, the Mahican were also increasingly aggressive with their
neighbors, encouraged and armed by their European trading partners. The
Mahican, along with other Algonquian-speaking allies from southern New
England and eastern New York, raided into Mohawk territory but were ultimately left behind by the expanding frontier (Trelease 1997). Their populations reduced by a series of epidemics, the Mahican fled with many of
the survivors of King Philip's War to Schaghticoke on the upper Hudson.

In the later colonial period, Indians continued to serve the English as
soldiers, especially in the French and Indian wars of the 1750s and 1760s,
and were active as well in the maritime trades. Within Indian communities,
life continued much as it had for nearly a century and a half after the arrival
of Europeans, the "colonial culture" of its native people nearly invisible to
non-Indian outsiders (Bragdon 2001).

The St. Lawrence Drainage and the Eastern Great Lakes

The populous villages typical of historic period Iroquoian-speaking peoples appear, from archaeological evidence, to have been an established settlement type along the St. Lawrence River by the early sixteenth century
A.D. In 1534, Jacques Cartier made the first recorded contact with the Iroquoians of the St. Lawrence at the Baie de Gaspé. Following the directions
of two captured sons of a local leader named Donnacona, Cartier discovered
the mouth of the St. Lawrence the following year, and visited Indian communities in the vicinity of modern Quebec and Montreal. Encouraged by
stories of a nation rich in precious metals, Francis I established two short-
lived colonies near Quebec between 1541 and 1543, but native hostility to
these and subsequent French exploring parties prevented further encroachments until Champlain's voyages, beginning in 1603.

Although undocumented in historical sources, this period between the
first contact and establishment of permanent French settlements at Quebec
and Montreal was crucial in native history. The fur trade, securely estab-

lished along the maritime coast, had repercussions far inland. The St. Lawrence Iroquoians had been destroyed and dispersed, and the area overrun by Mohawk, Montagnais, and Algonquin (Trigger 1978, 346). Trigger suggests, however, that the surviving St. Lawrence Iroquoian groups may have entered into an alliance against Iroquoian peoples to the south, to their mutual benefit in the growing fur trade (346). At the same time, an alliance among Algonquian-speaking peoples north of the St. Lawrence, in opposition to the Iroquois to the south and west, set the stage for future conflict in the region.

The Huron, a populous agricultural people who occupied the territories north and east of Lake Huron, were trading with Algonquin to the east for European goods as early as 1580. Long before the Huron laid eyes on white men, trade goods had acquired importance in their ritual, and stimulated a trade in indigenous luxury goods such as gourds and marine shells from the south (Trigger 1978, 347). Eager to access the rich fur-producing regions in the west and shake loose the stranglehold of Montagnais and Algonquian middlemen, the French, under Samuel de Champlain, established the French settlement at Quebec in 1608. Champlain joined several Montagnais and Algonquian expeditions against the Mohawk, who soon turned their attention south in favor of trade relations with the Dutch.

Between 1615 and 1629, Huron traveled yearly across Lake Nipissing and the Ottawa River to the St. Lawrence to trade with the French. Tens of thousands of furs changed hands during this period, to the mutual benefit of both groups. Complex relations among the Huron, the Ottawa, and the Neutral—true to their name—were pivotal in trade networks involving the Huron and other Iroquoian groups to the south. After 1633, the Society of Jesus exercised control over the French settlements on the St. Lawrence, and thus over trade relations with the Huron and other remote peoples. In the succeeding decades, the Jesuits established a mission in Huron territory, where a concerted effort to convert them to Christianity began. At the same time, epidemics raged through Iroquoia, causing losses of up to 50 percent among the Mohawk, Huron, Petun, Wenro, and Neutral.

Overhunting of beaver in the most populous regions of northern Iroquoia led to shortages that threatened all Indian participants in the fur trade as early as 1640. Mohawks and their Oneida allies began attacking Huron villages, and later Mahican, Abenaki, and Maliseet communities, in their efforts to control the trade. Trigger suggests that the outcome of these raids and the subsequent abandonment of these territories by their former inhabitants was the regeneration of the beaver population, making these territories the primary hunting grounds exploited by the members of the Iroquois con-

federacy after 1670 (1978, 353). Mohawk strategy included the destruction
of Huronia and the securing of French neutrality, in order to establish hegemony in the region as well as control over the trade. By 1650, therefore,
the Huron had been dispersed, and soon after, the Neutral fell to Seneca
aggression. The way was clear then for direct access to the Great Lakes. In
spite of temporary alliances, hostilities between the French and the Iroquois
confederacy continued throughout the seventeenth century, complicated by
Dutch and Swedish intervention among the Susquehannock and Mohawk.
Raids and counterraids in Erie territory and the Ohio Valley were thus also
a feature of the latter half of the seventeenth century.

The displaced Huron, Petun, Neutral, Erie, and other St. Lawrence Iroquoians appear to have been absorbed by various other Iroquoian groups.
Trigger and Pendergast argue, for example, that the St. Lawrence Iroquoians
were adopted into Mohawk communities or moved westward to join the
Ottawa Valley Algonquians (1978, 361). The Huron, defeated and dispersed
by 1649, joined the Petun, Neutral, and Erie. Some Huron settled near
Lorette, on the St. Lawrence, establishing a distinctive Christian community
there (Morissonneau 1978). Similarly, the Petun and Wyandot, who had
strong trade alliances with the Ottawa, may have joined their communities
as well. Neutral, Wenro, and Erie were later dispersed, although Neutral
survivors are recorded among the Seneca (White 1978, 410), and a group
of 600 Erie surrendered to the Iroquois on the Virginia frontier in 1680
(416).

The Northern Iroquois in the Early Contact Period

Although the impact of European settlement felt by the Iroquois in the
Northeast was blunted by their inland location, they found themselves active participants in European expansion nonetheless. The Mohawk, whose
territories centered around the Mohawk River Valley, sometimes claimed
rights to lands as far north as the St. Lawrence and south to the Susquehanna. The first documented contact between the Mohawk and Europeans occurred early in the seventeenth century, with the establishment of
the Dutch trading post at Fort Nassau in Mahican country. The Mohawk
and their western allies—the Oneida and Onondaga, the Cayuga and Seneca—undertook to establish dominance in the French fur trade, embarking
on the so-called "Beaver Wars" (1649–57), which resulted in the dispossession or destruction of most of the St. Lawrence Iroquois and those of the
eastern Great Lakes region. Mohawk raiding parties penetrated well into

New England, driving Mahican, Abenaki, and other Algonquian peoples eastward, evidently in an effort to monopolize the trade centering around the Dutch post at Albany and to control the northern route to Montreal as well.

Others of the Five Nations, especially the Seneca and the Cayuga, struck to the south, attacking Susquehannock settlements and forging southeast in pursuit of trade with the Swedish settlements in Delaware and the English colonies of the Chesapeake Bay. Victory over the Susquehannocks opened the way for expansion into the Illinois and Ohio valleys in the late seventeenth century. Iroquois victories in this region made the Siouan- and Algonquian-speaking peoples of the Virginia Piedmont, as well as the Cherokee, Catawba, and other southern Indian nations, vulnerable to Iroquois attack as well (Englebrect 1995).

The formidable Iroquois were also the target of French missionary efforts. By 1667, Jesuits had established missions in each of the five nations. Although expelled by New York's Governor Dongan in 1683, they were replaced soon after by Protestant missionaries funded by the Society for the Propagation of the Gospel, which established a mission among the Mohawk early in the eighteenth century (Richter 1992a).

The late seventeenth century also saw the outbreak of war between the French and the Five Nations, exacerbated by the hostilities between the French and English known as King William's War (1689–97) (Trelease 1997). Retreating before advancing French troops, many Iroquois were displaced and forced to burn their villages rather than defend them. Once resettled, particularly in communities west of the Appalachians, Iroquois communities were often densely nucleated, defensible settlements on high ground (but, see Dennis 1993).

The period of King William's War was one of terrible population loss among the Iroquois as well. Some scholars estimate that nearly half the population was displaced or destroyed by disease. Iroquois relocated during the Beaver Wars were adopted into many Five Nations communities to replace those who had died, and the "Mourning Wars" staged by many communities brought additional captives, who were subsequently adopted into Iroquois communities.

The League of the Iroquois

That most famous of native North American confederacies, the League of the Iroquois, was established sometime during the sixteenth century and was probably, in part, a response to the new pressures and motivations governing Indian communities in the wake of the establishment of the fur trade. The league, made up originally of the five nations—Mohawk, Oneida, Onondaga, Cayuga, and Seneca—is unique in native North America for its profound impact, longevity, and political success (Richter 1992; Aquila 1997; Fenton 1998).

Iroquois tradition states that Deganawida or Hiawatha (or perhaps both) sought to convince the leaders of each of the five nations that a Great Peace should be established. The first Great Council established the rules of the League, marked by "rule among equals," in which consensus among all the nations' representatives was sought. Clearly in operation before 1630, it is possible that the League began in the mid-sixteenth century, and some Iroquois traditions place its origin much earlier (Tooker 1978, 420; Englebrecht 1985). The diplomatic protocol of the league required that all important statements or treaties be accompanied by the presentation of wampum, often in the form of a belt, as a record of the events that had taken place (Brandao 1997; Brandao and Starna 1996). Wampum became increasingly common in Iroquois diplomacy in the seventeenth and eighteenth centuries, as Europeans exchanged great quantities of it for furs.

The League in its mature form had well-established protocols, which had important ritual and symbolic significance as well. Each tribe was represented at council meetings by its chief, with each succeeding chief taking on the name of his predecessor. Fifty chiefs (the Roll Call of the Chiefs) were said to serve on the Council at any one time (Brandao and Starna 1996, 424). By Iroquois custom, names are the properties of specific clans (groups of individuals related to a distant, common ancestor, often designated eponymously). Thus, by requiring that chiefs take on the names of prior council members, even representation of each clan was ensured. The tribes were also organized into moieties (a division of a society into two "sides"). The Mohawk, Onondaga, and Seneca made up one moiety; the Oneida, Cayuga, and later, the Tuscarora, made up the other. Within Iroquois communities, opposite moieties had the responsibility of mourning the deceased of the other "side." Thus, in the League, responsibility for mourning chiefs of one moiety fell to the other.

Among the many important functions of the League was that of negotiating agreements advantageous to the League's members with all the European powers in turn. The diplomatic skill evidenced by the League's chiefs in the fur trade has become legendary, and the Iroquois successfully played off French and English interests to their own benefit throughout the seventeenth and eighteenth centuries. This function of the League was manifest in the famous "Covenant Chain," the alliance forged between the English and the League for their mutual benefit (Jennings 1989; Jennings et al. 1985).

THE COVENANT CHAIN

During King Philip's War, Governor Edmond Andros of New York sought to avoid a general Indian uprising, first by inciting the Mohawk to war with their New England enemies, hastening their defeat at the hand of the English colonists there, and by offering refuge to the displaced Susquehannock among the Delaware. When peace was restored in 1677, Andros was instrumental in promoting an extensive Indian-white alliance, known as the Covenant Chain. This arrangement linked several colonies, headed by New York, with a number of allied Indian nations, led by the Iroquois. Although the Susquehannock were forced to submerge their distinctive tribal identity with that of the Delaware and Iroquois, they in turn persuaded their Indian allies to make war against their former enemies in Maryland and Virginia. These tribes were ultimately forced to accept tributary status to the Iroquois alliance.

The Algonquians of the Middle Atlantic

Explorers from many parts of Europe, including England, France, and Spain, visited the middle Atlantic coast. Verrazano recorded his impressions of these people in 1524, and Spanish explorers, coasting north from Florida, noted their visits as well. It was a Spanish expedition that captured the young Don Luis, son of a chief of the York or James River in Virginia, carrying him to Spain in 1559–60. Don Luis returned to the York River with a Jesuit party in 1571, where he helped to destroy the mission, returning finally to his people (Lewis and Loomie 1953).

The ill-fated English Roanoke colony, established in 1584, was destroyed early the following year, and none of its residents were ever located. It is possible that some of these settled with surrounding Indian communities. The Jamestown colony, settled in 1607 in the heart of the Powhatan confederacy, soon disrupted native settlement and political relations as far north as the Potomac River. At the same time, Susquehannock raids into the middle Atlantic territories were harassing Piscataway and Wicomisse. Dutch settlements along the lower Delaware River in 1631 were dispersed by Munsee-speaking peoples living there, but Swedish colonists who settled at Fort Christina in 1638 were, for the most part, unmolested.

Occupying territories stretching north as far as the Hudson River drainage and western Long Island, south to the Delaware Bay, and west possibly as far as the Susquehanna River Valley, the historic Delaware were a group of linguistically related communities speaking languages now known as Munsee (in the north) and Unami (in the south). Verrazano describes a meeting with Delaware chiefs in New York harbor in 1524, but it is likely that they were already familiar with Europeans and their goods at that time (Goddard 1978a, 220). Like many of their coastal neighbors, the Delaware enjoyed early the benefits of the fur trade, and even after the local fur supply was depleted, Delaware men secured furs during long hunting expeditions to the interior. The Delaware's principle trading partners were the Dutch, who vigorously defended their expanding settlements against Delaware depredations. Land cessions to the Dutch and later the English in the New York region left many Delaware with no choice but to move farther westward, where they settled along the Hudson. Missions established by the Swedes and Moravians among the Delaware provided some measure of protection from increasing English settlement. Among displaced Munsee speakers were the Esopus and Minisink, as well as the Wappinger.

Northern Unami were also displaced by the infamous "Walking Purchase" of 1737. In collusion with the League of the Iroquois, who claimed the Delaware as tributaries, the colony of Pennsylvania expropriated vast holdings in the Lehigh Valley through this fraudulent purchase. Unami subsequently moved westward to the Susquehanna and the upper Schuylkill and Brandywine rivers. There they joined the Shawnee, who had previously emigrated to this region and with whom they now allied themselves. By 1750, southern Unami settled the Allegheny and upper Ohio valleys, forming the nucleus of the historic Delaware tribe (Goddard 1978c, 222). Others, including some Munsee and northern Unami, allied themselves with the Six Nations, moving with them to the Six Nations Reserve in Ontario following the Revolution (222). Other Delaware joined the Mahican at Stockbridge, or survived in scattered communities in present-day New Jersey. Some joined the Brothertown movement, settling eventually in Wisconsin.

The Nanticoke and their neighbors, whose territories spanned the region between the Potomac and the Chesapeake Bay, fared little better than the Delawares (Feest 1978a). Complex chiefdoms at the time of European colonization (Potter 1993), the Nanticoke and the Potomac River polities had "emperors" who controlled several tributary villages. The Accomac and Potomac peoples knew of the English colony at Roanoke and the Spanish mission on the York River, and were soon embroiled in Powhatan-English affairs after the founding of Jamestown in 1607. Trade relations in the Maryland region were profitable to all concerned, and the Algonquian speakers of the region joined together in alliance against the Massawomeck and Susquehannock, supported by the Jesuit mission there. Although numerous treaties between the Indians of Maryland and the colonial government were signed, English settlement continued to expand into their territories (Fausz 1985). Some communities became tributary to the Iroquois; others joined reserves in isolated areas of their former territories (Feest 1978a, 243). The majority of the Conoy moved west to the Susquehanna, along with a body of Nanticoke. Some were later sponsored by the Cayuga of the Six Nations. Others moved west with the Delaware, first to Kansas and later to Oklahoma.

Algonquians of Virginia and North Carolina

South of the Potomac, in territories extending west to the fall line of the Virginia Piedmont and north of the Dismal Swamp, the Virginia Algonquian peoples, most of whom had been united into the remarkable Powhatan Confederacy at the time of contact, made their home. Bounded to the west by hostile Siouan groups and to the southwest by the southern Iroquoian speakers, the Powhatans exemplified the effects of "social circumscription" (Carniero 1970; Hantman 1990). With abundant harvests and rich ecological resources available to them, the peoples united in the Powhatan Confederacy presented a formidable obstacle to English colonization. Their contacts with Europeans, however, predated the establishment of Jamestown by at least a generation (Feest 1978b). In 1560, an Indian from a York River community was captured by Spanish explorers, and later educated in Cuba and Spain. Baptized Don Luis, he was ultimately returned home, where he immediately led a raid on the mission established there, killing all but one of the Spanish in 1571. In 1584, Roanoke colonists also exchanged hostilities with the Virginia peoples before their own colony was dispersed.

The territories of the York River were inherited by Wahunsanacock (Powhatan), who may have been Don Luis's sister's son or another maternal relation (Rountree 1989). Powhatan consolidated his family's holdings in the following decades, such that by 1607, he controlled thirty separate native communities of the James and York rivers, excluding only the Chickahominy. Powhatan and his advisors were ambivalent in their early overtures to the English, sometimes showing willingness to trade, other times withdrawing with suspicion. Powhatan acquiesced to the betrothal of a favorite daughter, Matoaka, or Pocahontas, to the Englishman John Rolfe (fig. 7). But by 1620 relations between the two groups were seriously threatened, and in 1622 the Powhatan, led by Powhatan's brother Opechancanogh, staged a well-planned campaign against the scattered English settlements, killing nearly 350 of the colonists in a single day.

Unable to forge an alliance with the Potomac or Rappahannock tribes and besieged by Siouan and Iroquoians to the north and west, the surviving Powhatan rose again in 1644. Although they sustained hostilities for two years, they were ultimately unable to oust the English from the Virginia peninsula, and were themselves finally confined to reserves in what is now King William County, Virginia. During Bacon's Rebellion of 1677, several communities of noncombatant Indians were attacked, but after peace was again established, relations between the Powhatan descendants and the colonial and state government were governed by treaty, still in force in the twentieth century.

Other than their names—Roanoke, Croatoan, Weapemeoc, and Secotan—very little of the language of the people of North Carolina was recorded by the earliest English settlers of the region. Probably familiar to Spanish explorers in the sixteenth century, the Algonquians of the Pamlico Sound region were hosts to the first English colony in North America, the doomed Roanoke settlements of 1586 and 1587 (Feest 1978c). The fate of these English colonists is uncertain; after being driven from Roanoke Island by the settlers, some Algonquians may have found refuge among the Croatoan, or made their way northward toward the Chesapeake. No trace of them remained when the English arrived at Jamestown in 1607. The North Carolina Algonquians succumbed to European-introduced diseases in the seventeenth century. Those who survived joined, in some cases, with the Tuscarora, and others gradually relinquished their territorial rights.

Tuscarora, Meherrin, and Nottoway

The Tuscarora, Meherrin, and Nottoway, Iroquoians of the Virginia and North Carolina coastal plain, were productive farmers who also relied heavily on hunting and collecting. The boundaries between them and the coastal Algonquians were marked both linguistically and ecologically, and because they remained remote from English settlement for much of the seventeenth century, less is known about them. Aside from their involuntary involvement in Bacon's Rebellion, these people were primarily engaged along the peripheries of the fur trade, and their settlements were to some extent a buffer between the English settlers of the region and the Five Nations to the north. The Meherrin and Nottoway were assigned small reservations, but during the eighteenth century lost many of their holdings to white settlers. Refugee groups from the coastal plain, including the Nansemond and Weanock, joined them in the mid-eighteenth century.

The Tuscarora came into conflict with English colonists in North Carolina by 1660. Treaties specified land cessions and forbade the presence of the Tuscarora within the bounds of English territories, especially south of the Neuse River. In 1713–14, nearly 1,500 Tuscarora joined their linguistic relatives of the Five Nations, forming with them the new Six Nations Confederacy. The remaining Tuscarora were ultimately settled on a reservation on the north side of the Roanoke River. Their leader, Tom Blount, led the Tuscarora against the Yamasee in 1711–13. Economic conditions for the Tuscarora remaining in Virginia and North Carolina worsened through the eighteenth century, and many more had joined the Iroquois by 1766. Their reservation was sold in 1804, and the funds provided allowed the remaining reservation residents to move north to Pennsylvania and New York.

There is a tendency to view the colonial history of the Northeast in terms of the specific colonies that emerged there at the end of the seventeenth century. Certainly the various colonial policies and strategies led to different kinds of relationships among settlers and native people. However, it is also clear that the entire northeastern region was enmeshed in complex networks of trade, warfare, and colonial rivalry. The northeastern peoples—"peoples of the first frontier"—thus were linked in their unwilling role in the "contingent events" (Sahlins 1985) of the contact period, and in the choices these events forced upon them.

3   The Expanding Frontier

Chapter 3 focuses on the late seventeenth and eighteenth centuries, and follows the frontier westward through the "transappalachian" region, into the Ohio and Illinois valleys as far as the Great Lakes. Although some of the native people of these regions were in indirect or direct contact with newcomers prior to this period, their experiences must also be understood in light of the competition for fur and territories in which many European colonial powers, as well as native confederacies such as the League of the Iroquois, were engaged.

Just as the period of initial contact had its themes and patterns, so too did the period of colonial expansion, beginning in the early eighteenth century and continuing throughout the middle decades of the nineteenth century. The displacement of Indian communities in the interior that grew more severe as coastal dwellers were themselves pushed westward; the intertribal hostilities engendered by the fur trade; the inexorable spread of disease—all these factors made this period in Indian history a very complex one. Many native communities either disappear from the historical record at this time, are reformed into different polities, or join other, more powerful groups, thereby losing their own separate identities.

Among the many common features of this period of movement and reformation was the rise of several millenarian or nativistic movements, often lead by charismatic men and women known as "prophets." While nativistic movements were not restricted to this period (some have interpreted King Philip's War, for example, as a nativistic movement), the prophets of the later time period were often able to effect great changes in the societies of which they were a part. In particular, Handsome Lake, the Seneca Council Chief whose visions formed the basis for the Longhouse religion still practiced in traditional Iroquois communities today, had a profound effect in his own time as well. Anthony Wallace recounts the "death and rebirth" of the Seneca following their defeat in the Revolutionary War, when alcoholism and despair seemed to signal the decline of Iroquois society (1969; Jacobs 1995). Handsome Lake had a series of visions in which he was told to urge piety, chastity, abstinence, and a return to the old ways upon his people. The way of life he advocated made many aspects of traditional Iroquois life possible, while allowing adjustments to be made to the Iroquois's diminished political role.

Similarly, the Shawnee prophet Tenskwatawa, who was the younger brother of Tecumseh, preached a return to traditional lifeways and a rejection of white people and their values. His influential teachings supported the confederation organized by Tecumseh, which, although nearly destroyed at the Battle of Tippecanoe, had a lasting impact on Indians in the Ohio and Great Lakes region and served as a model for Indian resistance in subsequent decades.

In contradistinction to this nativism was the creation, in many regions, of an economic interdependence between Indians and frontier settlers that Richard White has called "the middle ground" (1991). Particularly in that region known as the "Old Northwest"—the Ohio and Illinois valleys and the eastern Great Lakes—the adaptations made by both groups created a distinctive regional culture, especially among the native peoples who played a long-standing role in the frontier economy. One interesting phenomenon of this rural culture was the frequent occurrence of native herbal curers, often called "doctors" or "doctresses," who traveled among rural communities in New England, serving as midwives and providing medical assistance to both Indians and non-Indians over a wide area.

Some of the most beautiful of objects were created and used by Indian people of the expanding frontier, especially the beaded and embroidered clothing and bags widespread throughout the Great Lakes. The art of block-stamped basketry was greatly elaborated, if not initiated, during this period as well. Today there are still thousands of those baskets in existence, woven and decorated by Indian men and women throughout the Northeast for sale as useful household objects or as souvenirs. In some native communities, such as the Passamaquoddy of Maine, such baskets are still made today.

Another feature of the expanding frontier was the growth among sophisticated easterners of the scholarly study of the purportedly "vanishing Indian." Thomas Jefferson, Albert Gallatin, and Wilhelm von Humboldt were foremost among a distinguished group of scholars who began to take an interest in native languages and who caused word lists to be collected in many northeastern communities. At the same time, native writers, especially the Pequot William Apess, began to express themselves and to represent the wrongs done to Indian people in published form.

The expanding frontier was thus as much a process as a place, and those who had been overtaken, especially the coastal Algonquian, continued to participate in the wider Indian historical experience through their connections to Indians farther west, or through their own migrations. At the same time, the experiences of the coastal native people were to some extent repeated among interior groups, who had escaped the earliest brutalities of contact but whose lands were ultimately overtaken and whose communities were threatened in much the same way those of the coastal peoples had been. Although the drama moves westward, many of the same dynamics— trade, disease, religious conversion, intercolonial rivalry—are operating. The fact that so much of the American "creation myth" is attributable to this period of hostility and accommodation speaks to its significance to Indians and non-Indians alike.

Behind the Frontier

The history of the native peoples who remained in Atlantic coastal regions, especially in New England, has been neglected by scholars, and the people themselves too often became invisible in the land that had once been theirs. But many native communities remained (Conkey et al. 1978); in northern New England, Indian people maintained a mobile existence with several loci of settlement (Calloway 1997). Some southern New England groups adopted Christianity and vernacular literacy (fig. 8). Others practiced traditional subsistence, intermarried, and governed themselves as before, and avoided the attention of officials (e.g., McBride 1991). Others gradually lost their remaining lands and joined other native communities in the region (e.g., Mandell 1996; O'Brien 1997). In the eighteenth century, several southern New England groups moved west under the direction of charismatic leaders who wished to protect their people from the dire influence of European colonists. Among these were the mixed Christian community led by Samson Occom (Love 1898), the Christian Oneida (Hauptman and McLester 1999), and the Housatonic Stockbridge (Cooley 1977). The native people of Virginia and North Carolina, although reduced to tributary status and confined to reservations, continued to practice traditional subsistence, intermarry with other Indians, and educate and govern themselves (fig. 9).

Transappalachia and Iroquois Territory

Transappalachia is a convenient term for the country that stretches west from the Mohawk and Susquehanna Valleys, across central and western New York and Pennsylvania to Lake Erie and the Ohio Valley. This region was a place of great foment and flux in the seventeenth and eighteenth centuries. During the late Woodland period, archaeologists believe that this region was occupied by northern Iroquoian-speaking people who practiced a seasonal round of hunting, foraging, and fishing, supplemented increasingly with agricultural products. These Iroquoian people lived in nucleated settlements comprised of up to 150 longhouses.

Monongahela

This culture complex, located in what is now northern West Virginia, southwestern Pennsylvania, and eastern Ohio from the period 1000–1600 A.D., shared many features with other late Mississippian cultures. Like Fort Ancient sites, many of the Monongahela communities were stockaded, and made up of a number of large, circular houses with bark-covered roofs. These sites included structures that may have had ceremonial functions similar to the historic period Delaware "Big Houses." Although trade goods appear on some sites, the identification of Monongahela sites with specific historic tribes has not been possible.

The first documented contact between residents of the Mohawk Valley and beyond and Europeans did not occur until 1634, although European trade goods were present on late Woodland period sites in the region dating a century earlier (Bradley 1987). Snow (1991) sees no significant changes from late prehistoric to historic populations in the region, suggesting that people of Mohawk origin were in situ prior to the period of contact. Dutch explorers and Jesuits visited Mohawk settlements beginning in the 1630s, reaching the site of modern Caughnawaga by the early 1660s. Iroquois traders, of course, had traveled to the coast many decades before, bringing European goods to their communities long before the Europeans themselves arrived. Populations in the region had already been disrupted, however, and archaeological evidence indicates that several principal settlements were moved in the early seventeenth century.

The Oneida, living west and north of the Mohawk, are their close linguistic relatives, and may have split from Mohawk populations in the late prehistoric period (Snow 1991). Like other Iroquois sites of the protohistoric period, Oneida communities were located on river bluffs and fortified, enclosing up to 80 longhouses. Also visited by the Dutch, Oneida peoples were also heavily involved in trade, as evidenced by the large numbers of trade items appearing on early seventeenth-century sites. Jesuit medals and rings also indicate contact with the French. Early historic records reveal that many Oneida men were slain in battles against the Huron, and later against the Erie, Susquehannock, Mahican, and other Algonquian-speaking peoples. The Oneida replenished their populations by adopting large numbers of Huron. During King William's War, many Oneida communities were sacked and destroyed, making them active in the negotiations that ended in the French-Iroquois peace accord of 1701.

Archaeologists also believe that the Onondaga, the "hearthkeepers" of the original Five Nations Iroquois, were living in their homelands for several hundred years prior to direct contact with Europeans, although the likelihood that Onondaga had links to St. Lawrence Iroquoians via Lake Ontario is strong. Changes in settlement patterns on sites otherwise showing no evidence of European influence suggest that Onondaga communities were nevertheless responding to changes brought about by warfare, disease, and economic restructuring that may have had its origins in the emerging fur trade. Other scholars suggest that the influence of the Mississippian collapse was a significant factor as well. French missionaries visited the Onondaga after 1654 and established a short-lived mission on Onondaga Lake, remaining friendly with the French until the attack on the Seneca in 1687 forced them to evict all the missionaries in the region.

The Cayugas of the Finger Lakes region of New York participated in the patterns of the protohistoric fur-trade economy, although no documented visits from Europeans to their region occurred before 1653, when French captive Pierre Esprit Radisson was taken to the cluster of three principal Cayuga settlements. Jesuits were also active among the Cayuga, and the English traveler Wentworth Greenhalgh reached them in 1677. Archaeologists working on Cayuga sites note the widespread seventeenth-century shift among the Iroquois from a subsistence farming economy to one based on trade, diplomacy, and warfare.

Finally, archaeological sites linked to the Seneca, "keepers of the Western Door," provide tantalizing evidence that Mississippian trade patterns, linking the Chesapeake Bay, the Great Lakes, and other regions, had been revived in the late sixteenth century. Some sixteenth-century sites contain European trade goods as well. The French *coureur de bois*, Étienne Brûlé, traveled among the Seneca, and Jesuit missionaries and explorers, including René-

Robert Cavelier and Sieur de La Salle, also encountered Seneca warriors in the 1660s, while several Seneca emissaries traveled east to English and Dutch settlements. Their originally populous communities were struck with a number of epidemics, however, and also suffered losses due to the constant hostilities that marked seventeenth-century Iroquois history.

By the end of the seventeenth century, the peace established between the Iroquois and the French at the Treaty of Montreal in 1701 marked the onset of "the golden age of Iroquois diplomacy." During this period, the Iroquoian peoples reached a high level of material prosperity and were able to rebuild communities ravaged by disease, warfare, and colonial competition. By permitting trading posts only on the borders of their domains, the Iroquois successfully held at bay the expanding colonial settlements to the east, while their Indian allies and tributaries, including the Delaware, Shawnee, Conoy, Tuteloe, and Susquehannock, protected their southern borders. The Tuscarora, forced northward from their original territories in North Carolina, became the sixth Iroquois nation in 1722.

Missionaries, traders, and colonial military officials also settled near Iroquois country, bringing innovations and forcing changes. Iroquois villages, formerly consisting of the large matrilineal longhouses, came to include log cabins and single-family homes. Some Iroquois began raising livestock— chickens, horses, cattle, and pigs—and to grow non-native crops, fruits, and grains. Beautiful objects of metal, modeled on traditional designs, were crafted. Clay tobacco pipes became increasingly elaborate. Splint baskets became common items in Iroquois homes.

The remarkable accommodation to European goods and resources had very little effect on Iroquois economy or cosmology. Some authors have suggested, in fact, that the peace afforded by Iroquois diplomatic success during this period led to a florescence of traditional Iroquois culture. In many ways, too, the Iroquois transformed their colonial allies, most significantly in their insistence on an elaborate diplomatic protocol accompanied by gifts, fur exchange, and military protection. Archaeological sites dating to the eighteenth century in Iroquoia are marked by a number of distinctive artifacts and substances: catlinite, the smooth reddish mineral from which ceremonial pipe bowls were carved; wampum from coastal New England and New York; gunflints and other gun parts; coins; German silver ornaments; metal tomahawks, peace medals, and amulets.

The riches and centrality of Iroquoia were prizes difficult for Europeans to resist. While settlers made consistent inroads along the eastern borders of their territories, French and British efforts to control the Great Lakes threatened the Iroquois to the west. Fort Hunter, on the Schoharie Creek, was established by the English within Mohawk territories; it was the thin edge of the wedge pushing English settlement north and west of Albany. French outposts at Detroit and Niagara also made inroads along the Mississippi possible. British forts along the Ohio were matched with French outposts in the same region. Warfare broke out between the two colonial powers in 1753. Known as the Seven Years' War, hostilities eventually spread to Europe.

Although officially neutral, various Iroquois nations favored one or the other power, creating rifts within their own confederacy. After the French defeat in 1760, the British refused to honor their promise to abandon former French forts. In retaliation, Seneca bands staged a rebellion now known as Pontiac's Rebellion. The Iroquois also failed to present a united front during the Revolution—a fatal mistake—with some communities and nations favoring the British and others supporting the Americans. Oneida warriors, for example, assisted American troops in the destruction of Susquehanna, Onondaga, Cayuga, and Seneca towns in 1778 and 1779. Other Iroquois retaliated by destroying American and Oneida settlements in New York and Pennsylvania (Mintz 1999). Devastated by the war and abandoned by their allies, many Iroquois people moved north to Canada or west to Oklahoma and Wisconsin. The descendants of those who remained live today on reservations in New York, negotiated for them in treaties following the Revolution (Campisi and Starna 1995), while others occupy reserves in Quebec, Ontario, Oklahoma, and Wisconsin.

The Ohio Valley

FORT ANCIENT

Archaeological evidence for the late Woodland period in the Ohio Valley indicates that societies there came to resemble Mississippian cultures elsewhere. A likely combination of cultural exchange and the actual migration of more southerly Mississippian peoples into the Fort Ancient area (what is now southern Ohio and northeastern Kentucky) permitted the spread of many Mississippian ideas and technological innovations, including temple-mound building, maize horticulture, and the use of the bow and arrow. The Ohio Valley in turn became a significant center for trade and expansion north to the Great Lakes, east to West Virginia and Pennsylvania, and across the Appalachian Mountains to the East Coast. It appears the populations of this region were largely continuous with earlier Adena and Hopewell peoples.

Fort Ancient communities were often fortified and organized around a central plaza area. Many sites had burial or temple mounds. Although scholars differ as to whether Fort Ancient societies were socially stratified, there is strong evidence of specialization of labor, especially in the production of bone tools and ornaments, ceramics, and stone pipes. This culture complex was still flourishing in the sixteenth and seventeenth centuries A.D., and European trade goods appear on many sites of the region. However, scholars have been unable to positively identify historically documented groups with any late Fort Ancient sites. It is likely that at least some were occupied by the historic Shawnee.

Archaeological sites in what is now western Pennsylvania and eastern Ohio indicate that European trade goods, including metal objects and glass beads, were widely available there by the early seventeenth century, although settlement patterns and house remains suggest that the peoples living there continued to practice many of the customs of their predecessors. Western Pennsylvania sites of this period are characterized by distinctive circular structures with underground storage areas, arranged around or inside plaza spaces. Objects owing their inspiration to Fort Ancient effigy figures, including beaver effigies, were made in imported metals, while shells from the mid- and northern Atlantic coast and Iroquois pots imply trading contacts with eastern native peoples. These people, sometimes referred to as Monongahela, disappeared by the 1640s, to be replaced by Delaware, Shawnee, and other displaced people.

Following the dispersal of the Ohio Valley's little-known original inhabitants, the Ohio Valley served for a time as hunting grounds for the Northern Iroquois, and later as home for a variety of Indian peoples displaced from their traditional homelands. Europeans entered the region by the mid-eighteenth century, although knowledge of the region and its people was current among the French and English for a century or more prior to the first explorations, and both groups competed for dominance over the region (McConnell 1992).

The first new inhabitants of the Ohio Valley for which there is solid evidence are the Wyandot, Iroquoians of the St. Lawrence region dispersed by the Northern Iroquois in the mid-seventeenth century. The Miami and Ottawa were among the earliest of the Algonquian-speaking peoples to resettle the area. The Wyandot were often in conflict with Ottawa and Shawnee there, and came under the influence of the English at Sandusky Bay.

The Miami, living on the southern shore of Lake Michigan in the late seventeenth century, also hunted in the Ohio Valley as far east as New York.

English and French traders and frontiersmen visited the Ohio Valley early in the eighteenth century, as Miami, Ottawa, and westerly Indians traveled east toward Albany. To the south of the great east-west route along Lake Ontario, two forts were established in Ohio country: Fort Augusta and Fort Louden, both built during the Seven Years' War.

Fox (Mesquakie) peoples joined displaced Delaware in the Ohio Valley in the early eighteenth century. They, like other native settlers in the region, sought protection from the Iroquois of the Five Nations, who controlled eastern access to the region, especially the Seneca, "keepers of the Western Door." The scattered Delaware united briefly under King Netawatwees, called Newcomer, in the 1760s. Later they moved westward again, joining with the Miami and others, some crossing the Mississippi prior to the Revolution.

Pontiac's Rebellion of 1763–64 drew most of the Indians of the Ohio region into its vortex, but Pontiac and his followers were unable to prevent the occupation of the region by English settlers (Parmenter 1997). The treaty of Fort Stanwix, signed in 1768, cemented an agreement by which the Iroquois ceded all their lands south of the Ohio River to the English. Another Stanwix treaty, signed after the Revolutionary War in 1784, ceded to the new nation all the Iroquois lands west of New York, and to Pennsylvania, all territories claimed by the Iroquois in that state. The Treaty of Fort McIntosh, signed in 1785, signified similar cessions by the Delaware and Wyandot. In the early nineteenth century, the conditions of the Treaty of Greenville (1795) were enforced. The remaining native residents of the Ohio Valley were forced to abandon most of their territories within the present state of Ohio. To facilitate white settlement of the region, the process of removing many of the natives resident in Ohio and southern Indiana to new territories in Oklahoma began by 1818 (Benn 1998).

The Illinois Valley

The Illinois Valley was also home to a number of societies with Mississippian characteristics in the late Woodland period. Among the the most important sites of the area are Cahokia, which contains many mound structures, including the largest manmade mound in North America; the Angel Site; and Kincaid, where ceremonial mound sites also occupy several acres. Archaeologists believe that each of these large centers controlled a surrounding countryside, but there does not appear to have been a centralized authority in the region (but, see Milner et al. 1991). Although many of these sites were occupied until at least the sixteenth century A.D., by the time French explorers reached the area, all these large mound sites had been abandoned. Archaeologists speculate that disease and other effects of European contact with Mississippian peoples in the southeast may have spread north to these communities, causing disruption that led to the decline of these complex centers. It appears that, just prior to the arrival of the French in the Illinois Valley, the region was controlled by the Algonquian-speaking Illinois Confederacy.

The so-called "Illinois Confederacy," made up of a number of related peoples named for their villages of Michigamea, Chepoussa, Espeminkia, Moingwena, Coiragamea, Tapouaro, Peoria, Tamaroa, Kaskaskia, Maroa, and Cahokia, shared the territories of the Illinois Valley, running south from the southern tip of Lake Michigan. Like the residents of the Ohio Valley, the people of Illinois country were hemmed in on the east by westward-moving tribes, and on the west by equally adamantine Siouan and Caddoan groups.

During the seventeenth century, Algonquian-speaking Sauk, Fox, Kickapoo, Mascouten, and Potawatomi shared the region with the Miami, Wea, and Piankashaw. Shawnee were also resident along its eastern borders. As the Miami moved west, the Neutral and Iroquois expanded into these territories as well. French influence in the region was strong in the late seventeenth and early eighteenth centuries, and missions were established along the heavily populated Kaskaskia River (Sleeper-Smith 1994). Iroquois raids and disputes with the Peoria caused the Kaskaskia to move westward to the Mississippi (Edmunds and Peyser 1993). Illinois people remained loyal to the French after their expulsion from Canada, and took the side of the colonists in the Revolutionary War.

Unlike their Illinois and Kaskaskia neighbors, the Miami, Wea, and Piankashaw cast their lot with the English, although they remained neutral during the Revolutionary War. Subsequently, however, white incursions into their territories fueled dissatisfaction among them, and land cessions to the increasing number of settlers began soon after 1800.

The Sauk, Fox, Kickapoo, and Mascouten, having been pushed south out of what was to become the state of Michigan, settled in the vicinity of the Fox and Chicago rivers. The Fox, steadfast enemies of the French, were nearly destroyed in the aftermath of their attack on Fort Ponchartrain (Detroit) in 1712, a series of skirmishes sometimes called the "Fox Wars" (Edmunds and Peyser 1993). In the 1730s, defeated on many fronts, the Fox requested refuge among their rivals, the Sauk, who, having taken them on, found themselves also vulnerable to attack. The combined peoples then settled on the banks of the Mississippi. The two groups split again in 1766, the Fox remaining near the Mississippi and the Sauk establishing their "Great Town" on the Wisconsin River. The Fox and Sauk chose different sides in many of the minor conflicts leading up to the Revolution, but their joint distrust of the Americans secured their loyalty to the British, with whom they fought in the War of 1812. Black Hawk's defeat at Bad Axe Creek signaled the end of the Sauk and Fox presence in Illinois; however, the Fox were successful in establishing a community near Tama, Iowa, where their descendants remain today (Gearing 1970) (fig. 10).

The Mascouten and Kickapoo followed the Sauk and Fox out of Michigan and joined the Miami and Wea on the Fox River in Wisconsin. The Mascouten and Kickapoo had similar histories in the early eighteenth century, and the Mascouten gradually lost their separate identity to the more numerous Kickapoo. Unlike many other tribes in the region, the Kickapoo were unwilling to conduct business or intermarry with non-Indians, although they had friendly relations with some of the Indian allies of the French, particularly the Illinois, and later joined the "Three Fires" of Potawatomi, Ottawa, and Chippewa in ousting the Peoria from the Illinois River.

After the defeat of the Peoria in 1769, the Potawatomi people who settled there became known as "Prairie" Potawatomi (Clifton 1978). The Potawatomi were allied with the British against the colonists in the Revolutionary War and the War of 1812, when they participated in the massacre at Fort Dearborn. The Potawatomi also supported the Sauk in Black Hawk's War.

Several different Kickapoo groups occupied the Illinois region in the eighteenth century, principally the "Prairie" Kickapoo of the Sangamon River, and the Kickapoo communities on the Wabash. They later joined forces with Tecumseh and were defeated with the Shawnee at the Battle of Tippecanoe in 1811. In 1832, most of the Kickapoo were removed to Kansas.

Far from their homelands, certain bands of Shawnee and Delaware also came to settle in the Illinois region. Allied with the French, the Shawnee served as a buffer against English expansion into the region in the 1740s. Delaware and Shawnee also settled on the Scioto River in 1760, and joined them in their move to Missouri in 1787. While the Delaware settled peaceably with the Kaskaskia, however, the Shawnee continued to move back and forth across the Illinois territories throughout the eighteenth and early nineteenth centuries.

The Upper Great Lakes

The French presence in the upper Great Lakes began early in the seventeenth century, when they secured a number of native allies, including the Potawatomi, Ottawa, and Chippewa. The fur trade caused enormous disruption in the upper Great Lakes, not least because the missionaries who followed the traders sought to attract people of many different ethnic backgrounds, further undermining territorial relations. The Ottawa and Wyandot were joined by Nipissing, Sauk, Fox, Potawatomi, Chippewa, and even Siouan groups near some missions, particularly at Sault Sainte Marie (Harp 1996).

After a brief respite in the 1690s, during which time French missions and forts were abandoned, the French refortified the upper Great Lakes in the early decades of the eighteenth century, extending westward into Manitoba, with centers at Michilimackinac and Fort Beauharnois. The inextricable involvement of all the native peoples of the upper Great Lakes in the French fur trade facilitated a rich amalgamation of various practices, creating the so-called "Upper Great Lakes" culture of the later historic period. Among the most notable features of the pan-Indian culture was the Midewiwin, a nativistic movement controlled by an organized and highly trained priesthood. Some Great Lakes groups took up new economic ventures, such as the Ojibwa's efforts to adopt agriculture (Rogers 1984), while others maintained a "traditional" subsistence into the twentieth century (Richards 1993).

Indians from the upper Great Lakes fought beside their French allies in the French and Indian War far to the east. However, after the French defeat, Indians dependent on the fur trade found themselves hostage to the new British trading system, wherein they frequently fell victim to the endless cycles of debt engendered by the trade. In spite of their dissatisfaction with the new system, however, most of the native people of the upper Great Lakes sided with the British in the Revolutionary War, and after their defeat were forced to cede much of their territories to the American "victors" (McLeod 1992; Sims 1992). Another interesting feature of this period is the growth of Meti (French/Indian or Scottish/Indian) populations, especially in Chippewa and Cree country.

At the same time, the Winnebago of Green Bay allied themselves to Algonquian-speaking groups, including the Sauk, Fox, and Potawatomi. Wabokieshiek, the Winnebago prophet, whose nephew was the Sauk leader Black Hawk, was resident at Prophetstown in 1832, and later joined Black Hawk on the Rock River (Willig 1996).

4 The Northeast: 1850 to the Present

Chapter 4 summarizes the important trends of modern Indian history in the Northeast, and emphasizes that, although the frontier moved beyond the region after the Civil War, native peoples of the Northeast continued to play an important role in American history, and have been especially active in modern Indian rights movements and cultural revitalization movements. The Northeast is especially significant as the locus of modern disputes over federal recognition and gaming.

The recent history of the native peoples of the Northeast is, in some ways, the least well known. The literal disappearance of some native peoples from the region, particularly the Beothuk, and the emigration or "removal" of many others (the majority of Unami and Munsee Delaware, many of the Mahicans, the native peoples of interior New England, and several of the native groups of the Illinois and Ohio valleys and upper Great Lakes) means that their histories became associated with other regions, especially "Indian Territory" in Kansas and Oklahoma, or with the many refugee communities and reservations in southern Canada.

Those native people who remained were increasingly isolated, both geographically and socially, from their non-Indian neighbors and often plagued by depressed economic opportunities, restricted mobility, and ever increasing governmental interference, as well as by a continuing vulnerability to many European-introduced epidemic and endemic diseases. The remaining native people had also learned the hard lessons of survival in an intolerant new world: to share no unnecessary information with outsiders and to be wary of government officials of any kind; in short, to become as "invisible" as possible (Baron et al. 1990).

Ironically, it was also early in this period when the first "modern" histories of the Northeast were written, notably Francis Parkman's monumental *France and England in North America* (1865–92). The first scientific anthropological and archaeological studies were conducted then as well. The mid-nineteenth century was also the period of the "rediscovery" of Indian languages of the Northeast, reflected in the work of James Hammond Trumbull and James Pilling (see part II).

At the same time that scholars and politicians regretted the "disappearance" of Indian people in the Northeast, and local communities celebrated their pioneer or colonial heritage in pageants and dramatic reenactments of historical events such as John Smith's rescue by Pocahontas, Philip's tragic defeat, or Squanto's meeting with the Pilgrims at Plymouth, native peoples of the region were participating in a number of institutions and movements that share several similar features over a broad region.

Guardians, Overseers, and Indian Agents

The native people of southern New England were among the first to be subjected to the system of oversight that later characterized federal Indian policy. By the late seventeenth century, several reservations were established in southern New England, including the Mashantucket or Ledyard reservation; the Stonington or Lantern Hill reservation; the Golden Hill Paugusset reservation in Connecticut; the Narragansett reservation in Charlestown, Rhode Island; and the reserve purchased for the Gay Head Indians by the Society for the Propagation of the Gospel (see table 1.3, chapter 1), as well as reserves in New York, New Jersey, and Virginia.

Typically these reserves were maintained by funds provided from the rent of property to non-Indian farmers, or through the sale of resources from the reservations, such as timber, clay, and salt marsh hay. Guardians or overseers managed these funds for the benefit of the tribe, providing monies for clothing, medicines, nursing, and burial expenses, and less frequently, for the purchase of seed, plowing, or building supplies. In many regions the guardians and teachers, whose salaries were paid for by missionary societies, were later supplanted by overseers appointed by the courts. The overseers provided a yearly accounting of their expenditures for the Indian communities in their charge and secured rental income on behalf of the Indian communities, or managed the monies allotted them by the state or local governments.

In the seventeenth and eighteenth centuries, Indian communities exercised some measure of self-governance through their participation in the selection of guardians and overseers, and the local Indian leaders continued to represent their people's interests to the overseer, or occasionally to the court or state legislature. Throughout southern New England, for example, the written petition became the preferred method of protest for Indian people, who often bypassed their guardians or overseers in their search for justice. In the early twentieth century, overseers were sometimes replaced by officers of newly established welfare departments. In Connecticut, the welfare department was in turn superseded by the Department of Parks and Recreation, which leased much of the desirable property to non-Indians for vacation homes.

The reservation system was deeply flawed; in exchange for the vast land cessions, the surviving Indian people of the Northeast were generally restricted to the least productive segments of their former territories, lands characterized by unproductive soils and inaccessibility to markets. On the reservations, elderly men, women, and children generally did whatever farming work was possible, while adult men were frequently absent from the reservations doing seasonal work, often in the maritime trades, farming, or the military. The limited funds available to the reservation communities were typically used only for the support of the helpless indigent or the terminally ill. It was inevitable that outsiders were adopted into Indian communities, especially as women married non-Indians as fewer and fewer Indian marriage partners were available. As social relations in New England and the South were increasingly defined by race, Indians reversed their early policy of acceptance of newcomers into their families and communities. Some reservation Indians took steps to prevent such intermarriage by restricting residence to people of Indian descent or by prohibiting marriage with non-Indians (Hutchins 1979; Mandell 1998).

The racialization of Indian politics was especially acute in Virginia, where remnants of the former Powhatan Confederacy and the independent Chickahominy tribe struggled to maintain some measure of sovereignty and to assert their distinct identities as Indians. Forced by the rigid biracial (white/colored) policies of Virginia's government to attend racially segregated schools, tribes such as the Pamunkey and the Mattaponi established their own reservation schools (Rountree 1990; 1992). Many of Virginia's Indians attended high school at Carlisle, Haskell, and even Chilocco, while others sent their children to high school, technical school, and college in other parts of the east, especially in Philadelphia. Meanwhile, residents on the reservations continued to hunt, fish, and farm as their ancestors had done. Little help was available to Indian people, who were consistently classified as colored, and subject to the de facto and de jure discrimination that characterized Virginia's policies toward nonwhites throughout the nineteenth and early twentieth centuries.

The upper Great Lakes saw the establishment of a similarly unsatisfactory—from the native point of view—system of Indian agents. Derived from the "factory" system of the American Fur Trading Company, established in the region after 1783, it strictly limited the ways Indians might trade. Generally, each community or post was assigned an agent, with whom the Indians in the region were required to do business. Natives no longer received gifts, as they had from the French, in exchange for their participation in the trade and their allegiance. Rather, Indians were "paid" only for furs, and often the payment took the form of "credit" in the factory-run stores. The traders were also the Indian agents, appointed by the territorial and state governments to distribute funds owed to each tribe, to manage their remaining lands, and to negotiate leases and sale of timber and other products.

The potential for abuse in this system, like that of the overseers in southern New England, is obvious to modern students of the period, but was less frequently noted in the nineteenth century. Many observers and administrators sincerely believed that Indians would be best served by weaning them from their former way of life, and by their dependency on the funds or lands set aside for them in numerous treaties. At the same time, some overseers and agents were unable to resist the temptation to sell off additional lands or to use Indian funds inappropriately or to benefit their own families and friends. Indians were left with few options but to endure dishonest or incompetent guardians, although their protests in the form of petitions and delegations sent to the state and federal governments were unceasing. Indians in the Great Lakes region also continued to emigrate to Kansas, Oklahoma, and other remote regions throughout the nineteenth century; their diminished reserves were ultimately sold off.

Labor Specializations in the Northeast

The territorial identifications of various Indian communities aside, Indian life in the nineteenth century remained mobile, especially for native men. Native whalers and sailors were present in most of the eastern ports, and significant percentages of Indian men in island communities on Martha's Vineyard, Nantucket, and Long Island were members of whaling crews, absent for months or years at a time. Interestingly, the men of the same community often shipped out together from the ports of New York, New Bedford, and elsewhere in southern New England. At the same time, maritime connections among the Indian communities of southern New England were marked by intermarriage and an interregional pattern of seasonal visits, especially during summer months, when several of these communities hosted "August meetings," harvest festivals, and religious remembrances. Over time, residents in a number of Indian communities on the islands and the mainland shared surnames, indicating a complex pattern of intermarriage in these communities. Shared military service, especially during the Revolutionary War, the War of 1812, and the Civil War, also bound the native men of southern New England together. Like fishing and whaling, military service was dangerous and demanding, and required long absences from home.

Itinerant labor and day labor, especially stonemasonry, was another adaptation of many Indian men of southern New England, and many of the surviving stone walls of Rhode Island and Connecticut were constructed in whole and in part by Indian men. Indian women worked as domestic servants, did laundry, and gathered and sold seasonally available berries, shellfish, and other fish at markets and door to door. Women also contributed to their families' incomes by weaving baskets, making brooms, and caning chairs. Nineteenth-century local histories of the region report that "wandering" families of Indians made yearly or seasonal appearances on farms in many rural communities, working for food and other goods.

Consolidation of the Upper Great Lakes Cultural Pattern

At the beginning of the nineteenth century, a complex regional interrelationship existed among many native peoples of the Great Lakes region, including the Menominee, Potawatomi, Iowa, Ottawa, Ojibwa, Delaware, and Iroquois, some of whom were later moved west of the Mississippi. The remaining communities, including the Winnebago in western Wisconsin, Potawatomi in Michigan, and Menominee, Ojibwa, and Ottawa in Minnesota, Wisconsin, and Michigan, were settled on reserves protected by treaty (Tanner 1987, 166–68). The surviving communities came to share an adaptation sometimes known as Upper Great Lakes culture (Quimby 1960, 147–57). All groups, for example, subsisted primarily as hunters and collectors, and shared many features of clothing style and decoration and other material objects. Common religious beliefs and practices, especially the Midewiwin, united the groups as well. Leadership was primarily through chiefs and elected councils.

Enfranchisement and Termination

Surprisingly, the earliest efforts to "detribalize" many Indian communities in the Northeast in the nineteenth century were centered not in remote areas but in Massachusetts, where the so-called "enfranchisement" movement of the 1850s reflected the growing concern of Indians and non-Indians that native peoples remained "uncivilized" (Nielsen 1985). Legislation adopted by the state of Massachusetts in 1870 required that Indian peoples relinquish their commonly held lands in favor of individual allotments, a move many thought would stimulate economic independence and initiative among the surviving Indian communities of the region. Gay Head and Mashpee, Massachusetts were thus divided, although a small parcel of commonly held land was retained at Gay Head. Predictably, lands then owned by Indian families were sold off or lost through debt or intestacy, such that by the early twentieth century much of Mashpee land was in the hands of non-Indian owners. The growth of the summer tourist industry in southern New England exacerbated this trend, and even remote Gay Head was feeling the pressures of development by the 1950s.

Perhaps the most notorious of the "termination" cases brought before the House in the 1950s was that of the Menominee. After successfully suing the federal government for mismanaging their reservation, the Menominee were threatened with termination by Arthur V. Watkins, one of the principal advocates of the new termination policy. A confusing vote was required of the tribe, in which they could access the funds granted them in their suit against the federal government only if they agreed to "the principle of termination." They were also required to use additional funds from the suit to administer the termination plan that had been forced upon them. Although the termination policy was later altered so that tribes were given more options, and was abandoned by the 1960s, the Menonimee languished. Mismanagement of their remaining funds and their remaining land holdings by the non-Indian run corporation, Menominee Enterprises, Inc., continued. High taxes on their newly acquired lands, medical costs, and low employment among the Menominee people caused many hardships in their community, but a grass-roots organization known as DRUMS (Determination of Rights and Unity for Menominee Stockholders) forced changes in the corporate structure of MEI and negotiated with the federal government for a reinstitution of federal status.

Boarding Schools

Schools for Native American students have a long history in the Northeast. John Eliot's "praying towns" often supported a native teacher, whose job it was to instruct Indian students in reading, writing, and the rudiments of the Christian religion. These schools, begun sometime after 1650, helped train a substantial percentage of the Indian population (close to 30 percent) to read and write. Students from these schools often themselves became teachers. Other Indians of Massachusetts studied at Harvard, although only one of these survived to graduate, Caleb Cheeschamuck, who died of disease soon after receiving his degree. These first boarding students, like the native boys who were present at the Indian School at the College of William and Mary in Virginia in the early years of the seventeenth century, had much in common with later boarding students—isolated from their families and communities, subject to harsh discipline and an unfamiliar diet, and vulnerable to the diseases that had little effect on their non-Indian fellows.

The missionary societies that funded the early Indian schools at Harvard and William and Mary also supported Eleazer Wheelock's Indian school, which was moved to the present Dartmouth College in the mid-eighteenth century. Students primarily drawn from southern New England communities, such as the Pequot, Mohegan, and Narragansett, were Wheelock's first students, and he also influenced the well-known native ministers and authors Samson Occom and William Apess.

Hampton Indian School, established in the late nineteenth century, drew many of its students from Lakota communities but also took students from New England and Virginia (Buffalohead and Molin 1996). Other natives studied at Carlisle, Pennsylvania or were sent west as far as the Haskell Indian school in Lawrence, Kansas and Chilocco in Oklahoma (Lomawaima 1994). Local boarding schools were also established, such as at Oneida (Jensen 1996).

The Meriam Report, which presented the results of an investigation of Indian boarding schools in 1928, found that Indian parents were correct in their concerns over the conditions under which their children were kept at these schools: the high incidence of disease and other illnesses; loneliness and low self-esteem; overwork; and poor training. Many of these schools were closed, although the Haskell School is now the Haskell Indian Junior College. They have been credited with the development of "pan-Indianism" in the Northeast and elsewhere, as Indians from many backgrounds met and exchanged ideas and experiences. Friendships and even marriages among students at these schools brought Indians from many regions together (Child 1996, 80).

Pan-Indianism

In 1907, William F. "Buffalo Bill" Cody's visit to the gravesite of Uncas in Mohegan, Connnecticut, was a dramatic gesture that helped fuel the growing revival of Indian awareness in that region and elsewhere that was part of the so-called "pan-Indian" movement. Local and regional Indian organizations increased during the 1920s and 1930s, some instigated by white lobbyists, others with Indian organizers. These organizations promoted native culture and pride in Indian origins, and hosted pageants and powwows to which non-Indians were invited. Native people began to research their own pasts, and to re-create or devise new regalia and ceremonials based on models from the Plains and elsewhere (Ciborski 1990). Older annual meetings, such as the Narragansett August festival, took on more of the characteristics of the western powwows, and eastern Indians adopted Plains-style music and dance as well (McMullen 1994).

The Indian Reorganization Act of 1934 encouraged many eastern Indians to create or revive Indian governmental structures, and to participate in inter-Indian organizations, Tribal museums were established at Mohegan and Narragansett, and non-Indian collectors such as Rudolph Haffenreffer of Providence, Rhode Island, amassed a large collection of regional objects and documentary sources for another museum, now the Haffenreffer Museum of Brown University. The revival of Indian crafts, especially pottery and basketry, and a new interest in native spirituality were other features of the early pan-Indian movement, as well as the protests staged at Plymouth Rock and the *Mayflower* in the early 1970s and the armed seizure of Ganienkeh by a group of Mohawks in 1974 (Landsman 1988).

Urban Indians

Many Indian people in the Northeast have, of necessity, chosen professions that take them off their reservations for some part or all of their lives. Beginning in the late nineteenth century, Mohawk and some other southern

New England native men have come to specialize in urban construction, especially the famous "high steel" workers of Syracuse, Rochester, and New York City (Hauptman 1986, 135). In the 1950s and 1960s, many Micmac began to congregate in Boston and other urban centers in the Northeast. Recent statistics suggest nearly 30 percent of the Micmac population was thus displaced (Guillemin 1975, 62).

Political Activism and Radical Politics, 1950 to the Present

The dislocation and disruption caused by general economic hardship and the ill-conceived termination policies of the 1930s through the 1950s created a mood of bitter resentment among many Indian people of the Northeast, a mood shared by other Indian people around the country (Goodman-Draper 1994). Coinciding with the growing civil rights movement among African Americans, the modern Native American rights movement had its inception (Deloria 1992). Rejecting the policies of accommodation advocated by previous generations of Indian leaders, Indian people came together at a number of public meetings beginning in the 1960s, in particular, the American Indian Chicago Conference, held at the University of Chicago in 1961. This conference saw the founding of the National Indian Youth Council, in which the Mohawk Shirley Hill Witt and the Winnebago Mary Natani (among others) were active. This group supported a number of Indian causes, especially the enforcement of native fishing rights. The publication of *Akwesasne Notes* (see below) dramatized the international disputes between the Mohawk and other Canadian and northeastern native groups. Another Mohawk, Richard Oaks, along with the group called Indians of All Tribes (IAT), helped to organize the occupation of Alcatraz Island in San Francisco Bay. The group inspired a number of similar "takeovers," but disbanded after Oaks was murdered in 1972. Other Iroquois-inspired resistance included the widely publicized Allegheny Seneca protest of the Kinzua Dam project (Bilharz 1998).

The American Indian Movement (AIM) was founded in Minneapolis in 1968 by a number of Anishinabes (as some Ojibwa people prefer to be called). Aided by the charismatic Russell Means (Oglala Lakota), AIM sponsored a number of dramatic protests, including the "capture" of the *Mayflower* replica in Plymouth Harbor on Thanksgiving Day in 1971. The march on Washington known as the "Trail of Broken Treaties" and the takeover of the BIA building in 1972 also drew national attention. Other native people of the Northeast have participated in nationwide organizations, especially the Indigenous Women's Network, which published the journal *Indigenous Woman*, and the International Indian Treaty Council (IITC), which was successful in helping to draft the Working Group on Indigenous Populations at the United Nations, and in drafting the Universal Declaration of the Rights of Indigenous Peoples in 1992.

Land Claims and Federal Recognition

In the 1790s the federal government passed a series of acts known as the Trade and Intercourse Acts, forbidding any but the federal government the right to negotiation with American Indian tribes for the sale of land. Through neglect, ignorance, or arrogance, most state and local jurisdictions in the Northeast violated these laws, and until the 1960s native protests and suits against state and local governments were generally dismissed by the courts, following the legal precedent known as "Thirteen Original States Doctrine" (Campisi 1984, 107; 1990a, 181, 1990b). The landmark case of the Oneida against the state of New York led to a Supreme Court decision in favor of that tribe, establishing that eastern Indians were, in fact, subject to the original Trade and Intercourse Acts and their provisions (Shattuck 1991).

Since 1974, many tribes in the Northeast have sought the federal recognition required to seek reparations for the misappropriation of their lands (Brodeur 1985). There are now several tribes in the Northeast who have received such recognition, including the Houlton Band of Maliseet, the Passamaquoddy, the Penobscot, the Gay Head Wampanoag, the Mohegan, the Mashantucket Pequot, and the Little Traverse band of Potawatomi (U.S. Senate 1994). The political and economic stakes of this process are extremely high, as many Indians involved in the process today can attest. The achievement of federal recognition, however, whether through the onerous process required of the Branch of Recognition and Acknowledgment of the Bureau of Indian Affairs or by congressional act, is an important step in securing federal benefits for Indian communities, and most who fit the rigid criteria established by the federal government for federal recognition are willing to undertake the years of effort and the enormous cost of the process.

The newly introduced "Traditional Cultural Properties" directives, a more recent initiative of the National Historic Preservation legislation enacted in the 1970s, may provide significant new support for Indian efforts to preserve landscape features and other sacred sites not now protected under current architectural guidelines. Indians are also allied with environmental action groups to protect wetlands and rivers from further development, as many such surviving resources are on or near Indian communities.

Gaming

Adding complexity to the federal recognition process is the sovereignty accorded by federal recognition, which permits, in special circumstances, the establishment of gaming enterprises on Indian reservations or on Indian-owned land. Many casinos are today operated by natives of the Northeast or their agents, but none probably more successfully than Foxwoods, the casino owned by the Mashantucket Pequot of Ledyard, Connecticut. Opened in 1992, it has provided jobs and opportunities for all tribal members, as well as a needed boost to the flagging economy of eastern Connecticut. The Mohegan Sun, which began operation in 1998 in nearby Norwich, Connecticut, is also an important economic asset to the region (Hauptman and Wherry 1990).

Predictably, the issues raised by gaming are very complex, and much debate in and out of "Indian country" concerns the social costs of gambling. In addition, Indian communities have in some cases allowed their governments to be influenced by the interests of non-Indian gaming consortiums, and non-Indian residents near gaming facilities complain about the disruption that the industry brings to their communities. Indians reply that gaming revenues bring many economic benefits to Indians and non-Indians alike, and that since gaming is a voluntary activity, no one need be harmed by it. More pointedly, they argue that federal recognition is not automatically followed by the establishment of new casinos, which are only permissible in strictly limited circumstances (West 1996).

Language and Cultural Revival

Concern about native language loss in the 1960s led many Indian communities in the Northeast to establish or seek funds for language preservation projects. The Passamaquoddy Bilingualism and Biculturalism Project is among the most successful of the programs developed at that time, producing curricular materials and beginning the Passamaquoddy-Maliseet Dictionary Project, still ongoing at present with more than 20,000 entries. At Akwesasne, a very successful "immersion" program at the Mohawk school has reintroduced the Mohawk language to young children, many of whom were unable to learn the language at home (Mithun and Chafe 1987). Dictionaries and grammars, including the Ojibwa dictionary and the current Wampanoag Dictionary Project, bring new awareness of and easier access to native languages of the Northeast, for the use of those studying ancestral populations and living speakers. Recently passed federal legislation provides limited funds for such projects as well (U.S. Senate 1992). Elsewhere, native spirituality is emerging after years of suppression (e.g., Pflug 1990).

Conclusions: The Northeast Culture Area Today

Native communities in the Northeast today are, in many ways, reflections of the four hundred years of their history that have followed the arrival of Europeans. Outwardly similar to surrounding non-Indian communities, largely English-speaking, and made up of people with a similar mix of politics, religious beliefs, and economic achievements, Indian communities still retain distinctive features. Native language use is still common among the Passamaquoddy and Maliseet, Mohawk, Ojibwa, and Menominee communities. Many Iroquois still practice the Longhouse religion (Shimony 1994). Native arts flourish in many Indian communities (fig. 11), and certain patterns of residence and diet still remain distinctively indigenous (Weinstein 1986, 1994; Strong 1996; Moretti-Langholtz 1999). Indian people often retain knowledge of traditional stories and sacred tales that are still shared in their communities (e.g., Simmons 1986).

Indian people of the Northeast are also different from *their* forebears. Like most Americans, they have adopted new technologies, developed new ways of organizing themselves politically, learned new languages, and for the most part, look, dress, and behave as twenty-first-century citizens. Many native people have adopted as their special mission, however, the preservation of alternative ways of being, seeing, and believing (Squire 1996). Through petitions for federal recognition, land claims cases, and other legal action, they continue to fight for native legal rights. Many Indians cooperate with public schools to improve the teaching of Indian history and culture. They also work to improve economic and social conditions for Indian people both on and off the reservations. They remain distinctly Native American, and contribute to the rich diversity of the northeastern region their own unique experience.

References for Part I

Apess, William. 1992. *On Our Own Ground: The Writings of William Apess*. Ed. Barry O'Connell. Amherst: University of Massachusetts Press.

Aquila, Richard. 1997. *The Iroquois Restoration: Iroquois Diplomacy on the Colonial Frontier, 1701–1754*. Lincoln: University of Nebraska Press.

Axtell, James. 1985. *The Invasion Within: The Contest of Cultures in Colonial North America*. New York: Oxford University Press.

———. 1995. *The Rise and Fall of the Powhatan Empire: Indians in Seventeenth-Century Virginia*. Williamsburg, Va.: Colonial Williamsburg Foundation.

Bailyn, Bernard. 1986. *The Peopling of British North America: An Introduction*. New York: Knopf.

Baker, Alex W. and Timothy R. Pauketat, eds. 1992. *Lords of the Southeast: Social Inequality and the Native Elites of Southeastern North America*. Washington, D.C.: American Anthropological Association.

Bakker, Peter. 1989. "The Language of the Coast Tribes Is Half Basque: A Basque-American Indian Pidgin in Use Between Europeans and Native Americans in North America, ca. 1540–ca. 1640." *Anthropological Linguistics* 31(3–4): 117–47.

Baron, Donna Keith, J. Edward Howd, and Holly V. Izard. 1990. "They Were Here All Along: The Native American Presence in Lower Central New England in the Eighteenth and Nineteenth Centuries." *William and Mary Quarterly* (1996) 53(3): 561–86.

Bauxar, J. Joseph. 1978. "History of the Illinois Area." In *The Northeast*, ed. Bruce

G. Trigger. Vol. 15 of *Handbook of North American Indians*, ed. William Sturtevant, 594–601. Washington, D.C.: Government Printing Office.

Benes, Peter, ed. 1991. "Algonkians of New England: Past and Present." *Annual Proceedings (Dublin Seminar for New England Folklife)* 16.

Benison, Chris. 1997. "Horticulture and the Maintenance of Social Complexity in Late Woodland Southeastern New England." *North American Archaeologist* (1997) 18(1): 1–17.

Benn, Carl. 1998. *The Iroquois in the War of 1812.* Toronto: University of Toronto Press.

Bennett, M. K. 1955. "The Food Economy of the New England Indians 1605–75." *The Journal of Political Economy* 63:360–96.

Bilharz, Joy A. 1998. *The Allegany Senecas and Kinzua Dam: Forced Relocation Through Two Generations.* Lincoln: University of Nebraska Press.

Binford, Lewis. 1980. "Willow Smoke and Dog's Tails: Hunter-Gatherer Settlement Systems and Archaeological Site Formation." *American Antiquity* 45(1): 4–20.

Blair, Emma Helen, ed. 1996. *The Indian Tribes of the Upper Mississippi Valley Region of the Great Lakes.* Lincoln: University of Nebraska Press.

Bock, Phillip. 1978. "Micmac." In *The Northeast*, ed. Bruce G. Trigger. Vol. 15 of *Handbook of North American Indians*, ed. William Sturtevant, 109–22. Washington, D.C.: Government Printing Office.

Bonvillain, Nancy Lee. 1992. *The Mohawk.* New York: Chelsea House.

Bourne, Russell. 1990. *The Red King's Rebellion: Racial Politics in New England 1675–1678.* New York: Atheneum.

Bourque, Bruce J. 1973. "Aboriginal Settlement and Subsistence on the Maine Coast." *Man in the Northeast* 6:3–20.

Bourque, Bruce J. and Ruth H. Whitehead. 1985. "Tarrantines and the Introduction of European Trade Goods in the Gulf of Maine." *Ethnohistory* 32:327–41.

Boyce, Douglas W. 1978. "Iroquoian Tribes of the Virginia–North Carolina Coastal Plain." In *The Northeast*, ed. Bruce G. Trigger. Vol. 15 of *Handbook of North American Indians*, ed. William Sturtevant, 82–289. Washington, D.C.: Government Printing Office.

Bradley, James W. 1987. "Native Exchange and European Trade: Cross-Cultural Dynamics in the Sixteenth Century." *Man in the Northeast* 33:31–46.

Bragdon, Kathleen. 1988. "The Material Culture of the Christian Indians of Massachusetts." In *Documentary Archaeology*, ed. Mary Beaudry. Boston: Cambridge University Press.

———. 1991a. "Native Christianity in Eighteenth-Century Massachusetts: Ritual as Cultural Reaffirmation." In *New Dimensions in Ethnohistory*, eds. Barry Gough and Christie Laird. Papers of the Second Laurier Conference on Ethnohistory and Ethnology, 117–26. Hull, Quebec: Canadian Museum of Civilization.

———. 1991b. "Vernacular Literacy and Massachusett World View 1650–1750." *Annual Proceedings (Dublin Seminar for New England Folklife)* 16:26–34.

———. 1996. *Native People of Southern New England, 1500–1650*. Norman: University of Oklahoma Press.

———. (In press.) *Colonial Native New England, 1650–1775*. Norman: University of Oklahoma Press.

Bragdon, Kathleen and William S. Simmons, eds. 1998. *The Eastern Pequots of Connecticut: A Petition for Federal Recognition as an American Indian Tribe*. Manuscript in the possession of the Eastern Pequot Tribe of Connecticut, Inc.

Brandao, Jose Antonio. 1997. *"Your Fyre Shall Burn No More": Iroquois Policy Toward New France and Its Native Allies to 1701*. Lincoln: University of Nebraska Press.

Brandao, J. A. and William A. Starna. 1996. "The Treaties of 1701: A Triumph of Iroquois Diplomacy." *Ethnohistory* 43(2): 209–44.

Brasser, T. J. 1971. "The Coastal Algonkians: People of the First Frontiers." In *North American Indians in Historical Perspective*, eds. Eleanor B. Leacock and Nancy O. Lurie, 64–91. New York: Random House.

———. 1978a. &ldquoEarly Indian-European Contacts." In *The Northeast*, ed. Bruce G. Trigger. Vol. 15 of *Handbook of North American Indians*, ed. William Sturtevant, 8–88. Washington, D.C.: Government Printing Office.

———. 1978b. "Mahican." In *The Northeast*, ed. Bruce G. Trigger. Vol. 15 of *Handbook of North American Indians*, ed. William Sturtevant, 198–212. Washington, D.C.: Government Printing Office.

Broadwell, George Aaron. 1995. "1990 Census Figures for Speakers of American Indian Languages." *International Journal of American Linguistics* 61(1): 145–49.

Brodeur, Paul. 1985. *Restitution: The Land Claims of the Mashpee, Passamaquoddy and Penobscot Indians of New England*. Boston: Northeastern University Press.

Buffalohead, W. Roger and Paulette Fairbanks Molin. 1996. "'A Nucleus of Civilization': American Indian Families at Hampton Institute in the Late Nineteenth Century." *Journal of American Indian Education* 35(3): 59–94.

Callender, Charles. 1978a. "Great Lakes–Riverine Sociopolitical Organization." In *The Northeast*, ed. Bruce G. Trigger. Vol. 15 of *Handbook of North American Indians*, ed. William Sturtevant, 610–21. Washington, D.C.: Government Printing Office.

———. 1978b. "Shawnee." In *The Northeast*, ed. Bruce G. Trigger. Vol. 15 of *Handbook of North American Indians*, ed. William Sturtevant, 622–35. Washington, D.C.: Government Printing Office.

———. 1978c. "Fox." In *The Northeast*, ed. Bruce G. Trigger. Vol. 15 of *Handbook of North American Indians*, ed. William Sturtevant, 636–47. Washington, D.C.: Government Printing Office.

———. 1978c. "Illinois." In *The Northeast*, ed. Bruce G. Trigger. Vol. 15 of *Hand-*

book of North American Indians, ed. William Sturtevant, 673–80. Washington, D.C.: Government Printing Office.

Callender, Charles, Richard K. Pope, and Susan M. Pope. 1978. "Kickapoo." In *The Northeast*, ed. Bruce G. Trigger. Vol. 15 of *Handbook of North American Indians*, ed. William Sturtevant. Washington, D.C.: Government Printing Office.

Calloway, Colin. 1990. *The Western Abenakis of Vermont, 1600–1800: War, Migration, and the Survival of an Indian People*. Hanover, N.H.: University Press of New England.

———. 1991. *Dawnland Encounters: Indians and Europeans in Northern New England*. Hanover, N.H.: University Press of New England.

———, ed. 1997. *After King Philip's War: Presence and Persistence in Indian New England. Encounters with Colonialism: New Perspectives on the Americas*. Hanover, N.H.: University Press of New England

Campisi, Jack. 1984. "National Policy, States' Rights, and Indian Sovereignty: The Case of the New York Iroquois." In *Extending the Rafters: Interdisciplinary Approaches to Iroquoian Studies*, eds. Michael K. Foster, Jack Campisi, and Marianne Mithun, 95–108. Albany: State University of New York Press.

———. 1990a. "The New England Tribes and Their Quest for Justice." In *The Pequots in Southern New England: The Fall and Rise of an American Indian Nation*, eds. Laurence M. Hauptman and James D. Wherry, 179–93. Norman: University of Oklahoma Press.

———. 1990b. "The Emergence of the Mashantucket Pequot Tribe, 1637–1975." In *The Pequots in Southern New England: The Fall and Rise of an American Indian Nation*, eds. Laurence M. Hauptman and James D. Wherry, 117–40. Norman: University of Oklahoma Press.

———. 1991. *The Mashpee Indians: Tribe on Trial*. Syracuse, N.Y.: Syracuse University Press.

Campisi, Jack and William A. Starna. 1995. "On the Road to Canandaigua: The Treaty of 1794." *American Indian Quarterly* (1995) 19(4): 467–90.

Carneiro, Robert L. 1970. "A Theory of the Origin of the State." *Science* 169(3947): 733–38.

Carpenter, Roger Merle. 1999. *The Renewed, The Destroyed, and The Remade: The Three Thought Worlds of the Iroquois and the Huron, 1609–1650*. Riverside: University of California Press.

Carter, Harvey. 1987. *The Life and Times of Little Turtle, First Sagamore of the Wabash*. Urbana: University of Illinois Press.

Ceci, Lynn. 1990. "Wampum as a Peripheral Resource in the Seventeenth-Century World System." In *The Pequots in Southern New England: The Fall and Rise of an American Indian Nation*, eds. Laurence M. Hauptman and James D. Wherry, 48–65. Norman: University of Oklahoma Press.

Champlain, Samuel de. 1907 [1604]. *Voyages of Samuel de Champlain, 1604–1618.* Ed. W. L. Grant. New York: Scribner's.

Ciborski, Sara. 1990. *Culture and Power: The Emergence and Politics of Akwesasne Mohawk Traditionalism.* Albany: State University of New York Press.

Claassen, Cheryl and Rosemary A. Joyce. 1997. *Women in Prehistory: North America and Mesoamerica.* Philadelphia: University of Pennsylvania Press, 87–99.

Clifton, James. 1978. "Potawatomi." In *The Northeast,* ed. Bruce G. Trigger. Vol. 15 of *Handbook of North American Indians,* ed. William Sturtevant, 725–42. Washington, D.C.: Government Printing Office.

Colee, Philip Sauve. 1977. *The Housatonic-Stockbridge Indians: 1734–1749.* Albany: State University of New York Press.

Conkey, Laura, Ethel Boissevain, and Ives Goddard. 1978. "Indians of Southern New England and Long Island: Late Period." In *The Northeast,* ed. Bruce G. Trigger. Vol. 15 of *Handbook of North American Indians,* ed. William Sturtevant, 177–89. Washington, D.C.: Government Printing Office.

Cook, S. F. 1970. *The Indian Population of New England in the Seventeenth Century.* Berkeley: University of California Press.

Cronon, William. 1983. *Changes in the Land: Indians, Colonists, and the Ecology of New England.* New York: Hill and Wang.

Crosby, A. W. 1986. *Ecological Imperialism: The Biological Expansion of Europe, 900–1900.* New York: Cambridge University Press.

Day, Gordon M. 1975. "The Mots Loup of Father Mathevet." *Publications in Ethnology* 8.

———. 1978a. "Western Abenaki." In *The Northeast,* ed. Bruce G. Trigger. Vol. 15 of *Handbook of North American Indians,* ed. William Sturtevant, 148–59. Washington, D.C.: Government Printing Office.

———. 1978b. "Nipissing." In *The Northeast,* ed. Bruce G. Trigger. Vol. 15 of *Handbook of North American Indians,* ed. William Sturtevant, 787–91. Washington, D.C.: Government Printing Office.

———. 1998. *In Search of New England's Native Past: Selected Essays.* Eds. Michael Foster and William Cowan. Amherst: University of Massachusetts Press.

Day, Gordon M. and Bruce G. Trigger. 1978. "Algonquin." In *The Northeast,* ed. Bruce G. Trigger. Vol. 15 of *Handbook of North American Indians,* ed. William Sturtevant, 792–97. Washington, D.C.: Government Printing Office.

Deloria, Vine, Jr. 1992. "The Application of the Constitution to American Indians." In *Exiled in the Land of the Free: Democracy, Indian Nations, and the U.S. Constitution,* eds. Oren R. Lyons and John C. Mohawk. Santa Fe, N.M.: Clear Light.

Dennis, Matthew. *Cultivating a Landscape of Peace: Iroquois-European Encounters in Seventeenth-Century America.* Ithaca, N.Y.: Cornell University Press.

Dimmick, Frederica R. 1994. "Creative Farmers of the Northeast: A New View of Indian Maize Horticulture." *North American Archaeologist* (1994) 15(3): 235–52.

Dincauze, Dena and Robert J. Hasenstab. 1989. "Explaining the Iroquois: Tribalization on a Prehistoric Periphery." In *Centre and Periphery: Comparative Studies in Archaeology*, ed. T. C. Champion, 67–87. London: Unwin Hyman. Originally published in *Proceedings of the World Archaeological Congress*, September 1986, part 4.

Dobyns, H. F. 1983. *Their Number Become Thinned: Native American Population Dynamics in Eastern North America*. Knoxville: University of Tennessee Press.

Doherty, Robert. 1990. *Disputed Waters: Native Americans and the Great Lakes Fishery*. Lexington: University Press of Kentucky.

Drake, James David. 1995. "Severing the Ties That Bind Them: A Reconceptualization of King Philip's War." Ph.D. diss., University of California–Los Angeles.

Earle, Timothy. 1987. "Chiefdoms in Archaeological and Ethnohistorical Perspective." *Annual Reviews in Anthropology* 16:279–308.

Edmunds, R. David and Joseph L. Peyser. 1993. *The Fox Wars: The Mesquakie Challenge to New France*. (Vol. 211 of Civilization of the American Indian Series.) Norman: University of Oklahoma Press.

Engelbrecht, William. 1985. "New York Iroquois Political Development." In *Cultures in Contact: The Impact of European Contacts on Native American Cultural Institutions, A.D. 100–1800*, ed. William Fitzhugh, 163–86. Washington, D.C.: Smithsonian Institution Press.

————. 1995. "Case of the Disappearing Iroquoians: Early Contact Period Superpower Politics." *Northeastern Anthropology* 50:35–59.

Erikson, Vincent O. 1978. "Maliseet-Passamaquoddy." In *The Northeast*, ed. Bruce G. Trigger. Vol. 15 of *Handbook of North American Indians*, ed. William Sturtevant, 123–36. Washington, D.C.: Government Printing Office.

Evans-Pritchard, Edward Evan. 1940. *The Nuer: A Description of the Modes of Livelihood and Political Institutions of a Nilotic People*. Oxford: Clarendon Press.

Faulkner, Alaric. 1991. "The Lower Bagaduce Historic Sites Survey Phase 3. Further Definition of St. Castin's Habitation, 1990–1991." Report on file. Augusta: Maine Historic Preservation Commission.

Faulkner, Alaric and Gretchen Faulkner. 1987. *The French at Pentagoet, 1635–1674: An Archaeological Portrait of the Acadian Frontier*. Augusta: The Maine State Preservation Commission; Saint John, New Brunswick: New Brunswick Museum.

Fausz, Frederick J. 1985. "Patterns of Anglo-Indian Aggression and Accommodation Along the Mid-Atlantic Coast, 1584–1634." In *Cultures in Contact: The European Impact on Native Cultural Institutions in Eastern North America, A.D. 1000–1800*, ed. William W. Fitzhugh, 225–70. Washington, D.C.: Smithsonian Institution Press.

Feest, Christian F. 1978a. "Nanticoke and Neighboring Tribes." In *The Northeast*, ed. Bruce G. Trigger. Vol. 15 of *Handbook of North American Indians*, ed. William Sturtevant, 253–70. Washington, D.C.: Government Printing Office.

————. 1978b. "Virginia Algonquians." In *The Northeast*, ed. Bruce G. Trigger. Vol. 15 of *Handbook of North American Indians*, ed. William Sturtevant. Washington, D.C.: Government Printing Office.

————. 1978c. "North Carolina Algonquians." In *The Northeast*, ed. Bruce G. Trigger. Vol. 15 of *Handbook of North American Indians*, ed. William Sturtevant, 271–81. Washington, D.C.: Government Printing Office.

————. 1990. "Pride and Prejudice: the Pocahontas Myth and the Pamunkey." In *The Invented Indian: Cultural Fictions and Government Policies*, ed. James A. Clifton. New Brunswick, N.J.: Transaction Publishers.

Feest, Christian F. and Johanna E. Feest. 1978. "Ottawa." In *The Northeast*, ed. Bruce G. Trigger. Vol. 15 of *Handbook of North American Indians*, ed. William Sturtevant, 772–86. Washington, D.C.: Government Printing Office.

Fenton, William N. 1978. "Northern Iroquoian Culture Patterns." In *The Northeast*, ed. Bruce G. Trigger. Vol. 15 of *Handbook of North American Indians*, ed. William Sturtevant, 296–321. Washington, D.C.: Government Printing Office.

————. 1998. *The Great Law and the Longhouse: A Political History of the Iroquois Confederacy*. (Vol. 223 of Civilization of the American Indian Series.) Norman: University of Oklahoma Press.

Fitting, James E. 1978. "Regional Cultural Development 300 B.C.–A.D. 1000." In *The Northeast*, ed. Bruce G. Trigger. Vol. 15 of *Handbook of North American Indians*, ed. William Sturtevant, 44–57. Washington, D.C.: Government Printing Office.

Fitzhugh, William W., ed. 1985. *Cultures in Contact: The European Impact on Native Cultural Institutions in Eastern North America, A.D. 1000–1800*, ed. William W. Fitzhugh. Washington, D.C.: Smithsonian Institution Press.

Flannery, Regina. 1939. *An Analysis of Coastal Algonquian Culture*. Anthropological Series 7. Washington, D.C.: Catholic University of America.

————. 1946. "The Culture of the Northeastern Indian Hunters: A Descriptive Survey." In *Man in Northeastern America* (vol. 3 of Papers of the Robert S. Peabody Foundation for Archaeology), ed. Frederick Johnson. Andover, Mass.: Phillips Academy, the Foundation.

Foster, Michael K., Jack Campisi, and Marianne Mithun, eds. 1984. *Extending the Rafters: Interdisciplinary Approaches to Iroquoian Studies*. Albany: State University of New York Press.

Garrad, Charles and Conrad E. Heidenreich. 1978. "Khionotaternonon (Petun)." In *The Northeast*, ed. Bruce G. Trigger. Vol. 15 of *Handbook of North American Indians*, ed. William Sturtevant, 394–97. Washington, D.C.: Government Printing Office.

Gearing, Frederick O. 1970. *The Face of the Fox*. Chicago: Aldine Press.

Ghere, David L. 1988. "Abenaki Factionalism, Emigration and Social Continuity: Indian Society in Northern New England 1725–1765." Ph.D. diss., University of Maine.

————. 1993. "The 'Disappearance' of the Abenaki in Western Maine: Political Organization and Ethnocentric Assumptions." *American Indian Quarterly* 17(2): 193–207.

————. 1997. "Myths and Methods in Abenaki Demography: Abenaki Population Recovery 1725–1750." *Ethnohistory* 44(3): 511–34.

Gleach, Frederic W. 1997. *Powhatan's World and Colonial Virginia: A Conflict of Cultures*. Lincoln: University of Nebraska Press.

Goddard, Ives. 1978. "Delaware." In *The Northeast*, ed. Bruce G. Trigger. Vol. 15 of *Handbook of North American Indians*, ed. William Sturtevant, 213–39. Washington, D.C.: Government Printing Office.

————. 1999. Early Pidgins and Creoles." In Edward Gray and Norman Fiering, eds., *Language Encounter in the Americas*. John Carter Brown Library.

Goddard, Ives and Kathleen J. Bragdon. 1988. *Native Writings in Massachusetts*. (Vol. 185 of Memoirs of the American Philosophical Society.) Philadelphia: American Philosophical Society.

Goodman-Draper, Jacqueline. 1994. "The Development of Underdevelopment at Akwesasne: Cultural and Economic Subversion." *American Journal of Economics and Sociology* 53(1): 41–56.

Graymont, Barbara. 1991. *The Iroquois*. Norman: University of Oklahoma Press.

Greenblatt, Stephen. 1976. "Learning to Curse: Aspects of Linguistic Colonialism in the Sixteenth Century." In *First Images of America: The Impact of the New World on the Old*, ed. Fred Chiappelli, 566–68. Berkeley: University of California Press.

————. 1991. *Marvelous Possessions: The Wonder of the New World*. Chicago: University of Chicago Press.

————. 1993. *New World Encounters*. Berkeley: University of California Press.

Griffin, James B. 1993. "Cahokia Interaction with Contemporary Southeastern and Eastern Societies." *Midcontinental Journal of Archaeology* 18(1): 3–17.

Grimes, Barbara F. *Ethnologue: Languages of the World*. 12th ed. Dallas: Summer Institute of Linguistics.

Grumet, Robert S. 1995. *Historical Contact: Indian People and Colonists in Today's Northeastern United States in the Sixteenth Through the Eighteenth Centuries*. Norman: University of Oklahoma Press.

Guillemin, Jeanne. 1975. *Urban Renegades: The Cultural Strategies of American Indians*. New York: Columbia University Press.

Hallowell, A. Irving. 1960. "Ojibwa Ontology, Behavior, and World View." In *Culture in History: Essays in Honor of Paul Radin*, ed. Stanley Diamond, 19–52. New York: Columbia University Press.

Hammell, George R. 1987. "Mythical Realities and European Contact in the Northeast During the Sixteenth and Seventeenth Centuries." *Man in the Northeast* 33:63–87.

———. 1992. "The Iroquois and the World's Rim: Speculations on Color, Culture, and Contact." *American Indian Quarterly* 16(4): 451–69.

Hankins, Jean Fittz. 1993. *Bringing the Good News: Protestant Missionaries to the Indians of New England and New York, 1700–1775.* Bridgeport: University of Connecticut Press.

Hantman, Jeffrey L. 1990. "Between Powhatan and Quirank: Reconstructing Monacan Culture and History in the Context of Jamestown." *American Anthropologist* 92(3): 676–90.

Hanzeli, Victor. 1969. *Missionary Linguistics in New France: A Study of Seventeenth- and Eighteenth-Century Descriptions of American Indian Languages.* The Hague: Mouton.

Harp, Maureen Anna. 1996. *Indian Missions, Immigrant Migrations, and Regional Catholic Culture: Slovene Missionaries in the Upper Great Lakes, 1830–1892.* Chicago: University of Chicago Press.

Harrington, Faith. 1985. "Sea Tenure in Seventeenth-Century New Hampshire: Native Americans and Englishmen in the Sphere of Coastal Resources." *Historical New Hampshire* 40(1–2): 18–33.

Hauptman, Laurence M. 1986. *The Iroquois Struggle for Survival: World War II to Red Power.* Syracuse, N.Y.: Syracuse University Press.

Hauptman, Laurence M. and L. Gordon McLester III, eds. 1999. *The Oneida Indian Journey: From New York to Wisconsin, 1784–1860.* Madison: University of Wisconsin Press.

Hauptman, Laurence M. and James D. Wherry, eds. 1990. *The Pequots in Southern New England: The Fall and Rise of an American Indian Nation.* Norman: University of Oklahoma Press.

Heidenreich, Conrad. 1978. "Huron." In *The Northeast*, ed. Bruce G. Trigger. Vol. 15 of *Handbook of North American Indians*, ed. William Sturtevant, 368–87. Washington, D.C.: Government Printing Office.

Henige, David. 1986. "Primary Source by Primary Source: On the Role of Epidemics in New World Depopulation." *Ethnohistory* 33:293–312.

Herrick, James W. and Dean R. Snow. 1995. *Iroquois Medical Botany.* 1st ed. Syracuse, N.Y.: Syracuse University Press.

Hickerson, Harold. 1970. The *Chippewa and Their Neighbors: A Study in Ethnohistory.* New York: Holt, Rinehart and Winston.

Hirsch, Adam J. 1988. "The Collision of Military Cultures in Seventeenth-Century New England." *Journal of American History* 74:1192.

Hoffman, Bernard G. 1967. "Ancient Tribes Revisited: A Summary of Indian Distribution and Movement in the Northeastern United States from 1534 to 1779. Parts I–III." *Ethnohistory* 14(1–2): 1–46.

Hoxie, Fred., ed. 1996. *Encyclopedia of North American Indians.* Boston: Houghton Mifflin.

Hutchins, Francis 1979. *Mashpee: The Story of Cape Cod's Indian Town.* West Franklin, N.H.: Amarta Press.

Ingstad, Helge M. 1969. *Westward to Vineland: The Discovery of Pre-Columbian Norse Housesites in North America.* Trans. Erik J. Friis. New York: St. Martin's.

Jacobs, Lyn Richard. 1995. "Native American Prophetic Movements of the Eighteenth and Nineteenth Centuries." *Social Science Review* [Syracuse University] 70(3–4): 243.

Jennings, Francis. 1975. *The Invasion of America: Indians, Colonialism, and the Cant of Conquest.* Chapel Hill: University of North Carolina Press for the Institute for Early American History and Culture.

———. 1978. "Susquehannock." In *The Northeast,* ed. Bruce G. Trigger. Vol. 15 of *Handbook of North American Indians,* ed. William Sturtevant, 362–67. Washington, D.C.: Government Printing Office.

———. 1984. *The Ambiguous Iroquois Empire: The Covenant Chain Confederation of Indian Tribes with English Colonies from Its Beginnings to the Lancaster Treaty of 1744.* New York: Norton.

Jennings, Francis, William Fenton, and Mary Druke, eds. 1985. *The History and Culture of Iroquois Diplomacy: An Interdisciplinary Guide to the Treaties of the Six Nations and Their League.* Syracuse, N.Y.: Syracuse University Press.

Jensen, Kathy, comp. 1996. "Oneida Boarding Schools: An Oral History." *Voyageur: Northeast Wisconsin's Historical Review* 12(2): 34–40.

Josselyn, John. 1988. *John Josselyn, Colonial Traveler: A Critical Edition of Two Voyages to New England.* Ed. Paul J. Lindholdt. Hanover, N.H.: University Press of New England.

Kaplan, Susan. 1985. "European Goods and Socio-Economic Change in Early Labrador Inuit Society." In *Cultures in Contact: The European Impact on Native Cultural Institutions in Eastern North America A.D. 1000–1800,* ed. William W. Fitzhugh, 362–67. Washington, D.C.: Smithsonian Institution Press.

Keesing, Felix M. 1939. *The Menomini Indians of Wisconsin.* (Vol. 10 of Memoirs of the American Philosophical Society.) Philadelphia: American Philosophical Society.

Kelly, Marc A., Paul S. Sledzik, and Sean P. Murphey. 1987. "Health, Demographics, and Physical Constitution in Seventeenth-Century Rhode Island Indians." *Man in the Northeast* 34:1–25.

Kidwell, Clara Sue. 1992. "Indian Women as Cultural Mediators." *Ethnohistory* 39(2): 97–107

Knowles, Nathaniel. 1940. "The Torture of Captives by the Indians of Eastern North America." *Proceedings of the American Philosophical Society* 82:151–225.

Koehler, Lyle. 1997. "Earth Mothers, Warriors, Horticulturists, Artists, and Chiefs: Women Among the Mississippian and Mississippian-Oneota Peoples, A.D. 1000 to 1750." In *Women in Prehistory: North America and Mesoamerica,* eds. Cheryl

Claassen and Rosemary A. Joyce, 211–26. Philadelphia: University of Pennsylvania Press.

Krech, Shepard, III, ed. 1981. *Indians, Animals, and the Fur Trade: A Critique of Keepers of the Game*. Athens: University of Georgia Press.

———. 1999. *Ecological Indian*. New York: Norton.

Kupperman, Karen. 1979. "'Nature's Rude Garden': English and Indians as Producers and Consumers of Food in Early New England." *Comparative Civilizations Review* 1:64–78.

———. 1980. *Settling With the Indians: The Meeting of English and Indian Cultures in America, 1580–1640*. Totowa, N.J.: Rowman and Littlefield.

———. 2000. *Indians and English: Facing Off in Early America*. Ithaca, N.Y.: Cornell University Press.

Landsman, Gail H. 1988. *Sovereignty and Symbol: Indian-White Conflict at Ganienkeh*. Albuquerque: University of New Mexico Press.

Lapomarda, Vincent A. 1990. "The Jesuit Missions of Colonial New England." *Essex Institute Historical Collections* 126(2): 91–109.

Leach, Douglas. [1958] 1992. *Flintlock and Tomahawk: New England in King Philip's War*. New York: Macmillan. Reprint, East Orleans, Mass.: Parnassus Imprints.

Leacock, Eleanor B. 1954. "The Montagnais 'Hunting Territory' and the Fur Trade." *Memoirs of the American Anthropological Association* 78.

———. 1978. "Women's Status in Egalitarian Society: Implications for Social Evolution." *Current Anthropology* 19:247–55, 268–75.

Leavitt, Robert M. and David A. Francis. 1984. *Kolusuwakonol: Peskotomuhkati-Wolastoqewi naka Ikolisomani Latuwewakon; Philip S. Lesourd's English and Passamaquoddy-Maliseet Dictionary*, ed. and rev. Robert M. Leavitt and David A. Francis. Fredericton, N.B.: Micmac-Maliseet Institute, University of New Brunswick.

LePore, Jill. 1998. *The Name of War: King Philip's War and the Origins of American Identity*. New York: Knopf.

Lewis, C. M. and J. J. Loomie. 1953. *The Spanish Jesuit Mission in Virginia, 1570–1572*. Chapel Hill: University of North Carolina Press for the Virginia Historical Society.

Lomawaima, K. Tsianina. 1994. *They Called It Prairie Light: The Story of Chilocco Indian School*. Lincoln: University of Nebraska Press.

Lurie, Nancy O. 1978. "Winnebago." In *The Northeast*, ed. Bruce G. Trigger. Vol. 15 of *Handbook of North American Indians*, ed. William Sturtevant, 690–707. Washington, D.C.: Government Printing Office.

MacLeod, D. Peter. 1992. "The Anishinabeg Point of View: The History of the Great Lakes Region to 1800 in Nineteenth-Century Mississauga, Odawa and Ojibwa Historiography." *Canadian Historical Review* 73(2): 194–210.

Malone, Patrick M. 1993. *The Skulking Way of War: Technology and Tactics Among the New England Indians.* Baltimore: Johns Hopkins University Press.

Mandell, Daniel R. 1996. *Behind the Frontier.* Lincoln: University of Nebraska Press.

———. 1998. "Shifting Boundaries of Race and Ethnicity: Indian-Black Intermarriage in Southern New England, 1760–1880." *Journal of American History* 1998 85(2): 466–501.

Martin, Calvin. 1978. *Keepers of the Game: Indian-Animal Relationships and the Fur Trade.* Berkeley: University of California Press.

McBride, Bunny and Harold Prins. 1996. "Walking the Medicine Line: Molly Ockett, A Pigwaket Doctor." In *Northeastern Indian Lives, 1632–1816,* ed. Robert Grumet, 321–48. Amherst: University of Massachusetts Press.

McBride, Kevin A. 1991. "'Ancient and Crazie:' Pequot Lifeways During the Historic Period." *Annual Proceedings (Dublin Seminar for New England Folklife)* 16:63–75.

———. 1993. "Dutch Exploration and Trade in Eastern Long Island Sound and the Connecticut River Valley." Paper presented at the annual meeting of the Northeastern Anthropological Association, Danbury, Conn., 27 March 1993.

McConnell, Michael Norman. 1992. *A Country Between: The Upper Ohio Valley and Its Peoples, 1724–1774.* Lincoln: University of Nebraska Press, xiv, 346.

McGee, Harold Franklin. 1974. "Ethnic Boundaries and Strategies of Ethnic Interaction: A History of Micmac-White Relations in Nova Scotia." Ph.D. diss., Southern Illinois University.

McGhee, Robert. 1984. "Contact Between Native North Americans and the Medieval Norse." *American Antiquity* 49(1): 4–26.

McMullen, Ann. 1991. "Native Basketry, Basketry Styles, and Changing Group Identity in Southern New England." *Annual Proceedings (Dublin Seminar for New England Folklife)* 16:76–88.

———. 1994. "What's Wrong with This Picture: Context, Conversion, Survival, and the Development of Regional Native Cultures and Pan-Indianism in Southeastern New England." In *Enduring Traditions: The Native Peoples of New England,* ed. Laurie Weinstein, 123–50. Westport, Conn.: Bergin and Garvey.

———. 1996. "Soapbox Discourse: Tribal Historiography, Indian-White Relations, and Southeastern New England Powwows." *Public Historian* 18(4): 53–74.

Milner, George R., Eve Anderson, and Virginia G. Smith. 1991. "Warfare in Late Prehistoric West-Central Illinois." *American Antiquity* 56(4): 581–603.

Mintz, Max M. 1999. *Seeds of Empire: The Revolutionary Conquest of the Iroquois.* New York: New York University Press.

Mithun, Marianne and Wallace Chafe. 1987. "Recapturing the Mohawk Language." In *Languages and Their Status,* ed. Timothy Shopen, 3–34. Philadelphia: University of Pennsylvania Press.

Mohegan Tribe of Connecticut. 1994. "Final Decision." Washington, D.C.: Bureau of Indian Affairs, Branch of Acknowledgment and Recognition.

Mooney, James. 1928. "The Aboriginal Population of America North of Mexico." *Smithsonian Miscellaneous Collections* 80(7): 1–40.

Morrison, Kenneth M. 1976. "The People of the Dawn: The Abenaki and Their Relations with New England and New France 1600–1727." Ph.D. diss., University of Maine.

Morissonneau, Christian. 1978. "Huron of Lorette." In *The Northeast*, ed. Bruce G. Trigger. Vol. 15 of *Handbook of North American Indians*, ed. William Sturtevant, 389–93. Washington, D.C.: Government Printing Office.

Morton, Thomas. 1838. *New English Canaan*. Reprinted in vol. 2 of *Tracts and Other Papers, Relating Principally to the Origin, Settlement, and Progress of the Colonies of North America, from the Discovery of the Country to the Year 1776* (1836–1846), ed. Peter Force. New York: P. Force.

Nassaney, Michael S. 1989. "An Epistemological Enquiry Into Some Archaeological and Historical Interpretations of Seventeenth-Century Native American–European Relations." In *Archaeological Approaches to Cultural Identity*, ed. S. J. Shennan, 76–93. London: Unwin-Hyman.

Nielsen, Donald M. 1985. "The Mashpee Indian Revolt of 1833." *New England Quarterly* 58:400–20.

O'Brien, Jean M. 1997. *Dispossession by Degrees: Indian Land and Identity in Natick, Massachusetts, 1650–1790*. Cambridge: Cambridge University Press

Parfit, Michael. 2000. "Hunt for the First Americans." *National Geographic* (Dec. 2000):40–67.

Parkman, Francis. 1865–1892. *France and England in North America: A Series of Historical Narratives*. 9 vols. Boston: Little, Brown.

Parmenter, Jon William. 1997. "Pontiac's War: Forging New Links in the Anglo-Iroquois Chain 1758–1766." *Ethnohistory* 44(4): 617–54.

Peregrine, Peter. 1996. *Archaeology of the Mississippian Culture: A Research Guide*. New York: Garland.

Pflug, Melissa Ann. 1990. "Contemporary Revitalization Movements Among the Northern Great Lakes Ottawa (Odawa) Indians: Motives and Accomplishments." Ph.D. diss., Wayne State University Press.

Pilling, James Constantine. 1888. *Bibliography of the Iroquoian Languages*. Smithsonian Institution, Bureau of [American] Ethnology (Bulletin no. 6). Washington, D.C.: Government Printing Office.

———. 1891. *Bibliography of the Algonquian Languages*. Smithsonian Institution, Bureau of [American] Ethnology (Bulletin no. 13). Washington, D.C.: Government Printing Office.

Porter, Frank, III, ed. 1987. *Strategies for Survival: American Indians in the Eastern United States*. New York: Greenwood Press.

Potter, Stephen Robert. 1993. *Commoners, Tribute, and Chiefs: The Development of Algonquian Culture in the Potomac Valley*. Charlottesville: University Press of Virginia.

Pring, Martin. 1603. *A Voyage Set Out From the Citie of Bristoll with a Small Ship and a Barke for the Discoverie of the North Part of Virginia*. Reprinted in *Early English and French Voyages, Chiefly from Hakluyt, 1534–1608* (1906), ed. Henry S. Burrage, 34–352. New York: Scribner's.

Prins, Harald E. 1990. "New England's Algonquian Cultures." *American Indian Quarterly* (1990) 14(3): 289–91.

Quimby, George. 1960. *Indian Life in the Upper Great Lakes, 11,000 B.C. to A.D. 1800*. Chicago: University of Chicago Press.

Radin, Paul. 1923. *The Winnebago Tribe*. In *Annual Report of the Bureau of American Ethnology* 37. Washington, D.C.: Government Printing Office.

Ranlet, Philip. 1988. "Another Look at the Causes of King Philip's War." *New England Quarterly* 61.

Reddy, Marlita A. 1995. *Statistical Record of Native North Americans*. 2nd ed. Detroit: Gale, lv.

Reid, John G. 1990. "Mission to the Micmac." *Beaver* [Canada] 70(5): 15–22.

Reynolds, Barrie. 1978. "Beothuk." In *The Northeast*, ed. Bruce G. Trigger. Vol. 15 of *Handbook of North American Indians*, ed. William Sturtevant, 101–108. Washington, D.C.: Government Printing Office.

Richards, Patricia B. 1993. "Winnebago Subsistence: Change and Continuity." *Wisconsin Archeologist* 74(1–4): 272–89.

Richter, Daniel K. 1983. "War and Culture: The Iroquois Experience." *William and Mary Quarterly* 40:530–34.

———. 1992a. *Ordeal of the Longhouse: The Peoples of the Iroquois League in the Era of European Colonization*. Chapel Hill: University of North Carolina Press for the Institute of Early American History and Culture, Williamsburg, Va.

———. 1992b. "'Some of Them . . . Would Always Have a Minister With Them:' Mohawk Protestantism, 1683–1719." *American Indian Quarterly* 16(4): 471–84.

Ritzenthaler, Robert E. 1978. "Southwestern Chippewa." In *The Northeast*, ed. Bruce G. Trigger. Vol. 15 of *Handbook of North American Indians*, ed. William Sturtevant. Washington, D.C.: Government Printing Office.

Robinson, Paul, Marc Kelley, and Patricia Rubertone. 1985. "Preliminary Biocultural Interpretations from a Seventeenth-Century Narragansett Indian Cemetery in Rhode Island." In *Cultures in Contact: The European Impact on Native Cultural Institutions in Eastern North America A.D. 1000–1800*, ed. William W. Fitzhugh, 107–30. Washington, D.C.: Smithsonian Institution Press.

Rogers, E. S. 1978. "Southeastern Ojibwa." In *The Northeast*, ed. Bruce G. Trigger. Vol. 15 of *Handbook of North American Indians*, ed. William Sturtevant, 760–71. Washington, D.C.: Government Printing Office.

————. 1994. "The Algonquian Farmers of Southern Ontario, 1830–1945." In *Aboriginal Ontario: Historical Perspectives on the First Nations*, eds. Edward S. Rogers and Donald B. Smith, 122–66. Toronto: Dundurn Press.

Rosaldo, Michelle. 1974. "Women, Culture, and Society: A Theoretical Overview." In *Women, Culture, and Society*, eds. Michelle Z. Rosaldo and Louise Lamphere, 17–42. Stanford: Stanford University Press.

Rountree, Helen C. 1989. *The Powhatan Indians of Virginia: Their Traditional Culture*. Norman: University of Oklahoma Press.

————. 1990. *Pocahontas's People: The Powhatan Indians of Virginia Through Four Centuries*. Norman: University of Oklahoma Press.

————. 1992. "Indian Virginians on the Move." In *Indians of the Southeastern United States in the Late Twentieth Century*, ed. Anthony Paredes, 9–28. Tuscaloosa: University of Alabama Press.

Sahlins, Marshall. 1985. *Islands of History*. Chicago: University of Chicago Press.

Salisbury, Neal. 1974. "Red Puritans: The Praying Indians of Massachusetts Bay and John Eliot." *William and Mary Quarterly*, 3d ser., 31(1): 27–54.

————. 1982. *Manitou and Providence: Indians, Europeans, and the Making of New England, 1500–1643*. New York: Oxford University Press.

————. 1987. "Toward the Covenant Chain: Iroquois and Southern New England Algonquians 1637–1684." In *Beyond the Covenant Chain: The Iroquois and Their Neighbors in Indian North America, 1600–1800*, eds. Daniel K. Richter and James M. Merrell. Syracuse, N.Y.: Syracuse University Press.

Salwen, Bert. 1975. "Indians of Southern New England and Long Island: Early Period." In *The Northeast*, ed. Bruce G. Trigger. Vol. 15 of *Handbook of North American Indians*, ed. William Sturtevant, 160–76. Washington, D.C.: Government Printing Office.

Sauer, Carl O. 1971. *Sixteenth-Century North America: The Land and the People as Seen by the Europeans*. Berkeley: University of California Press.

Schoolcraft, H. R. 1851–1857. *Historical and Statistical Information Respecting the History, Condition and Prospects of the Indian Tribes of the United States*. Philadelphia: Lippincott, Grambo.

Seaver, James E. [1824] 1992. *A Narrative of the Life of Mrs. Mary Jemison*. Canandaigua, N.Y.: Bemis. Reprint, Norman: University of Oklahoma Press.

Shattuck, George C. 1991. *The Oneida Land Claims: A Legal History*. Syracuse, N.Y.: Syracuse University Press.

Shimony, Annemarie. 1994. *Conservatism Among the Iroquois at the Six Nations Reserve*. Syracuse, N.Y.: Syracuse University Press.

Shoemaker, Nancy. 1991. "The Rise or Fall of Iroquois Women." *Journal of Women's History* 1991 2(3): 39–57.

Shoemaker, Nancy, ed. 1995. *Negotiators of Change: Historical Perspectives on Native American Women*. New York: Routledge.

Simmons, William S. 1976. "Southern New England Shamanism: An Ethnographic

Reconstruction." In *Papers of the Seventh Algonquian Conference*, ed. William Cowan, 217–56. Ottawa: Carleton University.

———. 1978. "Narragansett." In *The Northeast*, ed. Bruce G. Trigger. Vol. 15 of *Handbook of North American Indians*, ed. William Sturtevant, 190–97. Washington, D.C.: Government Printing Office.

———. 1986. *The Spirit of the New England Tribes*. Hanover, N.H.: University Press of New England.

Simmons, William S. and George F. Aubin. 1975. "Narragansett Kinship." *Man in the Northeast* 9:21–31.

Sims, Catherine A. 1992. *Algonkian-British Relations in the Upper Great Lakes Region: Gathering to Give and to Receive Presents, 1815–1843*. London, Ontario: University of Western Ontario.

Sleeper-Smith, Susan. 1994. *Silent Tongues, Black Robes: Potawatomi, Europeans, and Settlers in the Southern Great Lakes, 1640–1850*. Lansing: University of Michigan Press.

Slotkin, Richard. 1973. *Regeneration Through Violence: The Mythology of the American Frontier, 1600–1800*. Middletown, Conn.: Wesleyan University Press.

Smith, John. 1986. *The Complete Works of Captain John Smith (1580–1631)*. Ed. Philip L. Barbour. Chapel Hill: University of North Carolina Press for the Institute of Early American History and Culture, Williamsburg, Va.

Snow, Dean R. 1978. &ldquoEastern Abenaki." In *The Northeast*, ed. Bruce G. Trigger. Vol. 15 of *Handbook of North American Indians*, ed. William Sturtevant, 137–47. Washington, D.C.: Government Printing Office.

———. 1980. *The Archaeology of New England*. New York: Academic Press.

Snow, Dean R. and Kim M. Lanphear. 1988. "European Contact and Indian Depopulation in the Northeast: The Timing of the First Epidemics." *Ethnohistory* 35(1): 15–33.

Speck, Frank. 1928. *Native Tribes and Dialects of Connecticut, a Mohegan-Pequot Diary*. In *Annual Report of the Bureau of American Ethnology* 43 (1925–1926). Washington, D.C.: U.S. Government Printing Office.

———. 1940. *Penobscot Man: The Life History of a Forest Tribe in Maine*. Philadelphia: University of Pennsylvania Press.

Speck, Frank G. and Alexander General. 1995. *Midwinter Rites of the Cayuga Longhouse*. Lincoln: University of Nebraska Press, xvi, 192.

Spindler, Louise S. 1978. "Menominee." In *The Northeast*, ed. Bruce G. Trigger. Vol. 15 of *Handbook of North American Indians*, ed. William Sturtevant, 708–24. Washington, D.C.: Government Printing Office.

Stanley, George F. G. 1991. "The Indians in the War of 1812." In *Sweet Promises: A Reader on Indian-White Relations in Canada*, ed. J. R. Miller, 105–24. Toronto: University of Toronto Press.

Starna, William A. 1992. "The Biological Encounter: Disease and the Ideological Domain." *The American Indian Quarterly* 16(4): 511–19.

Stewart-Smith, David. 1998. "The Pennacook Indians and the New England Frontier, Circa 1604–1733." Ph.D. diss., Union Institute, School of Interdisciplinary
Arts and Sciences (Cincinnati).

Strong, John. 1989. "Shinnecock and Montauk Whalemen." *Long Island Historical
Journal* 2(1): 29–40.

———. *"We are still here!": The Algonquian Peoples of Long Island Today.* Interlaken,
N.Y.: Empire State Books, 108.

Szasz, Margaret Connell. 1988. *Indian Education in the American Colonies, 1607–
1783.* Albuquerque: University of New Mexico Press.

———. 1994. *Between Indian and White Worlds: The Cultural Broker.* Norman:
University of Oklahoma Press.

Tanner, Helen Hornbeck, ed. 1987. *Atlas of Great Lakes Indian History.* Norman:
University of Oklahoma Press.

Thomas, G. E. 1975. "Puritans, Indians, and the Concept of Race." *New England
Quarterly* 48(1): 3–27.

Thomas, Peter. 1976. "Contrastive Subsistence Strategies and Land Use as Factors
for Understanding Indian-White Relations in New England." *Ethnohistory*
23(1): 1–18.

———. 1985. "Cultural Change on the Southern New England Frontier, 1630–
1665." In *Cultures in Contact: The European Impact on Native Cultural Institutions in Eastern North America A.D. 1000–1800,* ed. William W. Fitzhugh,
131–62. Washington, D.C.: Smithsonian Institution Press.

Thwaites, Reuben G., ed. [1616] 1959. *The Jesuit Relations and Allied Documents:
Travel and Explorations of the Jesuit Missionaries in New France, 1610–1791:
The Original French, Latin, and Italian Texts, with English Translations and
Notes.* 73 vols. Cleveland: Burrows Brothers, 1896. Reprint, New York: Pageant,
1959.

Tooker, Elisabeth. 1970. *The Iroquois Ceremonial of Midwinter.* Syracuse, N.Y.: Syracuse University Press.

———. 1978a. *The Indians of the Northeast: A Critical Bibliography.* Newberry
Library. Bloomington: Indiana University Press.

———. 1978b. "The League of the Iroquois: Its History, Politics, and Ritual." In
The Northeast, ed. Bruce G. Trigger. Vol. 15 of *Handbook of North American
Indians,* ed. William Sturtevant, 418–41. Washington, D.C.: Government
Printing Office.

———. 1979. *Native North American Spirituality of the Eastern Woodlands.* New
York: Paulist Press.

———. 1991. *An Ethnography of the Huron Indians, 1615–1649.* Syracuse, N.Y.:
Syracuse University Press, xiv, 183.

Trelease, Allen W. [1960] 1997. *Indian Affairs in Colonial New York: The Seventeenth
Century.* Bison book ed. Lincoln: University of Nebraska Press.

Trigger, Bruce G. 1976. *Children of Aataentsic: A History of the Huron People to 1660*. 2 vols. Montreal: McGill-Queen's University Press.

———. 1978a. Introduction to *The Northeast*, ed. Bruce G. Trigger. Vol. 15 of *Handbook of North American Indians*, ed. William Sturtevant, 1–3. Washington, D.C.: Government Printing Office.

———. 1978b. "Cultural Unity and Diversity." In *The Northeast*, ed. Bruce G. Trigger. Vol. 15 of *Handbook of North American Indians*, ed. William Sturtevant, 798–804. Washington, D.C.: Government Printing Office.

———. 1978c. "Early Iroquoian Contacts with Europeans." In *The Northeast*, ed. Bruce G. Trigger. Vol. 15 of *Handbook of North American Indians*, ed. William Sturtevant, 344–56. Washington, D.C.: Government Printing Office.

———. 1985. *Natives and Newcomers: Canada's "Heroic Age" Reconsidered*. Montreal: McGill-Queen's University Press.

———. 1991. "The Jesuits and the Fur Trade." In *Sweet Promises: A Reader on Indian-White Relations in Canada*, ed. J. R. Miller, 3–18. Toronto: University of Toronto Press.

Trigger, Bruce G. and Gordon M. Day. 1994. "Southern Algonquian Middlemen: Algonquin, Nipissing, and Ottawa, 1550–1780." In *Aboriginal Ontario: Historical Perspectives on the First Nations*, eds. Edward S. Rogers and Donald B. Smith, 64–77. Toronto: Dundurn Press.

Trigger, Bruce G. and James F. Pendergast. 1978. "St. Lawrence Iroquoians." In *The Northeast*, ed. Bruce G. Trigger. Vol. 15 of *Handbook of North American Indians*, ed. William Sturtevant, 357–61. Washington, D.C.: Government Printing Office.

Tuck, James A. 1978. "Regional Cultural Development, 3000 B.C. to 300 B.C." In *The Northeast*, ed. Bruce G. Trigger. Vol. 15 of *Handbook of North American Indians*, ed. William Sturtevant, 28–43. Washington, D.C.: Government Printing Office.

U.S. Senate. 1992. Select Committee on Indian Affairs. *Assisting Native Americans in Assuring the Survival and Continuing Vitality of Their Languages: Report (to Accompany S. 2044)*. Washington, D.C.: Government Printing Office, 12.

———. 1994. Select Committee on Indian Affairs. *Pokagon Band of Potawatomi Indians Act and the Little Traverse Bay Bands of Odawa Indians and the Little River Band of Ottawa Indians Act: Hearing Before the Committee on Indian Affairs, United States Senate, One Hundred Third Congress, Second Session, on S. 1066, to Restore Federal Services to the Pokagon Band of Potawatomi Indians and S. 1357, to Reaffirm and Clarify the Federal Relationships of the Little Traverse Bay Bands of Odawa Indians and the Little River Band of Ottawa Indians as Distinct Federally Recognized Indian Tribes, February 10, 1994*. Washington, D.C.: Government Printing Office.

———. 1995. Select Committee on Indian Affairs. *Federal Recognition Administra-*

tive Procedures Act: Hearing Before the Committee on Indian Affairs, United States Senate, One Hundred Fourth Congress, First Session, on S. 479, to Provide for Administrative Procedures to Extend Federal Recognition to Certain Indian Groups, July 13, 1995. Washington, D.C.: Government Printing Office.

Van Lonkhuyzen, Harold W. 1990. "A Reappraisal of the Praying Indians: Acculturation, Conversion, and Identity at Natick, Massachusetts 1646–1730." *New England Quarterly* (1990) 63(3): 396–428.

Vaughan, Alden T. 1965. *New England Frontier: Puritans and Indians 1620–1675.* Rev. ed. New York: Norton, 1979.

Waldman, Carl and Molly Braun. 2000. *Atlas of the North American Indian.* Rev. ed. New York: Checkmark Books.

Wallace, Anthony. 1958. "Dreams and Wishes of the Soul: A Type of Psychoanalytic Theory Among the Seventeenth-Century Iroquois." *American Anthropologist* 60(2): 234–48.

———. 1969. *The Death and Rebirth of the Seneca.* New York: Knopf.

———. 1978. "Origins of the Longhouse Religion." In *The Northeast,* ed. Bruce G. Trigger. Vol. 15 of *Handbook of North American Indians,* ed. William Sturtevant, 442–48. Washington, D.C.: Government Printing Office.

Walsh, Martin W. 1992. "The 'Heathen Party': Methodist Observation of the Ohio Wyandot." *American Indian Quarterly* (1992) 16(2): 189–211.

Washburn, Wilcomb. 1978. "Colonial Indian Wars." In *The Northeast,* ed. Bruce G. Trigger. Vol. 15 of *Handbook of North American Indians,* ed. William Sturtevant, 89–100. Washington, D.C.: Government Printing Office.

Weinstein, Laurie. 1986. "We're Still Living on Our Traditional Homeland: The Wampanoag Legacy in New England." In *Strategies for Survival: American Indians in the Eastern United States,* ed. Frank W. Porter III. Westport, Conn.: Greenwood Press.

Weinstein, Laurie, ed. 1994. *Enduring Traditions: The Native Peoples of New England.* Westport, Conn.: Bergin and Garvey.

West, Richard. 1996. "Gaming." In *Encyclopedia of North American Indians,* ed. Frederick E. Hoxie. Boston: Houghton Mifflin.

White, Marion, 1978a. "Erie." In *The Northeast,* ed. Bruce G. Trigger. Vol. 15 of *Handbook of North American Indians,* ed. William Sturtevant, 412–17. Washington, D.C.: Government Printing Office.

———. 1978b. "Neutral and Wenro." In *The Northeast,* ed. Bruce G. Trigger. Vol. 15 of *Handbook of North American Indians,* ed. William Sturtevant, 407–11. Washington, D.C.: Government Printing Office.

White, Richard. 1991. *The Middle Ground: Indians, Empires and Republics in the Great Lakes Region, 1650–1815.* Cambridge: Cambridge University Press.

Williams, Roger. [1643] 1936. *A Key Into the Language of America.* 5th ed. Providence: The Rhode Island and Providence Plantations Tercentenary Committee.

Willig, Timothy D. 1996. "Prophetstown on the Wabash: The Native Spiritual Defense of the Old Northwest." *Michigan Historical Review* 23(2): 115–58.

Witthoft, John. 1949. "Green Corn Ceremonialism in the Eastern Woodlands." *Occasional Contributions from the Museum of Anthropology of the University of Michigan* 13.

Wolf, Eric R. 1982. *Europe and the People Without History*. Berkeley: University of California Press.

Wood, William. [1634] 1997. *New England's Prospect*. Ed. Alden Baughan. Amherst: University of Massachusetts Press.

Part II

People, Places, and Events in
Northeast Native History

Abenaki, Eastern ("People of the Dawnland" or "Easterners")
Originally claiming the territories extending between the Saco and Penobscot rivers, the numerous Eastern Abenaki were a foraging people who participated actively in the colonial fur trade and the French-English rivalry
that ensued in that region. Throughout the colonial era, European epidemics ravaged the numerous Abenaki. Although the Abenaki resisted any alliance with either the English or the French, they maintained a better relationship with the French, partly because of the greater land encroachment
perpetrated by English settlers. As the colonial wars intensified in North
America, the Abenaki were increasingly drawn into the conflict as French
allies, and they participated in raids into New York, New Hampshire, and
Maine. The most famous Abenaki raid was on Deerfield, Massachusetts in
1704. But the cumulative toll of warfare and disease dislocated many Abenaki and forced them into Canada. By 1805 the British government set aside
land to accommodate the influx. During World War II, many Abenaki men
served as soldiers, and it was largely their experiences and disappointments
upon returning that fueled Abenaki efforts in the 1950s and 1960s to seek
treaty rights promised them. Currently the main body of Eastern Abenaki
people live on the reservation at Old Town, near Orono, Maine.

Abenaki, Western
Those Abenaki people who occupied territories west of the Saco River and
north of the related Pennacook and Pawtucket of north central New England. Similar to their Eastern Abenaki cousins in technology and world-

view, the Western Abenaki were in early contact with French missionaries, but disappeared from view early in the eighteenth century as they migrated north and west.

Akwesasne
Uniquely situated on the border between Canada and the United States, the Mohawk town of Akwesasne is also known as the St. Regis Reservation. Akwesasne was founded in 1755 near a Jesuit mission site, at a confluence of the Salmon, Grass, St. Regis, Raquette, and St. Lawrence rivers. Politically sophisticated leaders at Akewesasne have successfully defended their community's rights, particularly during the construction of the St. Lawrence Seaway, which polluted the rivers nearby and caused major health problems in that community. Forced by circumstances into activist politics, the community also supports the publication of *Akwesasne Notes*, which has kept Indians informed of issues of pan-Indian concern.

American Fur Company
The company was chartered in 1808 by John Jacob Astor to challenge rival fur companies in Canada. The company gained a virtual monopoly in the Great Lakes fur trade. As the frontier expanded west, the American Fur Company extended its operations into the Missouri Valley and Rocky Mountains.

American Indian Defense Association (AIDA)
In 1923 this organization was formed, composed of people advocating Indian rights. One of its original members, John **Collier**, later became Commissioner of Indian Affairs under Franklin Roosevelt. In later years, AIDA merged with the National Association of Indian Affairs to form the Association of American Indian Affairs, still operating today.

American Indian Freedom of Religion Act (1978)
This act declared that Indian religious freedom was provided by the First Amendment of the United States Constitution.

American Indian Movement (AIM)
Founded in 1968 by Dennis Banks, Eddie Benton Banai, Clyde Bellecourt, and George Mitchell, and later often represented by Russell Means, AIM sought to protect the rights of urban Indians. Since its inception, AIM has supported many American Indian causes, many of them controversial. AIM

members participated in the occupation of Alcatraz Island (1969–71), a take-over of BIA headquarters in Washington, D.C. (1972), and the 1973 occu-pation at Wounded Knee, South Dakota.

Apess, William (1798–1839)

Pequot scholar and author who wrote several important Indian histories of New England. By exploring Anglo-Indian relationships, Apess became one of the first American historians to present the perspective of American In-dians, particularly the Pequot. His most famous work is *A Son of the Forest: The Experience of William Apess: A Native of the Forest* (1829).

Arnold, Benedict (1741–1801)

Arnold was the infamous hero-turned-traitor of the American Revolution whose betrayal so personally wounded General Washington. In 1775, with the outbreak of hostilities, Arnold captured Fort Ticonderoga and from there launched a daring winter campaign to capture Montreal and Quebec from the British. While the campaign only narrowly failed, Arnold's Herculean efforts were made possible only because of the participation of Abenaki war-riors. These warriors contributed to the campaign by leading the force through the blizzards and harsh terrain of upper New England and Quebec.

Atwater, Caleb (b. 1778)

A talented and versatile man, Atwater had many and varied occupations throughout his life: Presbyterian minister, state legislator, education re-former, newspaperman, law student, businessman, author, and railway/canal advocate. Atwater moved to Ohio after declaring bankruptcy, and he became fascinated with the prehistoric mounds. He wrote several works on the mound builders, including *Descriptions of the Antiquities Discovered in the State of Ohio and Other Western States* (1829). That same year President Jackson appointed Atwater one of three commissioners to conduct the treaty negotiations at Prairie du Chien in Wisconsin. Afterward, Atwater became increasingly interested in Indian affairs and advocated labor and vocational training in schools to solve the "Indian problem."

Aubery, Joseph (1673–1755)

French Jesuit who worked at the St. Francis mission from 1709 through 1755. Author of two important Abenaki-French dictionaries, Aubery also provided important ethnographic information about the peoples of the up-

per Connecticut River and the New England interior in the early eighteenth
century.

Aupaumut, Hendrick (d. 1830)

A Mahican who served as the chief sachem of the Stockbridge Indians,
Aupaumut began urging his fellow Mahican to continue to emigrate west,
away from the negative influences of the Oneida and frontier whites. Aupaumut scouted west into territories already settled by the displaced Delaware and Munsee. He also served as an emissary between **Tecumseh** and
the federal government. After the war of 1812, Aupaumut finally succeeded
in sending a New Stockbridge contingent west under the leadership of John
Metoxen, who, after further travels, settled in Wisconsin in 1828 along with
another Mahican band under the leadership of John **Quinney**. The remaining Stockbridge arrived in Wisconsin in 1828, two years before Aupaumut's death.

Bacon, Nathaniel (1646–76)

After leaving England to avoid charges of fraud, Bacon purchased a plantation above Jamestown, Virginia. With neighboring planters he participated
in trading ventures with Indians. But, like many frontier residents, Bacon
was alarmed by a Susquehannock raid on the Virginia frontier and exasper-
ated by the response of Governor **Berkeley**. The discontent spilled over into
an armed insurrection known as **Bacon's Rebellion**, in which Bacon declared himself "General by Consent of the People." After attacking friendly
Pamunkey and Occaneechee Indians, his soldiers defeated loyalist forces
and burned Jamestown. Although the governor fled to the eastern shore, the
uprising collapsed when Bacon died of dysentery.

Bacon's Rebellion (1675–76)

Indian policy in the colony of Virginia was increasingly divided as the Crown
(represented by the colonial governor, William **Berkeley**) attempted to con-
ciliate local Indian communities, while settlers demanded access to Indian
lands and freedom to protect themselves from perceived threats. Local hostilities turned serious when Virginia militiamen mistakenly murdered a
group of noncombatant Susquehannock and then, when the Susquehannock agreed to a parley, murdered their representative chiefs. In retaliation,
the Susquehannock began a series of raids on outlying English settlements.
Fearing that the local dispute might erupt into a widespread Indian war,
Berkeley sought a reconciliation but was thwarted by the actions of Na-

thaniel **Bacon**, who organized raiding parties that struck among peaceful and tributary tribes within the colony, without official sanction. Leading to civil war and the destruction of Jamestown, Bacon's Rebellion ended with the death of Nathaniel Bacon and the arrival of 1,000 troops from England, and was largely the result of unjustified hostilities against Virginia's Indian allies.

Bashebes (fl. 1605)
Leader of a confederation of Indian communities that extended from Penobscot Bay to Massachusetts in the early years of the seventeenth century. Also known as Betsabes or Bashaba, he may have been a Penobscot Abenaki. In competition with English traders and other native peoples for control of the early coastal trade, his raiders terrorized the coastal peoples of southern New England. Bashebes was likely killed by the English in retaliation for these raids (see Smith 1614, Wood 1634).

Bender, Chief (1883–1954)
Charles Albert "Chief" Bender was an Ojibwa professional baseball player, considered one of the greatest pitchers of his era. Bender played for Philadelphia from 1903 through 1914. Bender was educated at the **Carlisle Indian School** and Dickinson College. Widely admired as an upstanding sportsman and teammate, he is currently the only American Indian to have been inducted into the Baseball Hall of Fame.

Berkeley, Sir William (1606–77)
Appointed Governor of Virginia by Charles I in 1642, Berkeley lobbied for improvements in the defenses of Virginia. He coordinated extensive reorganizations and intensified militia training, which also included the exclusion of slaves and indentured servants. In 1675, the aging Berkeley underestimated dissatisfaction with his Indian policies and his refusal to retaliate for Susquehannock raids. During the ensuing **Bacon's Rebellion**, Berkeley lost control of the militia, which either remained neutral or sided with Nathaniel **Bacon**. Berkeley and his loyalists were defeated near Jamestown and withdrew to the eastern shore until Bacon's death. Berkeley then organized waterborne raids and crushed the rebellion.

Biard, Pierre (1676–1722)
French Jesuit at the mission of the failed Port Royal settlement, circa 1611–16. Biard's descriptions of the local Algonquian (especially Micmac) peo-

ples of Nova Scotia (now collected in the *Jesuit Relations*) are valuable sources of information about their cultures and about the history of French-Indian relations on the northeastern frontier.

Big House Ceremony

An important Delaware ritual that evidently evolved out of an annual fall harvest ceremony, the Big House Ceremony consisted of the recitation of puberty visions by older men, who took turns running counterclockwise around a central fire. Each participant sang songs acquired during his vision, and all participants joined in an accompanying dance as the reciter paused in his recitation. Younger men and women recited on the last evening of the twelve-night cycle. The last known ceremony was performed in 1924.

Big Tree, Treaty of (1797)

The treaty negotiations convened at Genesee, New York. The treaty stipulated that the Six Nations relinquish their claim to ancestral lands, with the exception of reservation lands.

Black Hawk (Makataimeshekiakiak, "Black Sparrow Hawk") (1767–1838)

Sauk war chief who fiercely opposed continued encroachments by American settlers. Greatly influenced while campaigning with **Tecumseh** during the War of 1812, Black Hawk unsuccessfully attempted a pan-Indian alliance. During the grueling Black Hawk War (1832–33), he and his followers, though outnumbered and poorly provisioned, evaded American troops. When his followers grew fatigued, he attempted to negotiate but was fired upon. Eventually, he surrendered and was imprisoned. After his release, he toured eastern cities and dictated his autobiography. After his death, his grave was looted and his bones displayed in tent shows and at a historical society.

Brainerd, David (1718–47)

Presbyterian missionary in Pennsylvania who, despite his chronic bad health and bouts with depression, traveled into the Wyoming and Susquehanna valleys to Christianize the Delaware and Mahican. His journal was later printed and issued as a handbook to Presbyterian missionaries in India and Africa during the nineteenth century.

Brant, Joseph (Thayendanegea, "He Places Together Two Bets") (1742?–1807)

Influential Mohawk leader who converted to Christianity as a young man and ministered to his people, translating a prayer book and the New Testament into Mohawk. During the American Revolution, his loyalist efforts and those of Sir William **Johnson** resulted in many American Indians supporting the Crown. He participated at Oriskany (1777) and in the Cherry Valley Massacre (1778). After the war he was unable to resolve Indian land claim disputes with the United States, but gained land and subsidies for the Mohawk in Canada. His death created a leadership vacuum that frustrated attempts to develop a coordinated resistance to American encroachments (fig. 12).

Brant, Molly (Degonwadanti) (1736–96)
An influential Mohawk who was the older sister of Joseph Brant and a member of Sir William **Johnson**'s household. She used her considerable influence to augment the efforts of Brant and Johnson to ensure that the Iroquois confederacy remained pro-British. She often provided Johnson and her brother with important intelligence and ran affairs in their absences. Although Brant married Johnson in a Mohawk ceremony and bore him eight children, he identified her as his housekeeper in his will.

Brothertown Indians
A community of Mohegan, Pequot, and Long Island Indians led by the native minister Samson **Occom**, who migrated west to Brothertown, New York to settle with the Oneida in 1775. Most of this community then moved west, along with the Stockbridge Indians, to Wisconsin in 1825, where their descendants remain today.

Brûlé, Étienne (d. 1633)
Among the best known of the early French *coureurs de bois*, Brûlé lived among the Huron between 1610 and 1633. He was murdered by Hurons who suspected that he was engaging in secret negotiations with the Seneca.

Bureau of Indian Affairs
Now a division of the Department of the Interior, the Bureau of Indian Affairs (BIA) is charged with administering the relationship between the many tribes and native groups of North America and the federal government. Because each tribe has a unique relationship with the federal government, determined by treaty, the administration of Indian affairs is complex and subject to misunderstanding on both sides. Indians have often accused the

Bureau of mismanagement and even fraud, while non-Indians resent the seemingly "privileged" status of Indian tribes. Since the 1978 passage of the Indian Claims Act, the BIA has been overwhelmed by the task of evaluating petitions for federal recognition submitted by hundreds of Indian communities, many from the Eastern Woodlands.

Cabot, John (Giovanni Caboto) (c. 1450–98)

A Genoan sailor and explorer in England's employ, who in 1497 made the first recorded European voyage of modern times. Searching for a water route to the East, Cabot sailed to the Grand Banks of Newfoundland, which was regularly fished by Basque, Breton, and Norman sailors. During his expedition Cabot encountered Indians of the Northeast. Cabot and his crew failed to return from their second voyage to the New World.

Carlisle Indian Industrial School

The first nonreservation Indian school in the United States, Carlisle was founded in 1879. Its first director, Richard Henry Pratt, sought to enculturate his native charges. Students were instructed in farming and industrial arts; the female students were taught domestic arts. Students were strictly forbidden to use their native languages, were required to cut their hair (if male), and to wear Western-style clothing. Most native students were unable to return home during summer vacations, and boarded instead with white families in the area. Although several thousand Indian students graduated from the school, it was closed for financial and political reasons in 1918.

Cartier, Jacques (1491–1557)

French explorer who made voyages to the New World between 1534 and 1541. His first two voyages were at the direct command of King Francis I. Cartier sailed first to Labrador and on to the Straits of Belle Isle and the Gulf of St. Lawrence. On his second voyage, Cartier landed at the future site of Quebec, then proceeded upriver to Montreal. Cartier made a third voyage in 1541, accompanied by the sieur de Roberval, and came into contact with many of the St. Lawrence Iroquoians. He exacerbated tensions by kidnapping the sons of Donnacona, the leader of Stadacona. Cartier also visited the large fortified community at **Hochelaga**, and wintered at Quebec. Cartier than kidnapped Donnacona himself, returning with him to France in the hope that Donnacona would convince Francis to finance a further expedition. Although Donnacona did not return, Cartier's third voyage resulted in the establishment of two short-lived French settlements near Quebec.

Cassasinamon, Robin (d. 1692)

The Pequot sachem immediately following the disastrous **Pequot War** (1636–37). In the aftermath of the annihilation of the Mystic River Pequot village, as well as the death and enslavement of so many Pequots, Cassasinamon drew together survivors into small settlements. Slowly the settlements increased as dispersed Pequots returned. Cassasinamon worked with the English, securing reservations and increasing autonomy, ensuring that his people would survive.

Caugnawaga

Established in 1667 by the French Jesuit Pierre Raffeix, who persuaded the Oneida Iroquois with whom he worked to establish a permanent residence at La Prairie across the St. Lawrence River from present-day Montreal. Joined by large numbers of Mohawk from New York, the community moved to its present location near St. Regis in 1755.

Cayuga ("Those of the Great Pipe")

The Cayuga, matrilineal Iroquoian speakers of New York, are one of the five tribes of the original Iroquois Confederacy. Bound by strong cultural, linguistic, and historic bonds with the Onondaga, Seneca, Mohawk, Tuscarora, and Oneida, the Cayuga occupied the smallest land of the Iroquois—between the territory of the Onondaga and Seneca. As a result of Iroquoian wars in the seventeenth century, the Cayuga were greatly depopulated. While the League of the Iroquois endeavored to maintain concerted policy, the American Revolution divided the legendary Iroquois unity. During the war, the Cayuga largely sided with the British. With British defeat, many Cayuga escaped to Canada, joined the Seneca, or relocated to Ohio. Currently, Cayuga still inhabit Canada, New York, and Oklahoma. During the 1980s the Cayuga challenged treaty violations of land rights, and received only a partial settlement.

Champlain, Samuel de (1567–1635)

The French explorer, navigator, trader, and colonial official who captained a two-year exploration of the West Indies and Mexico in 1599. He proposed a canal across Central America to link the Pacific and Atlantic oceans. Afterward, he concentrated his efforts along the St. Lawrence and the coast of eastern Canada. In 1608, Champlain founded a settlement at Quebec and spent time with the Algonquin and Huron Indians, exploring the area. His contact established vital trade alliances with these peoples but also alienated the powerful Iroquois, against whom he participated in raids. He was appointed Lieutenant General of New France, but was imprisoned when England captured Quebec. Champlain returned to his post until his death, when Canada was returned to France. He wrote an invaluable work, *Des Sauvages* (1603), which describes the customs and Indians of New France.

Chickahominy ("Crushed-Corn People")

The Chickahominy are an Algonquian-speaking people of eastern Virginia. When Jamestown was founded, the populous and warlike Chickahominy were one of the few Tidewater peoples not paying tribute to **Powhatan**. As conflict with the English settlers increased and European diseases reduced their numbers, the Chickahominy and Powhatan cooperated ever more closely in an intricate relationship of trade and mutual defense. As a result of the **Tidewater Wars** and attacks by the League of the Iroquois, the Chickahominy were increasingly fragmented and disorganized. By the early eighteenth century, the Chickahominy were so few in number that they could not protect their reservation. By 1900 Chickahominy numbers had begun to rebound and they increasingly asserted their "Indian-ness." In 1983 the state of Virginia recognized the Eastern and Western Chickahominy.

Cloud, Henry Roe (Wa-Na-Xi-Lay) (1884–1950)

Henry Roe Cloud was born on the Winnebago reservation in Nebraska, and educated at government boarding schools in Nebraska and on the Santee Indian reservation. Cloud converted to Christianity as a young man, and was later admitted to the Mount Hermon preparatory school in Northfield, Massachusetts. Cloud was admitted to Yale in 1906. While at Yale, Cloud met the Roes, missionaries to the Arapaho and Cheyenne, with whom Cloud was to become very close, adopting their name as part of his own. Cloud took up many native causes as he continued his education, receiving a B.A. from Yale in 1910 and a degree in theology from Aubern Theological Seminary in 1913, where he was also ordained a Presbyterian minister. He also received a master's degree in anthropology from Yale in 1912. Cloud later married Elizabeth Bender, a prominent Minnesota Ojibwa and sister of Charles "Chief" **Bender**. Cloud was a respected activist and Indian expert, appointed to the Meriam Commission, and a trusted advisor of Commissioner of Indian Affairs John **Collier**. Awarded many honors by Indian and non-Indian organizations, Cloud became superintendent of the Umatilla Agency near Pendleton, Oregon, and later became a member of the BIA staff in Portland, Oregon.

Code of Handsome Lake

Based on the teachings of the Seneca prophet **Handsome Lake** (1735–1815), whose visions when seriously ill became the foundation of the Iroquois. Handsome Lake's third vision included instructions from the Creator that became known as the Code of Handsome Lake and included a call to renounce alcohol, to practice witchcraft only to heal, to forswear love medicine, and to cherish the blessings of marriage, family, and children.

Cody, William F. (Buffalo Bill) (1846–1917)

A scout, soldier, Pony Express rider, and famous American entertainer, Cody was one of the most colorful figures of the Old West. After the Civil War he served as a buffalo hunter and scout during campaigns against Indians. In 1883, he staged the first of his famous Wild West Shows, in which he presented reenactments of western battles and Indian societies. He became a spokesman for and supporter of Indian rights. In 1890, as tensions mounted with the Sioux during the Ghost Dance frenzy, he was sent by General Nelson Miles to meet with Sitting Bull. Indian Agent James McLaughlin refused to allow this. Shortly thereafter Sitting Bull was killed by his guards, and the Ghost Dance was quelled at Wounded Knee.

Collier, John (1884–1968)

A former social worker who was appointed Commissioner of Indian Affairs in 1933, John Collier worked to reform the **Bureau of Indian Affairs** and make its policies more equitable and beneficial to Indian people. Collier opposed allotment of Indian lands and, supported by Roosevelt's New Deal, helped to improve conditions on Indian reservations and provide funds for Indian education. He was also instrumental in the passage of the **Indian Reorganization Act**.

Commuck, Thomas (d. 1856?)

A resident of Brothertown, Wisconsin, who published a list of words taught to him by his Narragansett grandmother (d. 1825). These words had been taught to her when she was a girl, by her mother. This contribution, along with the writings of Roger **Williams**, added considerably to the recovery of aspects of the Narragansett language, which had all but ceased to be spoken.

Condolence Ceremony

A major ceremony to commemorate or "condole" deceased hereditary chiefs of the League and to appoint their successors is still practiced among traditional Iroquois communities, especially at Onondaga and Tonawanda in the United States and at the Six Nations and Oneida communities in Canada. Included in this lengthy ceremony is a recitation of the history of the League and a roll call of the chiefs, as well as the beautiful "Requickening Address," designed to comfort the grieving. Iroquois communities are organized according to moieties, dual groupings that perform the Condolence Ceremony for the opposite moiety. Thus, the Older Brothers (Mohawk, Onondaga, and Seneca) host the Condolence Ceremony for chiefs of the Younger Brothers (Oneida, Cayuga, and Tuscarora), and vice versa.

Cornplanter (Kaiiontwa'ko, "By What One Plants") (c. 1735–1836)
The son of English and Seneca parents, Cornplanter was a Seneca statesman who aided the British by leading raids in New York and Pennsylvania during the American Revolution. After the war, he adopted a conciliatory stance toward the United States and signed the divisive Second Treaty of **Fort Stanwix** (1784), as well as numerous other treaties ceding Seneca lands. He also led his people to support the United States during the War of 1812. For his efforts in dissuading Iroquois support of Shawnee and British efforts, Cornplanter was granted land on the Allegheny River.

Dawes Severalty Act (General Allotment Act) (1887)
Passed by the United States Congress, this act authorized the allotment of 160-acre parcels to the heads of Indian families. Proponents believed that Indians would develop and farm the lands, thus becoming independent, economically motivated landowners. After the allotment of reservation lands, the excess property was available to non-Indians. Many Indians did not utilize their allotments, while others, such as the Cherokee and Choctaw, refused allotment. In 1928, after a two-year study, a report by The Brookings Institution declared the allotment system a dismal failure.

Deganawida ("Two River Currents Flowing Together") (fl. 1560–70)
According to Iroquois tradition, Deganawida was a spiritual leader, possibly a Huron or a Mohawk, who with the aid of **Hiawatha** founded the Iroquois confederacy. Deganawida and Hiawatha also established the laws, regulations, and principles that guided the confederacy. The League ended incessant warfare among the Mohawk, Oneida, Onondaga, Cayuga, and Seneca, and enabled them to pursue collectively vital policy goals.

Delaware (Lenni Lenape, "Real People")
The Delaware inhabited vast stretches of land along the middle Atlantic coast and the Delaware River, and were comprised of three large groups.

The Algonquian-speaking Delaware maintained a diffused, unstructured political framework, and are considered one of the oldest tribes, respectfully called "grandfather" by many Woodland Algonquians. Because of their coastal habitation, the Delaware had early contact with European sailors and explorers at the beginning of the sixteenth century. After the English gained control of Dutch settlements in New York, the Delaware began an unorganized migration westward, but they remained in Pennsylvania and Ohio until the early nineteenth century. Because of their long interaction with Europeans, large and scattered populations, and linguistic skills, the Delaware often functioned as diplomats, negotiators, and translators between Indians and colonists. During the 1960s the United States Supreme Court awarded the Oklahoma Delaware an award of more than $12 million from the Indian Claims Commission. Unfortunately, the dialects historically spoken by the Delaware are seldom spoken today.

Edwards, Jonathan (1703–58)
A prominent Puritan theologian best known for his influential writings. His preaching during the period 1735–37 inspired a noted revival movement. He was dismissed from his pastorate in 1750, and served for six years as a missionary to the Housatonic Indians at Stockbridge. In 1758, Edwards arrived in Princeton during an epidemic to assume the presidency of the College of New Jersey (now Princeton), but died shortly after his arrival.

Eliot, John (1604–90)
Puritan teacher and missionary who was received by the Massachusett people in 1646. Eliot established a series of **"praying towns"** to educate and teach Puritan values to Christian Indians. Eliot's missionary program brought together the Massachusett, Pokanoket (or Wampanoag), and Nipmuck into praying towns, where he became known as the "Indian Apostle." He translated and printed a Massachusett translation of the Bible—not only one of the first Indian translations but also one of the first books published in America. **King Philip's War** ended Puritan support, and most of the praying towns were abandoned.

Erie
An Iroquoian-speaking people who lived orbitally near what is now Buffalo, New York, but were dispersed in 1657 in the competitive era of the early fur trade. Historical records suggest that some Erie joined a Carolina group known as the Westo. Others merged with the Seneca, resettling the Ohio Valley in the 1740s.

False Face Society
A popular voluntary society among the Iroquois; its members wear wooden masks carved to represent beings seen in visions or in the forest. While wearing the masks, False Face Society members are thought to have enhanced physical abilities, and members visit households in the community once or twice a year to rid people and places of disease.

Feast of the Dead
The Huron ceremony described by seventeenth-century French missionaries, in which the decomposed bodies of individuals who had died in all the communities of a region were disinterred and reburied with elaborate grave goods in communal ossuaries.

Fort Stanwix, Treaties of (1768, 1784)
After the defeat of the French by British forces in 1763, the Iroquois found themselves unable to maintain a position of dominance in their diplomatic and trade relationships. The first treaty of Fort Stanwix coerced the Iroquois into the sale of all their lands west of the Alleghenies and south of the Ohio, undermining their influence over their tributaries to the west, including the Delaware and Wyandot. The Second Treaty of Fort Stanwix, at the end of the Revolutionary War, stripped the confederacy of all its territories in western Pennsylvania and Ohio and forced each tribe to negotiate a separate peace with the federal government. The outcome was the additional sale by each tribe of the majority of their remaining lands, maintaining only small reservations surrounding existing villages.

Gallatin, Albert (1761–1849)
The Swiss immigrant who became a distinguished anthropologist, linguist, diplomat, and Secretary of the Treasury to President Jefferson. Key government officials such as Lewis Cass, Lewis and Clark, and Thomas McKenny provided Gallatin with invaluable linguistic information. In 1826 he published A *Table of Indian Languages of the United States* and *Synopsis of the Indian Tribes of North America* (1836). His linguistic research suggested that Indian languages evolved from one people that were neither European nor biblical. Gallatin was a proponent of assimilation, and opposed large land payments to Indians as well as annual annuities.

General, Alexander (Shao-hyowa, "Great Sky") (1889–1965)
Alexander General was born on the Grand River Reserve in Ontario to conservative Oneida/Cayuga parents. Raised by the tenets of the **Longhouse**

religion, General and his siblings attended the annual cycle of ceremonies and assisted their parents in agricultural work. Although responsible for his younger brothers and sisters after his parents' early deaths, General studied the Longhouse religion and its voluminous oral tradition, becoming a well-respected speaker. Together with his brother, Levi General—who was elected Deskahe, one of the fifty hereditary chiefs of the Iroquois Confederacy Council—Alexander General fought for the sovereignty rights of the Iroquois, opposing the Canadian government's efforts to impose a new electoral council form of government on the reserve. Upon Levi's death in 1925, Alexander General was elected Deskahe in his turn. Traveling in 1930 to England to plead the Confederacy Council's case to the king, General used an Iroquois-issued passport. General also became active in the Indian Defense League, supporting in particular the provisions of the Jay Treaty of 1794, which allowed American Indians the right to travel freely over the Canadian border from the United States. General also took his role as interpreter of Iroquois culture seriously. He generously worked with many anthropologists, especially Frank **Speck**, and linguists, and helped produce the annual Iroquois historical pageant.

General Allotment Act: *see* **Dawes Severalty Act.**

Godfroy, Francis (Palonswa) (1788–1840)
A Miami whose father was a French trader, Godfroy occupied tribal lands in Indiana and built a successful trading post near Mount Pleasant, at the mouth of the Mississinewa River. Godfroy acted as an intermediary between the Miami and the federal government, securing favorable treaties and payments for Miami lands in treaties negotiated in the 1820s and 1830s. Although many Miami were forced to emigrate during the period of removal, Godfroy's efforts preserved a small remnant community, whose ancestors remain in Indiana today.

Green Corn Ceremonial
A first-fruits harvest festival celebrated by a number of Eastern Woodland societies, which shared a number of common features. Prominent among these was the construction of brush shelters or arbors on which grains and fruits were hung, along with other items of wealth. Special dances, prayers and foods were enjoyed during these rituals, in honor of the first harvest of corn.

Greenville, Treaty of (1795)

This crucial treaty established peace between the new United States government and a number of warring Indian groups in the Ohio region. In addition,
it ratified the cession of all lands in Ohio south and east of the Greenville
treaty line, land making up nearly two thirds of the present state. With this
and the treaty of Fort Industry (1805) and the Detroit treaty of 1807, the
Wyandot and other Ohio Indians ceded the bulk of their remaining territories
as far west as the Auglaize River. Historians also recognize this treaty as establishing the ensuing legal relationship between the federal government and
Indian tribes, a fiduciary relationship based on the reservation system.

Hampton Institute

Originally named the Hampton Normal and Agricultural Institute, it was
established in 1870 for the education of freedmen. However, Kiowa captives
were sent to the institute in 1878 in an experimental program, and Indian
students continued to attend until 1923, when the native program was dis-
continued. Hampton Institute continued to flourish, however, and became
Hampton University in 1984, retaining the name Hampton Institute for its
undergraduate division.

Handsome Lake (Sganyadai'yo) (c. 1735–1815)

The Iroquois spiritual leader and half-brother of **Cornplanter**. He developed
the **Code of Handsome Lake**, and preached family values, sharing, community, and maintenance of costumes such as those used with songs and
dances, and encouraged Seneca children to attend schools to learn the ways
of the whites. His message contained Christian components most likely
adopted from contact with Quakers.

Hendrick (Tiyanoga) (c. 1680–1755)

Known by various English names, Hendrick was an influential Mohawk
leader allied to Sir William **Johnson**. He commanded a contingent of warriors during the initial phase of the French and Indian War (1754–63). In
1755, Hendrick participated in an English campaign to repel the French
offensive along the Lake Champlain waterway. Hendrick and many of his
warriors were killed in an ambush during the chaotic Battle of Lake George.

Hewitt, J. N. B. (1859–1937)

Ethnologist and linguist J. N. B. Hewitt was born on the Tuscarora Indian
reservation in western New York State, the son of Harriet Brinton and David

Brainerd Hewitt. His father was a white man who had been adopted into the Tuscarora tribe as a boy. Educated by his parents and unable to speak fluent Tuscarora until he entered school at age eleven, Hewitt was prevented by poor health from completing his studies at the union school at Lockport, New York. Hewitt returned to the reservation, where he farmed and worked part-time as a newspaper correspondent. In 1880, Erminie A. Smith, a researcher from the Bureau of American Ethnology, hired Hewitt as a linguistic consultant. At Smith's death, Hewitt applied for a position at the Bureau, where he completed their joint project, a Tuscarora-English dictionary. Hewitt was promoted to the position of ethnologist at the Bureau, where he remained for more than fifty years. While there, Hewitt investigated the histories and genetic relationships of numerous Native American languages, and wrote a number of important scholarly papers on Iroquois ethnology. Hewitt made lasting contributions to the field of ethnology through his translations of Iroquois ritual speeches and traditions. He also served as president of the Anthropological Society of Washington, and was a charter member of the American Anthropological Association.

Hiawatha (Heowenta, "He Makes Rivers") (fl. 1560–70)

According to Iroquois tradition, Hiawatha, a Mohawk, and **Deganawida**, a spiritual leader, cofounded the Iroquois confederacy. With Deganawida he established the laws, regulations, and principles that guided the confederacy. The League of the Iroquois ended incessant warfare among the Mohawk, Oneida, Onondaga, Cayuga, and Seneca. The Iroquois confederacy enabled them to pursue vital policy goals more effectively. Because Deganawida considered himself a poor speaker, Hiawatha most often appeared publicly with their message of unity.

Hochelaga (c. 1534)

A heavily stockaded Iroquois village located on the banks of the St. Lawrence River. When **Cartier** explored the river valley during his 1534 expedition, he found many large, populous villages like Hochelaga. The presence of so many Indians, many of them hostile to encroachment, was one of many deterrents to French settlement in the region. When **Champlain** visited the St. Lawrence in the early seventeenth century, he found many of the village sites uninhabited and the Iroquois gone, presumably from epidemics. Montreal was founded on the former site of Hochelaga.

Hole in the Day (Bugonageshig) (1828–68)

This remarkable Ojibwa leader was born at Sandy Lake in Minnesota. His mother and father were descendants of civil and military leaders, who traditionally shared power in Ojibwa society. Hole in the Day advocated the adoption of agriculture among the Ojibwa, which he believed would free the tribe from dependence on government aid. However, he fought the disastrous Treaty of 1855, negotiated by civil leaders of the tribe, which provided only a tiny allotment to each tribal member in exchange for vast land cessions. Instead, he sought alliances with non-Indian traders and the influential Meti community, and in 1862, declared war on the United States. In 1864 the treaty was renegotiated, allowing Ojibwa additional funds and lands to make their agricultural transformation possible. Hole in the Day was married to at least four women and had several children. His marriages, designed to cement alliances between communities, also included one to a white woman, Ellen McCarty, whom he met in a hotel in Washington, D.C. He was assassinated by members of the Ojibwa community who feared his power, or the influence of warriors generally, on June 27, 1868.

Hudson, Henry (fl. 1607–11)

Commissioned by the Muscovy Company to find a northern passage to China, Henry Hudson's first voyage to the New World (1607–11) brought him to eastern Greenland. In 1609, sponsored this time by the Dutch East India Company, Hudson discovered the Hudson River. Finally, in 1610 he explored Hudson's Bay, this time in service to the English. Hudson's crew mutinied on the return voyage, and abandoned him and others to die.

Huron (Wendot, "Island People" or "Peninsula Dwellers")

The Huron Confederacy likely formed in the early sixteenth century when four Iroquoian-speaking peoples formed a cohesive alliance. The Huron numbered approximately 30,000 people by 1600, and occupied vast, fertile lands east of Lake Huron. When the Huron, which meant "boar" or "savage" in French, first encountered Samuel de **Champlain** in 1609, they forged lasting trade, religious, and military alliances with the French that irreversibly altered their culture. In the wake of epidemics and protracted warfare with the Iroquois, the Huron were decimated. Other Indians, including the Iroquois, adopted many Huron survivors. The Huron subsisted as farmers but supplemented their diet with fishing, hunting, and gathering wild plants. Canada currently maintains a Huron reservation at Wendake Reserve.

Illinois ("The People")

Centered in the vicinity of the prehistoric mounds at Cahokia, the Illinois Confederacy was a group of independent tribes speaking an Algonquian-Wakashan language and sharing a common culture. They numbered more than 10,000 people in the seventeenth century; rivalry with Iroquois and Great Lakes tribes virtually exterminated the Illinois by the nineteenth century. The Great Lakes tribes used the assassination of Pontiac by an Illinois as justification to dispossess the Illinois of much of their traditional land. The United States recognized the Illinois as the Confederated Peoria in 1854, and in 1907 the United Peoria and Miami became citizens of the state of Oklahoma.

Indian Reorganization Act (Wheeler-Howard Act) (1934)

The United States Congress passed this legislation to end the previous policy of assimilation and allotment. The act contained many provisions to encourage formal self-government and increased individual freedoms and opportunities for Indians. The act promoted tribal constitutions and the establishment of justice systems, granted religious freedom, expanded educational opportunities on reservations, advocated the hiring of Indians by the Bureau of Indian Affairs, and returned unsold allotted lands to tribes.

Indian Rights Association (IRA)

Formed by prominent Philadelphians in 1882, this organization was dedicated to promoting Native American interests and to guaranteeing their equal protection under the law. The IRA served as a watchdog group for the Bureau of Indian Affairs, and was instrumental in passing the **Dawes Severalty Act** and other legislation prior to 1900. As public and Indian sentiment came to reject the principles behind the allotment movement, the IRA declined in influence.

Jemison, Mary (Dehgewanus, "Two Falling Voices") (c. 1742–1833)

Jemison was captured in 1758 by French and Shawnee raiders in southwestern Pennsylvania and sold at Fort Duquesne. She married a Seneca, and after the French and Indian War successfully resisted repatriation. She had at least two Seneca husbands and bore eight children. She also helped to negotiate the Treaty of **Big Tree** (1797). Her experience is related in *A Narrative of the Life of Mrs. Mary Jemison* (1824).

Johnson, Pauline (Tekahionwake) (1861–1913)

Johnson was born on the Grand River Reserve of the Six Nations, the daughter of Mohawk chief George Henry Martin Johnson and an Englishwoman, Susanna Howells. Her grandfather, John "Smoke" Johnson, was a hero in the War of 1812. Her father, an activist who opposed the sale of alcohol and timber on the reservation, was the subject of violent harassment, and was severely injured in an attack in 1878. After his death in 1884, the family moved to Brantford, Ontario, and took the name Tekahionwake. Pauline wrote and read poetry to increasingly wide audiences, traveling to London in 1894, and published a book of poems, *The White Wampum,* in 1895. A second, less successful book of poetry, *Canadian Born,* was published in 1903. An important artistic influence on her work was her later collaboration with Squamish chief Joe Capilano, with whom she published *The Legends of Vancouver.* She died in 1913 of tuberculosis.

Johnson, Sir William (1715–74)

An Irish colonist in New York who, as a trader and land speculator, learned the Mohawk language and customs. Married to Molly **Brant** and befriended by **Hendrick**, Johnson became critical to maintaining Iroquois support for England during the French and Indian War. Although he cautioned Crown officials about mounting tensions preceding Pontiac's Rebellion, these warnings were unheeded. He was knighted and appointed Superintendent for Indian Affairs, and became one of the most influential Indian diplomats and frontier entrepreneurs.

Kellogg, Minnie (1880–1949)

Born to farming parents on the Oneida reservation near Green Bay, Wisconsin, Minnie Kellogg had an illustrious ancestry; included in her lineage were many of the prominent Oneida leaders who had followed the Reverend Eleazer Williams from their reservation in New York to Wisconsin. Kellogg was educated locally, and also studied at Barnard, Cornell, Stanford, and the University of Wisconsin. Combining remarkably a great gift for linguistics with an extraordinary talent as a storyteller, Kellogg lectured on the history of the League of the Iroquois and published a number of plays, political tracts, and articles on women's rights. In 1911, Kellogg helped to form the Society of Native Americans, where she remained critical of the policies of the BIA. She married a non-Indian, attorney Orrin Joseph Kellogg, in 1912, and spent many years organizing a complex land claims case on behalf of the Iroquois with him. Claims of fraudulent use of funds collected for the suit, which had come from Indian people all over the United States and Canada, undermined Kellogg's reputation, and she and her causes gradually lost favor with the Indian community. Her whereabouts during the last years of her life and the exact date of her death are unknown.

Kenekuk ("Putting His Foot Down") (c. 1790–1852)

Kickapoo chief and spiritual leader of a Kickapoo faction that refused to relocate westward following the Treaty of Edwardsville (1819), which ceded the last of their Illinois lands. Kenekuk preached avoidance of whites and a return to ancestral lifestyles. He combined elements of Kickapoo ceremonialism with Christianity to encourage his people to abandon their clan bundles and abstain from alcohol. He forestalled the forced removal of the Kickapoo with his feigned promises to willingly move westward. The end of the **Black Hawk** War brought American reassertions, and Kenekuk's Kickapoos were forced west.

Keokuk ("Watchful Fox") (1783–1848)

Sauk orator who rose to prominence during the War of 1812 as the opposition leader to **Black Hawk**. Keokuk advocated accommodation and concession with the Americans, which led to federal recognition that he was the legal leader of the Sauk nation. He utilized gifts, treaty goods, and annuities from Indian agents to cement his leadership. He continued to cede lands until the Fox and Sauk were forced onto reservations in Kansas, where he died largely alienated from his people.

Kickapoo ("He Who Moves About, Standing Now Here, Now There")

As their name suggests, the Kickapoo have lived over a wide area of the United States, from as far east as New York to Alabama and Missouri. Although participants in the early fur trade, the Kickapoo adamantly resisted missionary efforts. After supporting **Tecumseh** and **Black Hawk** in their wars of resistance, small bands of Kickapoo migrated westward—like many tribes internally divided as to how best to respond to American encroachments. One band even relocated to the Santa Rosa Mountains of Mexico. By the close of the nineteenth century, most Kickapoo had congregated in Oklahoma. Historically, the Kickapoo have strongly resisted efforts at acculturation, education, and allotment. While their tribal heritage and language have been largely retained, their low educational achievements have contributed to unusually high levels of poverty, unemployment, and substance abuse. As late as the 1980s, the Kickapoo adult population worked primarily as migrant laborers.

King Philip's War (1675–76)

The first widespread war between English colonists and Indians in New England. The war is named for King Philip, the son of **Massasoit** and chief of the Wampanoag (see **Metacom**). His Wampanoag name was Metacom or Metacomet. Upon the death (1662) of his brother Wamsutta (Alexander), whom the Indians suspected the English of murdering, Metacom became sachem and maintained peace with the colonists for a number of years. Hostility eventually developed over the steady succession of land sales forced on the Indians by their growing dependence on English goods. In 1667, when the town of Swansea, within Metacom's territories, was opened to white settlement without his consent, Metacom took an increasingly threatening stance. Suspicious of Metacom, the English colonists in 1671 questioned and fined him, and the Wampanoag, acceding to the colonists' demands, surrendered their arms. In 1675, John Sassamon, a Christian Indian who had been acting as an informer to the English, was murdered, probably at Metacom's instigation. Three Wampanoags were tried for the murder and executed. Incensed by this act, the Indians in June 1675 made a sudden raid on Swansea. Other raids followed; towns were burned and many whites— men, women, and children—were slain. Unable to draw the Indians into a major battle, the colonists resorted to similar methods of warfare in retaliation and antagonized other tribes. The Wampanoag were joined by the Nipmuck and by the Narragansett (after the latter were attacked by the colonists), and soon all the New England colonies were involved in the war. Metacom's cause began to decline after he made a long journey west in an unsuccessful attempt to secure aid from the Mohawk. Metacom was unable to assemble an effective Indian alliance against the English. Although initial engagements and heavy colonial losses favored Metacom, his forces were ultimately overwhelmed by the numerical superiority and firepower of the colonists, who adopted Indian tactics and widely employed Mohegan, Pequot, Niantic, and "praying Indians" against Metacom. In 1676 the Narragansett were completely defeated and their chief, Canonchet, was killed in April of that year; the Wampanoag and Nipmuck were gradually subdued. When the fighting ended, virtually all hostile sachems, including Metacom, were dead, along with thousands of their people. Metacom's wife and son were captured, and in August 1676 he was killed by an Indian in the service of Capt. Benjamin Church after his hiding place at Mt. Hope (Bristol, Rhode Island) was betrayed. His body was drawn and quartered and his head exposed on a pole in Plymouth. The war, which was extremely costly to the colonists in people and money, resulted in the virtual extermination of tribal life in southern

New England and the disappearance of the fur trade. The New England Confederation then had the way completely clear for white settlement.

Kirkland, Samuel (1741–1808)
A Presbyterian "New Light" missionary and Indian agent. Abandoning his collegiate studies, Kirkland established a mission among the Iroquois. Kirkland preached a highly individualistic fundamentalism that did not impose Western values (unless they requested it), since he believed that it would disrupt the indigenous societies. His message appealed to the Oneida warrior faction that was increasingly at odds with traditional Iroquois leadership. By 1770, Oneida loyalties were divided between Kirkland and Sir William Johnson, which deprived the British of valuable warriors during the American Revolution. With the assistance of Alexander Hamilton, Kirkland established the Hamilton Oneida Academy to teach classics and Calvinism to literate Oneida.

Little Turtle (Mishikinakwa) (c. 1747–1812)
Miami chief noted for his military tactics and skillful diplomacy, which he employed to embarrassingly defeat U.S. armies in 1790 and 1791. When General Anthony Wayne invaded the Ohio country, Little Turtle advocated peace. His pleas for negotiation were ignored, and the Indian alliance was defeated at Fallen Timbers (1794). Little Turtle reluctantly signed the Treaty of Greenville (1795), which ceded most of Ohio. Little Turtle further alienated himself from the Miami by ceding additional lands and refusing to join Tecumseh in his attempts to form a pan-Indian confederation.

Longhouse religion
After the Revolutionary War, many Iroquois communities suffered great losses. Not only had the power of the League been broken, but those who did not move north into Canadian territories found themselves restricted to tiny reservations within their formerly vast territories and increasingly vulnerable to the depredations of white settlers, alcoholism, and disease. In 1799, Handsome Lake, brother of Allegheny Seneca leader Cornplanter, fell into an illness during which he experienced a series of visions, which became known as the Code of Handsome Lake, the foundation of the Longhouse religion. Handsome Lake preached his beliefs fervently, especially against the practice of witchcraft, and also advocated education and the adoption of agriculture. Handsome Lake died in 1815, but his teachings lived on the preachings of his grandson, Jimmy Johnson, at Tonawanda, and

were eventually written down in 1845 by Ely S. **Parker**. The center of the Longhouse religion has remained the Tonawanda Longhouse, where each fall representatives of all Iroquois communities are invited to participate in the recitation of the Code of Handsome Lake. Recitations are then conducted in a "circuit" of other tribal longhouses. Other ceremonies associated with the Longhouse religion include the Maple, Thunder, Midwinter, Seed-planting, Bean, Little Corn, and Green Corn ceremonies, as well as the Four Sacred Rituals (the Feather Dance, the Thanksgiving Dance, the Personal Chant, and the Bowl Game).

Mahican ("The Place Where the Waters Are Never Still")

The Mahican, Algonquian speakers who lived along the upper Hudson River, are related to the Delaware and Mohegan. Because of the novel *The Last of the Mohicans*, many confuse the Mohegan and Mahican. It is estimated that the Mahican lost nearly 92 percent of their precontact population to European epidemics. After disastrous encounters with the Dutch, the Mahican became shrewd participants in the array of colonial trade and warfare. Nevertheless, by the seventeenth century they were driven from the fur trade by the Mohawk and relocated in Massachusetts, where they were known as the Stockbridge. English settlers drove them into Pennsylvania, and after the American Revolution many resettled with the Oneida. During the nineteenth century, the Mahican moved to Wisconsin and Kansas, but finally returned to Massachusetts as the Stockbridge-Munsee Band of Mahican Indians in 1934. In the 1990s the Mahican have endeavored to protect graves imperiled by development and joined tribes of the upper Great Lakes to oppose a copper mine on the Wolf River.

Maliseet (Wula'stegwi'ak, "Good River People")

Traditionally, the Maliseet inhabited territory in New Brunswick, Quebec, and northern Maine. Even the earliest French estimates of the size of the Maliseet were rather small, so that European epidemics and colonial warfare had a severe impact on them. After meeting Samuel de **Champlain** in 1603, the Maliseet allied themselves with the French. Most of the Maliseet were displaced by the English after the War of American Independence to accommodate loyalists from the United States. The loss of so much of their traditional homeland initiated a cultural transition whereby traditional values and culture were increasingly replaced by European, colonial, and other Native American elements. In the twentieth century, significant Maliseet communities emerged in Connecticut, Massachusetts, and New York. The

Maliseet speak an Eastern Algonquian language closely related to Passa-maquoddy.

Mashpee
Known in the seventeenth century as the "South Sea Indians," the Mashpee settled in their western Cape Cod community as English settlers increasingly occupied the lands formerly held by their people, known as Pokanoket or Nauset and, later, as **Wampanoag**. The Mashpee community was predominantly Indian until the nineteenth century, when non-Indian vacation-home owners demanded participation in local elections, gradually taking over political control of the town. The loss of self-determination spurred political action at the state and federal level, culminating in a suit brought by the Mashpee against the New Seabury corporation in 1975, in which the tribe claimed several million dollars in damages and the right to federal recognition as an Indian tribe. Defeated in this landmark case, the Mashpee are currently appealing the decision.

Massachusett ("At the Range of the Hills")
During the early years of English settlement, the Algonquian-speaking Massachusett were one of the most influential tribes in New England. While the question is yet unresolved, some scholars and historians believe the Massachusett led a confederacy that included the Nauset, Nipmuck, and Wampanoag. The Massachusett were also very closely related to the Narragansett and Pequot linguistically. The Massachusett lived in Massachusetts and Rhode Island, on land granted to the Virginia Company by King James I. If not for repeatedly devastating epidemics that virtually annihilated the Massachusett and other tribal populations, the Puritans might have encountered the organized resistance experienced at Jamestown and during the **Tidewater Wars**. By the 1640s few Massachusett remained, and most of those converted to Christianity. It was in the 1660s that John **Eliot** translated the Bible into Massachusett, and also composed a grammar and primer to assist in the education, conversion, and ordainment of Massachusett men. His writings have helped to preserve Massachusett language and history.

Massasoit (c. 1580–1661)
The powerful chief of the Wampanoag who allied himself with the Plymouth Colony in their disputes with the Massachusett. This alliance initially enhanced Wampanoag power and prestige, which had been impaired by severe population decline as a result of decimating epidemics. Massasoit

befriended Roger **Williams**. **Squanto** served Massasoit as a knowledgeable advisor.

Matinnecock

A native community living in the northwestern portion of Long Island in the seventeenth century. Dispossessed by the Dutch and English settlers of the island, the Matinnecock joined a community of whites and free blacks at the village of Success near Manhasset in 1829. The tribe was formally reincorporated in 1958.

Mattaponi

Commonly known as the Mattaponient, the Mattaponi are a small Algonquian-speaking tribe who belonged to the **Powhatan Confederacy**. When the confederacy attacked the English colonies during the Second Tidewater War (1644–46), the Mattaponi abandoned their ancestral home and moved west (see **Tidewater Wars**). Not until 1646, after the confederacy had collapsed, did the Mattaponi return to the Piscataway Creek and the Rappahannock River; however, the eruption of **Bacon's Rebellion** (1675–76) interrupted the migration. Later in the seventeenth century, the Seneca attacked a large Mattaponi village, slaughtering many and scattering the survivors. Many Mattaponi joined the Pamunkey and Chickahominy. The Mattaponi and Pamunkey are the only tribes recognized by Virginia that maintain reservations in the state.

Menominee ("Wild Rice Gatherers")

Known primarily for their rice cultivation and forest management techniques, the Algonquian-speaking Menominee live in the upper Great Lakes. Descendants of a single precontact village, the Menominee were dramatically reduced by smallpox epidemics following contacts with Europeans. Like other tribes of the region, the Menominee were closely allied to the French for trade and military reasons during the colonial wars; however, intraclan rivalries often undermined Menominee attempts to fully mobilize warriors. By the War of 1812, Menominee leadership had fractured, and few of them openly participated in the fighting. During the nineteenth century, the Menominee ceded land to the United States and other landless tribes, repeatedly relocating across Wisconsin. Although a few warriors participated in the **Black Hawk** War and the Santee Sioux fighting, the Menominee officially sought a policy of reconciliation with the United States. During the Civil War, the Menominee sent volunteers to join the Union Army, and they received the honor of guarding the assassination conspirators of President Lincoln during the trial and execution. During the 1950s, though, the Menominee were forced to sell prime lakefront real estate to developers. In recent years, the Menominee have struggled to recover lost hunting and fishing rights. They have also placed an emphasis upon education by opening the College of the Menominee Nation, which specializes in health care, forestry management, and gaming administration.

Mesquakie/Fox ("Red-Earth People")

Along with the Sauk, the Mesquakie are the only native group surviving in modern Iowa. These Algonquian-speaking people live on lands purchased from the state in 1857 near the town of Tama. First described in writing by French explorers of the Great Lakes, the Mesquakie were horticultural people also heavily dependent on fish and game. Gaining prominence in the eighteenth century through their control over the portages linking the Great Lakes and the Mississippi, the Mesquakie allied themselves with the closely related Sauk and Kickapoo. In the nineteenth century, Mesquakies were forced west into Kansas; however, a large group returned to Iowa and purchased the lands where the main body of the tribe lives today.

Metacom (or Metacomet; King Philip) (c. 1639–76)

Son of **Massasoit**, Metacom succeeded his brother Wamsutta (Alexander) as Wampanoag sachem, and came to embody Indian resistance to colonial power in New England. Metacom was raised during the period in which native people of southern New England struggled with the combined problems of massive population loss, the huge influx of English settlers to the region, and increasingly hostile relations with surrounding Indian groups, all struggling to compete in the fur and wampum trade and to maintain their sovereignty. With his people and their lands wedged between the Massachusetts Bay and Plymouth colonies, Metacom became increasingly suspicious of the English colonists and frustrated by their attempts to influence Wampanoag politics and land sales. When Puritans executed three Wampanoag for murder, Wampanoag rage erupted into war. Combined Puritan, Mohawk, and Narragansett forces overwhelmed Metacom. Metacom's death in August 1676 marked the end of Indian independence in Massachusetts and Rhode Island, although Connecticut's Mohegans, who had served the English during the war, retained a measure of independence. See also **King Philip's War**.

Miami ("Peninsula People")

Although the Algonquian-speaking Miami numbered perhaps 25,000 in the mid-seventeenth century, approximately 2,000 remained a hundred years later. Culturally related and politically allied to the Kickapoo, the Miami were almost always at war with the Chickasaw and Iroquois. Like most tribes of the western Great Lakes region, the Miami became bound to the French by military and trade alliances. With mounting losses from epidemics and warfare, the Miami migrated to Ohio, where they maintained a close-knit, brotherly status with the Shawnee. Although the Miami were largely uninvolved during the American Revolution, they played a pivotal role in the years immediately afterward. A Miami leader, **Little Turtle**, led a cohesive coalition of tribes from the Ohio country and Great Lakes against the fledgling United States. Utterly destroying the militia and regulars troops sent to force the tribes from Ohio, Little Turtle inflicted the worst defeat the United States Army ever suffered during the Indian Wars. While Indian resistance in Ohio lasted several more years, it collapsed with the Battle of Fallen Timbers (1794). In the years that followed, the Miami were forced west into Indiana and Oklahoma.

Miantonomi (c. 1600–43)
The Narragansett sachem during the turbulent **Pequot War** (1636–37). He and Narragansett warriors joined the expedition of Captain John Mason and participated in the annihilation of the Pequot on the Mystic River. As tensions increased with rising colonial populations, Miantonomi concluded that his people could not peacefully coexist with the English. He unsuccessfully called for Indian unity against the English. During the Narragansett-Mohegan conflict, Miantonomi was executed by Uncas.

Micmac
Traditionally, the Micmac inhabited the Maritime Provinces of Canada, and they represent numerous subtribes collectively named and treated by the French. The Micmac may have been the first American Indians to encounter European fisherman in the fifteenth century. It's probable that the Micmac also encountered Viking settlers and explorers in the eleventh century. From their first meeting with **Cartier** in 1534, the Micmac were closely bound to the French by the fur trade. Speaking an Algonquian language related to Abenaki and Passamaquoddy, the Micmac were primarily hunter-gatherers who cultivated tobacco. Throughout the colonial period the Micmac maintained a rivalry with the Abenaki that the French could not mediate. After the American Revolution, the English granted Micmac territory to loyalists fleeing America and forced the Micmac into semisedentary settlements. Not until the pan-Indian movement of the 1960s did the Micmac began recovering some of their economic independence.

Midewiwin (Grand Medicine)

A traditional Ojibwa healing society that remained relatively unknown until the 1930s. Only the most senior and experienced Ojibwa healers belonged to the society. In addition to serving a lengthy apprenticeship, candidates were required to be honest, brave, and humble members of the community.

Mingo

A corruption of the Algonquian term *mingwe*, said to mean "treacherous." The Mingo were members of an Iroquois-speaking group made up of displaced Shawnee, Seneca, Wyandot, Conestoga, and Delaware people who lived in western Pennsylvania in the mid-eighteenth century. The Mingo pursued a separate policy from that of the Six Nations, and moved westward after the Revolution. In 1817 they were joined by the Cayuga, whose land in New York had been sold. Although successful farmers, the Mingo were forced westward again during the period of Indian Removal, and the community was reestablished on a reservation near Neosho, Oklahoma. In 1937 they took the official name Seneca-Cayuga.

Mohawk (Haudenosaunee, "People of the Longhouse")

The Iroquoian-speaking Mohawk of New York were the easternmost tribe of the Iroquois confederacy. The Mohawk share strong cultural, linguistic, and historic bonds with the tribes of the confederacy: Onondaga, Cayuga, Seneca, Tuscarora, and Oneida. After becoming increasing involved in the fur trade and drawn into resulting conflicts, the Iroquois confederacy made peace with France in 1701. While the League endeavored to maintain a concerted policy, the American Revolution divided Iroquois unity, and the Mohawk sided with the British. Joseph **Brant**, a war chief, played a prominent role leading raids against the farms and villages of the rebelling colonists. After the British defeat, Brant led many Mohawk into Canada. Throughout the twentieth century the Mohawk have struggled to reclaim ancestral lands in New York with remarkable success. Nevertheless, because Mohawk live in New York, Ontario, and Quebec, issues of competing jurisdictions and legitimacy are serious obstacles for the tribe and the various governmental authorities.

Mohegan

Traditionally, the Mohegan lived along the upper Hudson River, but they had migrated into Connecticut by the time English settlers arrived. Historical accounts of the Mohegan are often contradictory; however, the Mohegan were closely and complexly involved with the Pequot. While not numerous,

Mohegan warriors joined the English in their war against the Narragansett and later in **King Philip's War**. In the early eighteenth century, a Mohegan, Samson **Occom**, emerged as a prominent Christian theologian. He founded the Mohegan-Pequot Brothertown, which promoted Christianity, farming, and individual ownership of property. Most of these Indians, however, lost their lands during economic fluctuations, and they joined other tribes. In 1994 the United States recognized the Mohegan, but the Brothertown Indian Nation has not yet been federally recognized.

Monacan ("Sword" or "Digging Instrument")

The Monacan, a confederacy of Siouan tribes, historically lived in the Piedmont region of Virginia, west of the powerful **Powhatan**. Although they were traditional enemies, the Powhatan and Monacan allied themselves against the English by 1611. European diseases and warfare decimated the Monacan, reducing them to virtual dependents of the English by 1665. By the end of the seventeenth century, the Monacan disappear from historical records, and may have joined the Saponi. Like many other Virginia Indians, the Monacan struggled throughout the nineteenth and most of the twentieth centuries to retain their lands and education, and to be recognized as a distinct culture. Although their Siouan language has been lost, the Monacan have been recognized since 1989 by the state of Virginia, and live primarily in western Virginia.

Morgan, Lewis Henry (Tayadawahkugh, "One Lying Across") (1818–81)

An early anthropologist and ethnographer whose groundbreaking work on the Iroquois established a methodological blueprint that many succeeding anthropologists followed. With the assistance and insights of Ely **Parker**, Morgan published *League of the Ho-de-no-sau-nee* (1851). It remains one of the best descriptions of the Iroquois. Morgan also studied kinship in 70 tribes of Hudson Bay and the upper Missouri River Valley.

Morse, Jedidiah (1761–1826)

A conservative Congregational minister and scholar who ministered to the Abenaki of coastal Maine. He also studied numerous Indian peoples and reported their condition to John C. Calhoun. He was a proponent of a separate state for Indians, and used his influence with President Jackson to advocate the formation of an Indian territory west of the Mississippi River.

Nansemond ("One Who Goes to Fish")

The Algonquian-speaking Nansemond traditionally lived along the banks of the Nansemond River in Virginia. Within twenty years of the settlement of Jamestown, the Nansemond splintered into two factions: Christian and native. Although the Nansemond, who lived south of the James River, had not participated in the First Tidewater War, the English launched raids against them. When the Second Tidewater War erupted in 1644, the Nansemond participated against the English (see **Tidewater Wars**). By 1786, the population of the native faction was so small that the reservation was sold and the members either joined the Christian faction or the Nottoway. In the seventeenth century the Christian faction intermarried with Europeans and adopted many aspects of English culture. Traditionally, the Nansemond were expert fisherman who harvested oysters and supplemented their crops by hunting. In 1984 the Nansemond petitioned for and received federal recognition.

Nanticoke ("Tidewater People")

The lands about the Nanticoke River are the ancestral territory of the Nanticoke tribe, who shared the eastern shore of Maryland with the Pocomoke and Choptank. The first extensive contact with Europeans for the Nanticoke was the arrival of John **Smith**. Although tensions increased when Lord Baltimore received a grant that included Nanticoke lands, the Nanticoke signed numerous peace treaties with the English. When the Nanticoke moved onto reserved lands, settlers continued to encroach, driving the Nanticoke and other tribes of the eastern shore into open hostility. With their defeat, the Nanticoke drifted into Pennsylvania and Delaware. Today the Nanticoke are largely dispersed across the United States and Canada, although some are concentrated on the Indian River in Delaware.

Narragansett

The Algonquian-speaking Narragansett inhabited portions of Rhode Island, Massachusetts, and portions of Connecticut. Archaeological evidence indicates that the Narragansett are one of the oldest tribes in North America. Among the first Indians of New England to interact with European sailors and explorers, the Narragansett were generally hospitable to Europeans, hosting da **Verrazano** in 1524 and welcoming an outcast Roger **Williams** in 1636. As a result of the influence of Williams, the Narragansett allied with the English during the **Pequot War** (1636–37). **Miantonomi** recognized the increasing threat the English posed, and tensions mounted as the English sought more land and interfered with intertribal politics. In 1675 the Narragansett allied with the Wampanoag against the Puritans, but the Battle of Great Swamp nearly annihilated them. Many survivors were sold into slavery or sought refuge with other tribes. In the 1920s the Narragansett began a long struggle to win back ancestral lands, which they realized in 1978. Five years later the Narragansett were awarded tribal status by the United States government.

Native American Graves Protection and Repatriation Act (NAGPRA) (1990)
Passed by Congress, NAGPRA provides for the protection of grave sites and the repatriation of American Indian remains and cultural artifacts back to the tribes.

Neolin ("Four") (1760–66)
Also known as the Delaware Prophet, Neolin blamed Europeans for the misfortunes of his people and advocated the rejection of white ways and alcohol use, and the return to native ritual, dress, and subsistence. Consistent with traditional beliefs about the role of supernatural spirits, Neolin's teachings promised that the rejection of nontraditional ways would restore the Delaware to favor. In the 1760s, Neolin was preaching to Indian peoples near his settlement at Cuyahoga River in Ohio, urging them to purge themselves of white ways and to expel the British from the region. Timely and persuasive, Neolin's message reached Indians as far west as the Illinois River and Michigan. The Ottawa chief Pontiac (see below) capitalized on this message in his assault on Detroit and the subsequent hostilities known as **Pontiac's Rebellion**. Scholars regard Neolin as more influential than his fellow Delaware prophet Wangomend (1752–75), and trace some of his ideas to the teachings of the famous Shawnee prophet **Tenskwatawa**.

New England Company
Formally known as the Society for the Propagation of the Gospel in Foreign Parts, this English Protestant missionary society was established in 1649 by the Long Parliament, and is still in operation today. The New England Company funded missionary work in northern and southern New England and eastern New York until the end of the colonial period.

Ninegret (c. 1600–1650s)
The leader of the Niantics during the **Pequot War** (1636–37). He joined

the expedition of Captain John Mason, along with the Narragansett, against the Pequots on the Mystic River. Like **Miantonomi**, Ninegret was awarded Pequot slaves by the victorious English.

Occom, Samson (1723–92)

Mohegan missionary, teacher, and author who became a devout Christian and attended school at the urging of his mother. He taught Indian children in New York and Connecticut, but his work was interrupted by the American Revolution. With the end of the war, he found immense satisfaction serving as the spiritual leader, teacher, advocate, and fund raiser of Brothertown. Occom's writings are a tremendous source of information still used by researchers today.

Ojibwa (Anishinabeg, "Original People" or "First People")

The Ojibwa, commonly referred to as Chippewa, are the largest tribe of Algonquian speakers. The French first encountered the Ojibwa in 1622, and they soon became heavily involved in the fur trade. Until the end of the Seven Years' War, the Ojibwa were crucial to the trade distribution and were allied with the French against the English. In the discontent that followed the French loss of Canada, they strongly supported Pontiac in his attacks on English garrisons. As a result of supporting resistance movements in the Ohio country, led by **Little Turtle** and **Tecumseh**, the Ojibwa lost much of their lands after the War of 1812. Throughout the remainder of the century, the Ojibwa relinquished numerous land claims in the United States, and some bands fled to Canada. Three Ojibwa founded the **American Indian Movement** (AIM) in 1968. The Ojibwa have also been involved in numerous court decisions during the twentieth century that contested forced removal and land use by the United States. Following important legal developments in the 1980s, the Ojibwa have used their fishing rights and gaming operations to boost reservation economies. Today the Ojibwa are the third largest group of American Indians, numbering more than 100,000.

Oneida ("People of the Stone Set Up")

The Oneida, matrilineal Iroquoian speakers of New York, are one of the five tribes of the original League of the Iroquois. Bound by strong cultural, linguistic, and historic bonds with the Onondaga, Seneca, Mohawk, Tuscarora, and Cayuga, the Oneida exploited their strategic location along the St. Lawrence River to become heavily involved in the fur trade. They maintained these trade networks nearly to the end of the eighteenth century. During the

American Revolution, the Oneida largely sided with the British. Afterward, the Oneida lost most of their land in the Treaty at Fort Herkimer (1785) and Treaty of Fort Schuyler (1788). During the nineteenth century, nearly 700 Oneida relocated to Wisconsin. Throughout the twentieth century, the Oneida of New York and Wisconsin have routinely resisted efforts by the United States to sell off tribal lands, and have both successfully operated gaming facilities that have funded extensive social assistance programs for their people and diversified business investments.

Onondaga ("People of the Hills")

The Onondoga, Iroquoian speakers of New York State, are one of the five tribes of the original League of the Iroquois, and held a revered status as keepers of the Council Fire. Bound by strong cultural, linguistic, and historic bonds with the other members of the confederacy, the Onondaga occupied lands in the middle of the confederacy. The skilled diplomacy of the Iroquois and their reputation as fierce warriors brought peace and prosperity to the Onondaga. During the American Revolution, the Onondaga and most of the Iroquois sided chiefly with the British. After the war, vast amounts of Iroquois land were taken by the United States, and many Onondaga relocated to Canada. What land remained was gradually reduced to satisfy the needs of settlers. Often portrayed as the most conservative of the Iroquois, the Onondaga have adamantly resisted attempts by the United States to undermine sovereignty in the twentieth century. Despite pressures in the 1940s, the Onondaga resisted organizing a representative government instead of their traditional structure. Most Onondaga live in Ontario or on the reservation near Syracuse, New York.

Opechancanough (c. 1550–1646)

The Pamunkey werowance and half-brother of **Powhatan**. Opechancanough succeeded Powhatan as paramount leader of his confederation. Concerned about the steady encroachment on lands and rights, Opechancanough departed from Powhatan's policy and secretly planned war against Jamestown. He coordinated the devastating March 1622 and April 1644 assaults against the unsuspecting settlements near Jamestown, which were designed to wholly eliminate the colony. Despite high English casualties and the abandonment of several outlying settlements in 1622, the attacks failed to annihilate the colony. In 1646, Opechancanough, frail and nearly blind, was captured and imprisoned in Jamestown, where he was shot in the back by his guards.

Ottawa

Closely related to the Ojibwa and Potawatomi, both culturally and linguistically, the Ottawa inhabited the lands of the upper Great Lakes. In 1653 the Ottawa and Huron fled before the assaults of the Iroquois during the devastating fur wars. Resettling in Michigan and Wisconsin, the Ottawa maintained a close military and trade alliance with the French. During the discontent that followed the surrender of Canada to the English, an influential Ottawa, Pontiac, rose to prominence, and coordinated an unsuccessful war against English garrisons and traders. In the 1830s Ohio and Michigan Ottawa ceded lands in return for a reservation in Kansas, which was eventually moved to Oklahoma. Although the Ottawa Tribe of Oklahoma lost federal recognition in 1956, it was reinstated in the 1970s, and within several years the Grand Traverse Bay Band of Ottawa and Chippewa gained federal recognition. Nevertheless, other Michigan bands are still struggling for federal recognition.

Pamunkey

In contrast to the Mattaponi, the Pamunkey were the most populous tribe of the Algonquian-speaking **Powhatan Confederacy**. While the origin of their name is unknown, it is associated with the Pamunkey River, on which the tribe has traditionally lived. When the Second Tidewater War ended in 1646, the Powhatan Confederacy had collapsed, and the population of the Pamunkey was greatly diminished (see **Tidewater Wars**). Like all other Indians of Virginia, the Pamunkey struggled ceaselessly in the nineteenth century and for most of the twentieth century against racism and attempts by whites to classify the Pamunkey as "colored." In the 1970s they actively participated in the pan-Indian movement. Today, the Mattaponi and Pamunkey are the only tribes recognized by Virginia who have reservations in the state.

Parker, Arthur C. (1881–1955)

Seneca anthropologist, ethnologist, and archaeologist who was a descendant of Ely Parker (see below). Befriended by Frederic Putnam and Franz Boas, Parker spent his summers excavating while attending Dickinson Seminary. Later he would hold important posts: archaeologist at New York State Museum; editor of *American Indian Magazine*; and Director of the Rochester Museum of Arts and Sciences. Parker's encouragement and collection of the work of Iroquois craftsmen and artisans helped preserve and encourage future artists.

Parker, Ely S. (Do-ne-ho-ga-wa, "Open Door") (1828–95)
Articulate Seneca sachem and engineer who became the military secretary
to General Ulysses S. Grant, and transcribed the terms of surrender at Ap-
pomattox Courthouse. He achieved the rank of brevet brigadier general, and
served on two Indian commissions prior to his appointment as Commissioner of Indian Affairs in 1869. Parker worked tirelessly to avoid war with
western tribes and intensified efforts to gather Indians on reservations so they
could be educated and introduced to agriculture. He was also an important
informant for the works of Henry Rowe Schoolcraft and Lewis Henry **Morgan**.

**Passamaquoddy ("Pollock-Spearing Place" or "Those of the Place Where
the Pollock Are Plentiful")**
The Passamaquoddy lived along coastal New Brunswick and Maine, and
were closely related to the Maliseet. The Passamaquoddy were members of
the Abenaki Confederacy who banded together in defense against the Iroquois. Near the end of the seventeenth century, the Passamaquoddy formed
an alliance with the French. In 1749, conflict with the Iroquois was resolved.
With the outbreak of the American Revolution, the Passamaquoddy supported the colonists. Within a few years of the Treaty of Paris (1783), Americans began pressuring the Passamaquoddy to convert to Christianity and
adopt farming. Reservations in their ancestral lands and good relations with
the state of Maine urged the Passamaquoddy onto reservations. The Passamaquoddy currently inhabit several reservations in Maine. Despite steady
demographic growth since 1900, the Passamaquoddy have struggled with
abject poverty. Several favorable court rulings and a settlement in a land
dispute case have encouraged them to return to the reservations.

Penobscot ("Many Stones" or "The Rocky Place")
The Penobscot were the largest tribe of the Eastern Abenaki, which included
the Passamaquoddy, Maliseet, and Pennacook. The Penobscot, Algonquian
speakers, traditionally inhabited large areas in central Maine along the Penobscot Bay and the Penobscot River. In 1749 the Penobscot left the confederacy and settled differences with the French and English. Although the
Penobscot attempted to remain neutral in European rivalries, the English
secured their alliance during the Seven Years' War and American Revolution. Conflicts with the state of Massachusetts in the eighteenth and nineteenth centuries reduced economic opportunities and deprived the Penobscot of much of their land. In the 1950s and 1960s many Penobscot left

reservations to seek opportunities elsewhere. In the 1970s the Penobscot and the Passamaquoddy sued the United States for land wrongfully taken from them. The resulting settlement not only gave federal recognition to the Penobscot but also provided the funding to begin businesses and create gaming facilities. The Penobscot are one of the few surviving tribes of New England; their reservation is composed of 146 islands in the Penobscot River plus the village of Old Town.

Pequot

Perhaps no single tribe in New England better represents the refusal of American Indians to vanish than the Pequot. Numbering as many as 15,000 at precontact, the Pequot inhabited much of Connecticut and became crucial, wealthy players in the wampum and fur trade. In 1637, when hostilities erupted with the Puritan settlement, a force of English and allied Indians attacked one of the two principal Pequot strongholds on the Mystic River. Hundreds of Pequots were massacred as the English fired the village and shot those who attempted to escape into the swamp. Many Pequots who surrendered elsewhere were sold into slavery among the allies of the English—Mohegan, Narragansett, and Niantic. Although scattered among the villages of other tribes, the Pequot and aspects of their culture endured. The Mashantucket Pequot Indian Claims Settlement Act (1983) federally recognized the Pequot and led to the dramatic economic change produced by the Foxwoods Casino. The success of the casino has created a resurgence of pride, and has brought many individuals of Pequot ancestry forward and enabled them to prove their lineage. Profits from the Foxwoods Casino enabled the Pequot to make generous gifts to the National Museum of the American Indian and to create a spectacular museum and research center dedicated to Pequot history.

Pequot War (1636–37)

One of the first successful colonial military campaigns against Indians, the Pequot War was a contest for hegemony in New England. Long-standing disputes and tension over lands between the powerful Pequot and the Puritans erupted into violence when colonists retaliated for the murder of an English trader. The Pequot conducted frontier raids and infested Fort Saybrook, but relatively few settlers were killed. Captain John Mason, along with Narragansett and Mohegan allies, surrounded the principal Pequot town on the Mystic River. Setting fire to the stockaded village, the colonists shot anyone who attempted to flee, annihilating the village. As the Pequot tried to regroup, the English launched attacks on other villages and their retreats. Approximately 200 Pequot survived to surrender. These were divided among the Indian allies of the English or sold into slavery in the Caribbean.

Philip: *see* **Metacom.**

Pocahontas (Matoaka) (c. 1596–1617)
One of the many daughters of paramount chief Wahunsunacock (known as **Powhatan**) of Virginia, Pocahontas became an important figure in the early history of Indian-white relations in the New World. A frequent visitor to Jamestown, she befriended its military leader, John **Smith**, and is said to have intervened when her father had decided to have Smith executed. Scholars now believe that Smith misunderstood the drama in which Pocahontas played a part, and that Powhatan wished to "adopt" Smith as an ally, in the native manner. As hostilities between the Powhatans and the English increased, Pocahontas withdrew from contact, but was kidnapped by the English captain Samuel Argall in 1613 and kept hostage at Jamestown for the following year. Remarkably, Pocahontas there converted to Christianity and took the English name Rebecca. Soon after, she married the English widower John Rolfe. Their marriage served as an excuse for both English and Indians to cease hostilities. Rebecca, John, and their infant son Thomas traveled to England in 1616, so that Rebecca could garner support for the English colony. She contracted a fatal illness within months of her arrival, and died in March of 1617. She is buried at the Church of St. George at Gravesend, Kent. Her son Thomas did not return to Virginia until 1640, by which time the power of the Powhatan Confederacy had been destroyed.

Pokanoket: *see* **Wampanoag.**

Pontiac (Obwondiyag) (c. 1720–69)
Ottawa war chief who rose to prominence during the widespread Indian discontent after the French and Indian War (1754–63). He encouraged opposition to the English, courted French officials, and traveled the Great Lakes region building support on the spiritual foundation established by **Neolin**, the Delaware Prophet. The skillful diplomacy of Pontiac and his convincing oratory fused with native discontent and ignited a widespread war against English garrisons and settlements. Despite overwhelming initial

Indian successes, Detroit and Fort Pitt withstood Indian assaults. The arrival of relief expeditions and dwindling Indian supplies compelled Pontiac to negotiate. Disgraced and exiled, Pontiac was murdered at Cahokia by a Peoria Indian, and reportedly buried in St. Louis.

Pontiac's Rebellion

The Ottawa leader Pontiac rose to prominence as a participant in the diplomatic negotiations between Indians and the British after the French defeat in 1760, but became increasingly frustrated by what he saw as English perfidy. He also came under the influence of the Delaware Prophet **Neolin**, and adapted Neolin's nativist doctrines to his own more specifically anti-English campaign. Assisted by French troops, Pontiac staged a siege against the British fort at Detroit in 1763 that, along with other Indian attacks against the British, came to be known as Pontiac's Rebellion. Pontiac's influence was never as widespread as he himself believed, however, and his increasing arrogance alienated his former allies among the Ottawa, Illinois, and Peoria. By 1769, Pontiac had been murdered, and the "rebellion" defused.

Poosepatuck (Unkechaug)

The Poosepatuck occupy a 50-acre reservation on Long Island, the remnant of lands designated for their use in the eighteenth century. Algonquian speakers, the Poosepatuck were allies of other island communities, and are still active in contemporary regional native networks.

Potawatomi (Neshnabek, "True People" or "Original People")

The Potawatomi are Algonquian speakers of the western Great Lakes who are closely related to the Ojibwa and Ottawa. Many scholars interpret their name as "people of the place of the fire" or "keepers of the sacred fire." By the beginning of the seventeenth century, the Potawatomi lived in regions of Wisconsin, Michigan, and Indiana. By maintaining close relations with the Ojibwa and Ottawa and also forging military and trade alliances with the French, the Potawatomi became influential throughout the region. Like most nations allied with the French in the Great Lakes area, the Potawatomi found themselves punished after the end of the Seven Years' War, and enthusiastically supported Pontiac in his war against the English. The Potawatomi were closely allied with the pan-Indian movements of the Ohio country during the late eighteenth century. During the removal phases of the nineteenth century, the Potawatomi were repeatedly uprooted and forced to relocate. During the 1950s the Prairie Band successfully resisted federal efforts to eliminate their tribal status. During the twentieth century, the Potawatomi have actively participated in the revival of native languages and cultural traditions. Today Potawatomi live on federal- and state-recognized reservations throughout Michigan, Indiana, Wisconsin, Kansas, and Oklahoma.

Powhatan (Wahunsunacock) (d. 1618)

Paramount chief of the confederacy of the same name, Powhatan was the native leader whose personal charisma and political skills created the largest native polity in the Northeast at the time of contact. The Powhatan chiefdom was made up of at least thirty communities, each with its own werowance, or ruler. Powhatan extracted tribute from each of these communities, and governed through a combination of coercion and kinship influence. As in most matrilineal societies, Powhatan inherited his position from his mother's brother, and passed it on in turn to his brothers Opitchapam and **Opechancanough**. Powhatan struggled to contain the aggressive English colonists at Jamestown, but his influence was evidently waning in the early years of the settlement, and he was succeeded by Opechancanough in 1614. He was discouraged by the loss of his daughter **Pocahontas**, by the epidemics that had swept through his territories, and by the knowledge that English control over the Tidewater was inevitable.

Powhatan Confederacy

Powhatan refers to Wahunsunacock (known to the English as **Powhatan**), a powerful leader whose name was given not only to an individual tribe but also to the confederacy of tribes he led. Joined by a common Algonquian language and leader, the Powhatan Confederacy was formed about 1570 in the Tidewater of Virginia. Powhatan inherited authority over six tribes. Through conquest and alliance he extended the confederacy to between thirty and forty tribes, which included the Powhatan, Chiskiack, Pamunkey, Mattaponi, and the Chickahominy from southern Virginia to the Potomac River. Although tensions existed and limited violence erupted, peace was largely maintained between the confederacy and the Jamestown settlement. But encroachments on Powhatan land fueled distrust. By 1646, after the end of two brutal **Tidewater Wars**, the power of the Powhatan and cohesion of the confederacy were broken, and English settlers overwhelmed the Powhatan. The Powhatan have not yet received state or federal recognition. However, in 1983 certain members of the confederacy did: the Chickahominy, Mattaponi, Rappahannock, and Nansemond.

Powhatan Uprisings: *see* Tidewater Wars.

Prairie du Chien, Treaty of (1825)

Negotiated by Indian Agent Lawrence Taliaferro, the treaty was designed to bring peace to the Indians of the western Great Lakes. The agreement is remarkable in that it did not involve land concessions by the signatory Indians. Instead, it attempted to establish peace and definable territories among the Sauk and Fox, Menominee, Iowa, Winnebago, Ottawa, Potawatomi, Sioux, and Ojibwa. The treaty designated the Red River as the major boundary; however, the rapid onset of settlers and deep-seated animosities quickly undermined the agreement.

Praying Towns

In 1660, John **Eliot** established seven "praying towns" in Massachusetts for Christian Indians seeking Puritan lifestyles. Converts renounced virtually every aspect of their native lives—languages, names, ceremonies, beliefs, customs, and dress—to become anglicized. Praying Indians were also taught English agrarian techniques. Eliot trained Indian males to travel as missionaries to their peoples. At their zenith, fourteen praying towns were inhabited, but most were abandoned after **King Philip's War.**

Quinney, John W. (1797–1855)

A Stockbridge Iroquois or Mahican who became one of the most successful bureaucratic warriors against the United States. Quinney was an adroit negotiator, working on behalf of the Iroquois. He accepted pressures from the United States to relocate the band to Green Bay, but secured market value for the lands lost. When whites and the Winnebago in Wisconsin complained, the Stockbridge Iroquois were moved again, but only after Quinney negotiated adequate payment for the improvements they had made to the land. After repeated moves, Quinney convinced Congress to grant the Stockbridge Iroquois 460 acres in their ancestral New York lands.

Rale, Pere Sebastien (1652–1724)

A French Jesuit missionary to the Abenaki whose mission was burned when New England colonists raided Norridgewock in 1722. With increasing violence and encroachments by New Englanders, Rale galvanized the Abenaki of the Kennebec River Valley. The successful retaliatory raid of the Abenaki prompted Massachusetts to offer exorbitant bounties for the scalps of Abenaki warriors. Assaults by New England militia bounty hunters wore down the Abenaki and finally killed Rale in 1724.

Rappahannock ("River Where the Tide Rises and Falls")
Often known as the Nantaughtacund, the Rappahannock historically lived in Virginia and were members of the **Powhatan Confederacy**. With the outbreak of the **Tidewater Wars**, the Rappahannock withdrew into the interior of the Virginia. When the Rappachannock returned at the cessation of hostilities, they found their land occupied by the English. Throughout the 1650s the Rappahannock waged war against these settlements, but by 1677, when **Bacon's Rebellion** collapsed, the Rappahannock and the other Algonquians of Virginia were defeated. Most of the Rappahannock adopted European dress and agriculture but still endured racism. A few resisted and fled into the swamps with other Indians and escaped slaves. In the early twentieth century, the Rappahannock began struggling for recognition. In 1983 the state of Virginia finally recognized the United Rappahannock, although they have no reservation and are not yet federally recognized.

Red Bird (c. 1790–1827)
Winnebago chief who supported **Tecumseh** and allied himself with the British during the War of 1812. In the 1820s, Red Bird resisted American intrusions and increasing pressure to relocate westward. With tensions high from trespassing farmers and miners, violence exploded in 1827 when warriors recaptured Winnebago women who had been abducted by Mississippi boatmen. Military columns converged on the Winnebagos. To prevent further violence, Red Bird surrendered himself. He died shortly thereafter, awaiting trial for murder.

Red Jacket (Segoyewatha, "Always Ready") (c. 1750–1830)
Seneca leader who after the American Revolution emerged as the principal spokesman of the Seneca. Although he adopted conciliatory policies with the United States and often ceded lands, Red Jacket was adamantly opposed to Christianity and the **Longhouse religion**. His religious stances were highly unpopular, and his opponents removed him from power. Discouraged and alcoholic, he died largely ignored by his people.

Richardville, Jean Baptiste (Peshewa) (1761–1841)
The Miami chief was the son of a French trader and Taucumwah, a member of a prominent Miami chief's family. His mother later remarried another

trader, and Richardville grew up with a strong interest in the trading business, learned from his father, mother, and stepfather. He married a Miami woman and came to emphasize his Indian heritage in public settings. Loyal to the British crown during the Revolution, in 1795 he was one of the signers of the Treaty of Fallen Timbers. An associate of Little Turtle, he also served as an emissary for the Miami, negotiating favorable terms for them during the period of their land cessions and removal.

Roanoke (1585–90)
The ill-fated English settlement attempted by Sir Walter Raleigh in 1584 on Roanoke Island. Located in the Carolina Outer Banks, Roanoke was swampy ground surrounded by Croatoan Indians. When Sir Francis Drake visited, he found the colonists starving and miserable. Relief ships with food, supplies, and additional settlers were prevented from arriving for several years by the outbreak of war with Spain. When a relief expedition arrived in 1590 at Roanoke, the colonists were absent. The word CROATOAN was carved in a tree trunk.

Sagard-Theodat, Gabriel (fl. early 17th century)
A Recollet missionary who lived among the Huron between 1623 and 1624, he wrote the earliest phrase book of the Huron language. Other descriptions of his stay constitute a valuable early source concerning the culture of the Huron people and their experiences during the fateful years of early French exploration and trade in New France.

Saponi ("Red-Earth People")
A small, semipermanent, matrilineal Siouan tribe of Virginia, first recorded as living in the vicinity of Lynchburg during the mid-seventeenth century. Harassed by sporadic warfare with English colonists and other tribes, the Saponi were joined by the Tutelo, Stuckanock, Meiponsky, and Occaneechi to form the Saponi Nation. In 1713, Governor Spotswood of Virginia established Fort Christianna, a reservation and trading post, and the Saponi Nation relocated. By mid-century, the Saponi Nation had allied itself with the Cayuga, and by 1771 the main body of the Saponi had relocated and were living with the Cayuga near present-day Ithaca, New York. Two bands of the Saponi Nation—the Occaneechi and Haliwa-Saponi—remained in North Carolina and southern Virginia. The Occaneechi adopted English names and, in some instances, were able to acquire title to their ancestral lands. Until 1957, the Haliwa-Saponi struggled with controversies con-

cerning access to schools and discrimination, and finally established their own school.

Sauk (Osakiwung, "People of the Outlet" or "People of the Yellow Earth")

Also known as the Sac, the Sauk are Algonquians closely related to the Fox and Kickapoo. Until the seventeenth century, the Sauk lived in Michigan; they were then forced out by the Ottawa. The Sauk resettled in Wisconsin, and in 1733 allied themselves with the Fox in order to capture territory from the Illinois. Like so many other American Indians, the Sauk became divided over how to respond to unrelenting pressures asserted by European and American settlers. In 1832, **Black Hawk** and his faction attempted to return to their traditional lands but were attacked and pursued by local militia. As a result of the Treaty of Chicago (1833), the Sauk ceded all their lands east of the Mississippi and moved to Iowa with the Fox. After several additional relocations and increased factionalization, most Sauk settled in Oklahoma. Since the 1930s the Sauk and Fox tribe has resided near Stroud, Oklahoma. While the Sauk farmed and hunted, they heavily relied upon buffalo for subsistence.

Seneca (O-non-dowa-gah, "People of the Great Hill")

The Seneca, an Iroquoian-speaking people of New York, were the western-most tribe of the League of the Iroquois. The Seneca share strong cultural, linguistic, and historic bonds with the other four tribes of the confederacy: the Onondaga, Cayuga, Mohawk, and Oneida. After becoming increasing involved in the fur trade and drawn into resulting conflicts, the Iroquois confederacy made peace with France in 1701. While members of the League participated in colonial warfare to varying degrees, the Seneca re-mained more sympathetic to the French, and supported Pontiac. The Sec-ond Treaty of **Fort Stanwix** (1784) reduced Seneca lands to several small reservations where they became increasingly reliant on the whites. During the nineteenth century, the Seneca were engaged in several struggles to maintain and protect their lands. Throughout the twentieth century the Seneca have strenuously opposed several massive construction projects and established important precedents in resolving land-lease disputes on tribal ground.

Shawnee (Sawanwa, "People of the South")

Renowned for their military prowess and staunch resistance to European and American encroachments, the Shawnee wandered through the woodlands of eastern America. Organized into five formal divisions, the Shawnee were patrilineal farmers and hunters. While the Shawnee spent much of the eighteenth century in Ohio and Kentucky, they also resided in Pennsylvania, Tennessee, South Carolina, and Missouri. From the defeat of General Braddock in 1754 through the War of 1812, the Shawnee aggressively organized and participated in regional coalitions against white encroachments. Despite the efforts of **Tecumseh** and **Tenskwatawa**, many Shawnee grew tired of warfare after the Treaty of **Greenville** (1795), which ceded Shawnee lands in Ohio. Although some warriors followed Tecumseh into the War of 1812 as British allies, most Shawnee had moved west to Missouri and eventually created three bands—Absentee Shawnee, Cherokee (or Loyal) Shawnee, and Eastern Shawnee. Although the Shawnee have purchased small tracts of land in Ohio, most reside in Oklahoma.

Shinnecock
The native people of eastern Long Island, the Shinnecock still occupy a reservation there. Pursuing a policy of accommodation to white settlement, the Shinnecock were famous whalers and sailors.

Smith, John (1579–1631)
English soldier and explorer whose accounts of Indians and maps of the Chesapeake were invaluable to English settlement. While fighting as a mercenary against the Turks, Smith was captured in Hungary. He escaped and returned to England through Russia in 1604. Because of his military experience, he was selected to accompany the Jamestown expedition (1607). As the colony struggled with dissent, food shortages, and hostile Indian relations, Smith was elected president of the colony's council. His austere leadership and improved relations with the **Powhatan Confederacy** stabilized the imperiled colony and enabled it to survive (see also **Pocahontas**). He returned to England to convalesce from severe powder burns.

Speck, Frank G. (1881–1950)
Prolific ethnographer and anthropologist, Speck published dozens of articles and books on the culture history of native peoples of the eastern United States and their descendant communities. In particular, Speck was interested in the survival of traditional culture traits, and recorded many such traits among the people with whom he worked. Less well known is Speck's active support for the modern descendants of Eastern Woodland people. Speck

helped to found Indian organizations in New England, and corresponded with officials in Congress and the Bureau of Indian Affairs over Indian rights issues.

Squanto (Tisquantum) (c. 1590–1622)

This remarkable Pokanoket (or Wampanoag) man was born in the village of Patuxet, later site of Plymouth Plantation. Cape Cod and the southern shores of Massachusetts Bay were visited by many explorers during the period of his youth, and in 1614, Thomas Hunt, who had accompanied John **Smith** in his explorations of the New England coast, took Squanto and several other native men and women captive, sailing then for Málaga, Spain, where many of them were sold. Rescued by priests who tried to convert them, Squanto and some companions eventually reached England, where he lived with the merchant John Slany, the treasurer of the Newfoundland Company. Sent on expedition to Newfoundland, Squanto then encountered Thomas Dermer, who took him back to England, where he met Sir Ferdinando Gorges, who agreed to finance a colonizing expedition to New England in 1619. Squanto returned to his village to find that nearly all its inhabitants had perished in the disastrous epidemics of the years 1614–19. Squanto interceded for Dermer with the powerful **Massasoit** of the Pokanoket (or the Wampanoag), but when Dermer was killed in a skirmish on Martha's Vineyard, Squanto himself was taken captive by Massasoit. In the spring of 1621, after Samoset, an Abenaki who was also familiar with the English, had reported their conditions to Massasoit, Squanto was dispatched to parley with the Pilgrims. He was famously credited with teaching the English to fertilize their crops with fish. Squanto assisted Massasoit, and the English, in negotiating favorable treaties with other local groups. Jealousies among some Indians and Squanto's own intrigue made him vulnerable to native reprisals, and some believe that his death in 1622 was an unnatural one. Historians credit him with an important role in preserving the infant Plymouth colony, although his reputation among native people remains an ambiguous one.

Stockbridge-Munsee

Possibly living on the Hudson River at the time of European contact, these people, then known as Mahican, accepted Protestant missionaries in the early eighteenth century, who then built a church and school at Stockbridge, Massachusetts. Although allied with the Americans, they were dispossessed after the Revolution and moved west to join the Oneida, who were also largely Christian converts. The Stockbridge ultimately settled in Wisconsin, and were joined there by other Munsee Delaware. Their reservation at Shawano, however, was dissolved in 1920 as an outcome of the **Dawes Severalty Act**. Reformed in 1934 under the provisions of the **Indian Reorganization Act**, the group now resides on a reservation in northeastern Wisconsin.

Susquehannock ("People at the Falls" or "Muddy Water People")

The Susquehannock lived along the Pennsylvanian River, which now bears their name. Traditional enemies of the Iroquois, the Susquehannock exploited their strategic location to establish a lucrative fur trade with the French. Noted for their hunting skills and martial prowess, the Susquehannock used the fur trade to acquire firearms and consolidate their influence. However, the cumulative toll of smallpox, warfare with the Iroquois, and hostilities with Maryland settlers decimated the Susquehannock by the end of the seventeenth century. In 1677, the Susquehannock entered into the Covenant Chain of the Iroquois, but they were virtual vassals to their traditional enemies. The last coherent band of Susquehannock settled at Conestoga, Pennsylvania, where they adopted Christianity and farming. The village at Conestoga was attacked and slaughtered en masse by Pennsylvania vigilantes. Although individuals and some families survived with other tribes, particularly the Mingo and Iroquois, the Susquehannock ceased to exist as a recognizable tribal entity. Also known as the Andaste and Minqua, the Susquehannock spoke an Iroquoian language.

Tecumseh ("Panther Crossing the Sky") (c. 1768–1813)

Shawnee leader renowned for his battlefield bravery, oratory skill, and humane treatment of prisoners. He repeatedly journeyed across the Great Lakes and as far south as the Gulf of Mexico to construct a concerted Indian resistance to throw back American settlers. Working with his brother, the Shawnee Prophet, he drew thousands of followers to Prophetstown. However, the defeat of the Shawnee Prophet in 1811, combined with unresolved inter-Indian disputes, eroded the efforts of Tecumseh. During the War of 1812, he was killed in Ontario while providing cover for the British flight from the Battle of the Thames (1813). The exact circumstances of his death and his burial are widely disputed. Throughout the nineteenth century many American politicians claimed to have slain Tecumseh.

Teedyuscung (1700–63)

Dispossessed as a result of the **Walking Purchase,** Teedyuscung and his family briefly accepted Moravian teaching, but in 1755 (during the Seven Years'

War), Teedyuscung was chosen chief of a confederacy of Delaware communities, drawn together in protest over Iroquois dominance in the region. Skillfully manipulating the colonial powers in a contest over his people and their lands, Teedyuscung parleyed with the pacifist Quakers, including the powerful William Penn, as well as William **Johnson**, the Royal Superintendent of Indian Affairs. Exposing the **Walking Purchase** for the fraud it was, Teedyuscung became a prominent Delaware leader, negotiating with the Iroquois League and the colonial government for reparations. He succeeded in establishing a new settlement on the Susquehanna River, but was evidently murdered when his new cabin was set on fire only a year later.

Tekakwitha, Kateri ("She Who Pushes All Before Her") (1656–80)

Mohawk woman whose life was recorded by Jesuit clergy in Canada. In 1660 she was her family's sole survivor of a smallpox epidemic; however, she was physically debilitated and remained nearly blind. From this ordeal and others, including mistreatment and social ostracism, she drew increasing strength from the Catholic faith of her mother. She was christened Catherine and went to live in the Christian Mohawk community at Sault St.-Louis near Montreal. Her steadfast devotion and constant penance, despite her frail condition, have been inspirational for generations of Roman Catholic Indians. She was beatified by Pope John Paul II in 1980.

Tenskwatawa ("The Open Door") (c. 1772–1836)

The younger brother of **Tecumseh** and the Shawnee spiritual leader commonly known as The Prophet. His message of Indian renewal through a return to traditional Indian lifestyles and repudiation of whites was an important cohesive element in Tecumseh's attempt to construct a pan-Indian confederation. He tried to eliminate internal dissent among the Shawnee by convening witch hunts. The Prophet established Prophetstown, where thousands of supporters convened. Alarmed by their success and aware that Tecumseh was absent, William Henry Harrison moved with an army against Prophetstown and goaded The Prophet into an ill-chosen confrontation. The Battle of **Tippecanoe** (1811) scattered most of the supporters, ending Tenskwatawa's prestige and significantly damaging Tecumseh's efforts.

Thorpe, Jim (1887–1953)

Jim Thorpe, widely regarded as one of the greatest American athletes of all time, was a Sauk and Fox Indian, born on the Sauk and Fox reservation in Oklahoma. His parents were of mixed Sauk and Fox, Menominee, Potawatomi, Kickapoo, French, and Irish ancestry. Educated at the **Haskell Institute** and **Carlisle Indian School,** Thorpe gained fame there as a football player. He won gold medals at the Olympic Games in Stockholm in 1912 in the decathlon and pentathlon, a feat no other athlete has since achieved. He was stripped of his honors because he had played semiprofessional baseball in the Rocky Mountain League, but Thorpe's medals have since been restored to his heirs.

Tidewater Wars (1622, 1644)

When **Opechancanough** succeeded **Powhatan** as paramount leader of the confederation, he secretly planned to war against the English colony at Jamestown due to steady land encroachments by the colonists. In 1622 and 1644 he coordinated widespread surprise attacks against the English settlements in an attempt to completely eliminate the colony. Although both ultimately failed, the 1622 attack was the most devastating to the English, who suffered high casualties and permanently abandoned several settlements. By the end of the second war, the confederation's power in the Tidewater was crushed and the elderly, beguiling Opechancanough was killed in Jamestown.

Tippecanoe, Battle of (1811)

The Battle of Tippecanoe was the culmination of strained relations between the aggressive governor, William Henry Harrison, and disaffected Indians led by **Tecumseh** and **Tenskwatawa.** Alarmed by the increasing success of the Shawnee brothers, Harrison organized a force of 1,000 men and marched on Prophetstown when his spies alerted him that Tecumseh was absent. Tenskwatawa inspired his outnumbered warriors with assurances they would be impervious to bullets and that they should kill Harrison. Their attack pressed Harrison's men, but his calm leadership rallied the Americans. The Indians retreated, then dispersed; Harrison set fire to Prophetstown.

Tiyanoga: *see* Hendrick.

Tuscarora

The Iroquoian-speaking Tuscarora currently reside on reservations near Lewiston, New York and Brantford, Ontario. Originally a loose and widespread confederation along the Atlantic, the populous Tuscarora were greatly reduced by smallpox epidemics and warfare with the Susquehannock and Seneca. After a particularly devastating war with settlers, the Tuscarora fled from the Carolinas and in 1722 officially joined the League of the Iroquois. While the other Iroquois tribes largely remained neutral or sided with the British during the American Revolution, many Tuscarora sided with the colonists. In the early twentieth century, many Tuscarora were farmers and factory workers. A Tuscarora leader, Clinton Rickard, formed the Indian Defense League in 1926, which championed and finally won the right for Indians to freely cross the U.S.-Canadian border.

Verrazano, Giovanni da (c. 1485–1528)

A Florentine navigator and explorer who encountered Indian peoples from North Carolina to Maine on his 1524 voyage. Although Europeans and American Indians had interacted previously, Verrazano produced the first written account of such an encounter.

Wabokieshiek ("White Cloud") (fl. 1800–33)

The Winnebago prophet, mystic, and medicine man known as White Cloud. As tensions mounted, the Winnebago Prophet preached resistance against white encroachment and kindled support for **Black Hawk** among the Winnebago, Potawatomi, and Kickapoo. Black Hawk and the Winnebago Prophet surrendered to end the Black Hawk War. White Cloud was pardoned and released by President Jackson.

Walking Purchase (1737)

The Walking Purchase is recognized as one of the most infamous land swindles perpetrated against Indians in the eighteenth century—a dubious distinction in an age of shady land deals. Pressed by creditors, Thomas and John Penn wanted land to sell to speculators and to the colony's increasing population. They produced an alleged 1686 land sale agreement that William Penn had negotiated with the Delaware. The Penn brothers then convinced the Delaware to accept the terms—that they would sell as much ground as a man could walk in a day and a half. Seasoned runners ran predetermined trails to maximize the land the Penns could purchase. Later, this 1686 document was again lost. This transaction seriously impaired frontier relations. Angry Delaware referred to it as "ye Running Walk."

Wampanoag (Wapanacki, "Easterner" or "Dawnlander")

The Wampanoag (known earlier as the Pokanoket or the Nauset) inhabited the coastal regions of Rhode Island and Massachusetts and spoke an Eastern Algonquian dialect known as Massachusett. Exposed to European diseases by sailors long before the establishment of permanent colonies, the Wampanoag population was greatly diminished. In 1621 the Wampanoag sachem, **Massasoit**, allied his people with the Puritans at Plymouth. Increasing tension and Puritan needs for land shattered the pact. In 1675, **Metacom** launched a violent, destructive war against the English; however, widespread regional support from Indians helped the Puritans to shatter the Wampanoag. By the beginning of the eighteenth century, the Wampanoag had increasingly converted to Christianity and moved onto plantations—early reservations. In the nineteenth and twentieth centuries many Wampanoag have worked as whalers, farmers, and soldiers.

Wheeler-Howard Act: *see* **Indian Reorganization Act.**

White Cloud: *see* **Wabokieshiek.**

Williams, Roger (c. 1603–83)
Persecuted because of his separatist notions and criticisms of Puritan settlements, Williams fled in the winter of 1636 to Rhode Island. He established Providence Colony, which was founded upon religious freedom and tolerance. Williams challenged the land claims of Puritans and respected the territorial claims of Indians. He carefully negotiated land purchases for his growing community from Rhode Island Indians. He became an interpreter and mediator, and wrote his invaluable *Key to the Indian Languages* in 1643. Williams used his considerable knowledge and esteem among Indians to repeatedly intervene on behalf of Puritan settlements, especially during the **Pequot War**.

Winnebago
The Winnebago are Siouan speakers from the upper Great Lakes who were divided into twelve clans, each with a distinct societal role. By 1700 the Winnebago had been decimated by epidemics, internal conflict, and rivalries with neighboring tribes. Having lost most of their ancestral lands, the Winnebago migrated west and allied themselves with the French. Severe pressures from lead miners and settlers ignited the brutal Winnebago War. In 1832 the Winnebago were forced to cede all former lands in Iowa. That same year a prophet, **Wabokieshiek** (White Cloud), persuaded the Winnebago to support the Sauk and Fox during the **Black Hawk** War. Further decimated by smallpox, the Winnebago relinquished all claims to their former Wisconsin lands. Throughout the remainder of the century, the Win-

nebago were repeatedly uprooted from their settlements. By the beginning of the twentieth century, many Winnebago had reassembled in Wisconsin and Nebraska, where they currently live. In 1975 the Winnebago of Nebraska were awarded $4.6 million by the Indian Claims Commission for lands ceded in 1837.

Zeisberger, David (1721–1808)

A Moravian missionary who founded communities for Christian Indians in Pennsylvania similar to **Eliot's praying towns**. Prior to the American Revolution, Zeisberger established several towns in the Ohio country along the Tuscarawa and Muskingham Rivers. Amid violent frontier raids and retaliations, Zeisberger kept his towns peaceful and used his influence to promote Indian neutrality. But Zeisberger secretly passed information concerning the strength and intentions of pro-British Indians to Forts Pitt and Henry. In 1782 almost one hundred Christian Delaware at his Gnadenhutten settlement were massacred by Pennsylvania militia and frontiersman. The many letters and detailed diaries of Zeisberger serve as important ethnographic and historical resources.

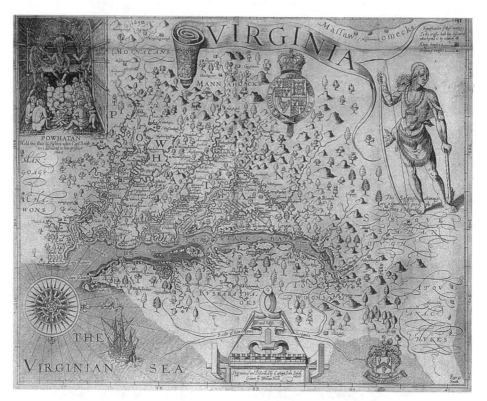

1. Map of Virginia, by John Smith. It depicts the extent of Powhatan's domain and the villages under his control.

2. Warrior of Secotan. Drawing by Theodore de Bry, 1590, based on drawings by John White.

3. Here Henry R. Schoolcraft illustrates a "specimen of Iroquois picture writing" of Onondaga origin, said to represent the "first Iroquois ruler under the Confederacy."

figure des sauuages almouchicois

4. "Almouchicois" man and woman. Champlain, 1604.

A KEY into the

LANGUAGE

OF

AMERICA:

O R,

An help to the *Language* of the *Natives*
in that part of A M E R I C A, called
N E W-E N G L A N D.

Together, with briefe *Observations* of the Cu-
stomes, Manners and Worships, &c of the
aforesaid *Natives*, in Peace and Warre,
in Life and Death.

On all which are added Spirituall *Observations*
Generall and Particular by the *Authour*, of
chiefe and speciall use (upon all occasions,)to
all the *English* Inhabiting those parts;
yet pleasant and profitable to
the view of all men:

BY ROGER WILLIAMS
of *Providence* in *New-England.*

LONDON,
Printed by *Gregory Dexter*, 1643.

5. Title page of *Key Into the Language of America* by Roger Williams, 1643.

6. Matoaka or Rebecca. From John Smith, *The Generalle Historie of Virginia, New England, and the Summer Isles*, 1624.

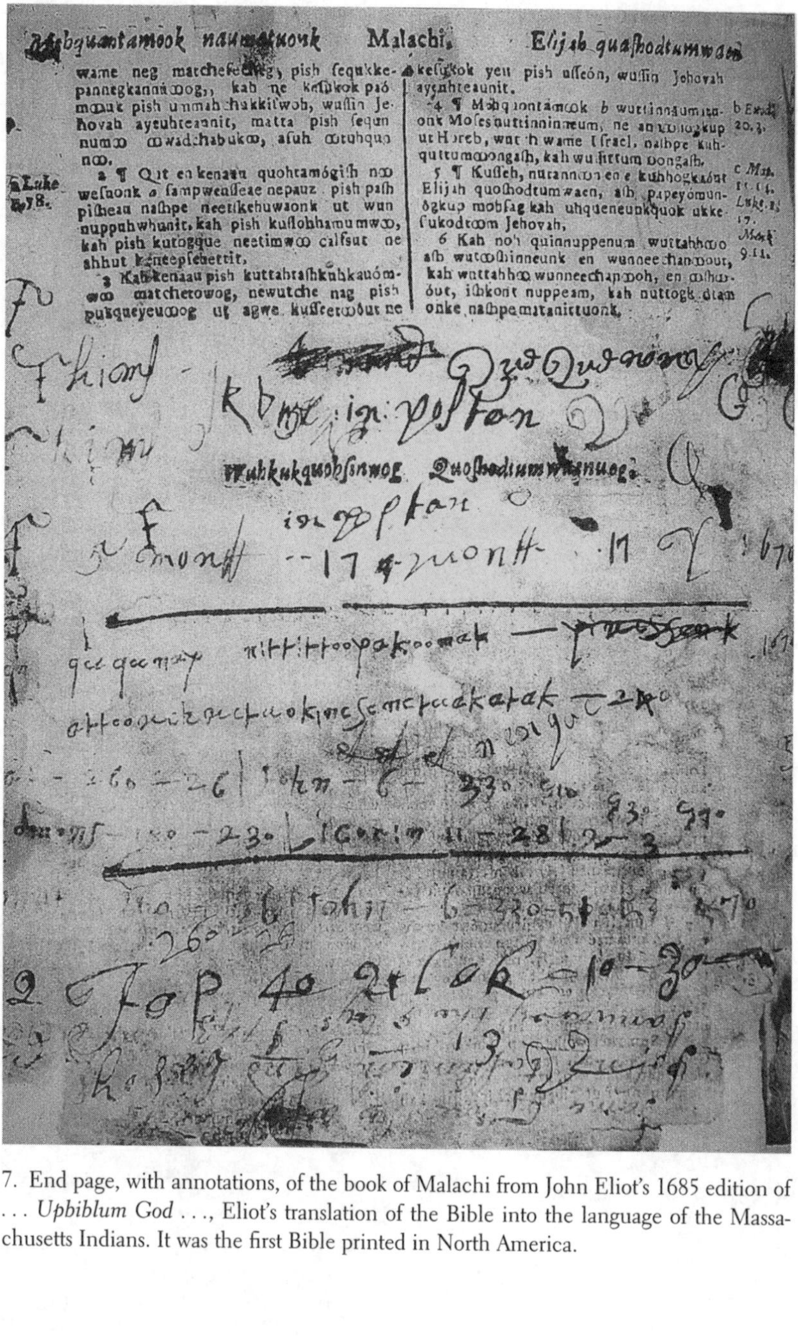

Mahquontamook naumatuonk Malachi. Elijah quashodtumwaen

wame neg matchekeeneg, pish sequkkepannegkannuwog,, kah ne kesukok paómouuk pish unnmahchakkitwoh, wussin Jehovah ayeuhteaunit, matta pish sequn numwo wwadchabukwo, asuh wtuhquonwo.
2 ¶ Qut en kenaau quohtamógish nwo wesuonk a sampweusseae nepauz pish pash pisheau nashpe neetukehuwaonk ut wunnuppuhwhunit, kah pish kussohhamumwo, kah pish kutogque neetimwo calfsut ne ahhut keneepsehettit,
3 Kah kenaau pish kuttahtashkuhkauómwo matchetowog, newutche nag pish pukqueyeuwog ut agwe kusseetwout ne kesukok yeu pish usseón, wussin Jehovah ayeuhteaunit.
4 ¶ Mahquontamook b wuttinnaumuonk Moses nuttinninneum, ne annoonogkup ut Horeb, wutch wame Israel, nashpe kuhquttumwongash, kah wussittum oongash.
5 ¶ Kusseh, nutannoonen e kuhhogkaóut Elijah quoshodtumwaen, ash papeyómundgkup mohsag kah uhqueneunkquok ukkesukodtoom Jehovah,
6 Kah noh quinnuppenum wuttahhoo ash wutooshinneunk en wunneechanooout, kah wuttahhoo wunneechanooh, en oshooout, ishkont nuppeam, kah nuttogk dtam onke nashpe matanittuonk.

a Luke 1.17.
b Exod. 20.3.
c Matt. 11.14. Luke 1.17. Mark 9.11.

Wuhkukquohsinwog Quoshodiumwagnuog.

7. End page, with annotations, of the book of Malachi from John Eliot's 1685 edition of . . . *Upbiblum God* . . ., Eliot's translation of the Bible into the language of the Massachusetts Indians. It was the first Bible printed in North America.

8. Two Indian women of Virginia. Beverley, 1705. Although the figure on the right is apparently a copy of the de Bry illustrations of John White's voyage to Roanoke, the woman on the left is shown wearing a "Duffield Matchcoat, bought of the English."

9. Sauk and Fox war dance.

10. Passamaquoddy basket maker Lillian Sockabasin, 1995.

11. Thayendanegea or Brant, "Great Captain of the Six Nations."

TECUMSEH.   Page 256

12. Tecumseh. Fanciful portrait by William V. Moore.

13. Ne-sou-a-quoit, a Fox chief.

14. Mattaponi fishing station, Mattaponi River, King William County, Virginia.

15. Amiskquew, a Menominee warrior.

16. Hoo-Wan-ne-ka, "Little Elk," Winnebago.

17. George Catlin illustrates four remarkable warriors of the Sac and Fox. His figure 283 is of Black Hawk; 284 is of Nah-se-us-kuk, "The Whirling Thunder," Black Hawk's eldest son; 285 is of Wah-pe-kee-suck, "The Prophet"; and 286 is of Wee-Sheet, "The Sturgeon's Head."

18. Sauk and Fox delegation with Louis Bogy, 1867.

19. Cornplanter.

Part III

Historical Timeline for the Northeast

Following are significant events in the history of the Northeast, listed in chronological order.

1497–98: John and Sebastien Cabot's voyages to "New-found-land"
Cabot's voyages marked the first contacts between Europeans and the native peoples of the northern maritime provinces.

1500–1501: Corte-Real explores northeastern coast; Basque fishermen begin annual visits
Fishermen began a pattern of seasonal trading visits to native people of the Northeast, and provided some of the earliest European loanwords in native languages.

1524: Verrazano visits the shores of Narragansett Bay and southern Maine
Verrazano's descriptions indicated that complex political organization was already a feature of southern New England native groups.

1534–41: Cartier explores the future "New France"
Cartier's voyages in the Bay of Gaspé and the St. Lawrence brought him into contact with the Iroquoians and Huron, and paved the way for the establishment of the French settlements at Quebec and Montreal.

1576: Frobisher's first North Atlantic voyage

Frobisher visited some of the northernmost of the northeastern maritime groups and returned with illustrations of their costumes, tools, and weapons.

1584: Raleigh's colony at Roanoke established

Although the colonists who had been left behind while other settlers returned to England eventually disappeared, John White's drawings of native people of the Pamlico Sound area are among the most celebrated of all early contact illustrations.

1602: Gosnold explores Cape Cod, the Elizabeth Islands, and Martha's Vineyard

Gosnold and his crew were among many who kidnapped and harassed the native people of southern New England, setting the stage for hostilities with the earliest English settlers there.

1603: The Dutch found New Amsterdam; Martin Pring explores New England coast

The Dutch explored many upriver Indian communities in what is now central Connecticut, establishing trade relations that remained important there throughout the seventeenth century.

1605: George Waymouth explores the coast of Maine

Waymouth's colony set the stage for future hostilities between the French, English, and their Abenaki allies.

1606: Settlement of Msr. de Poutrincourt at Port Royal, New France

The French settlement established trade relations and provided a staging point for Jesuit missionaries to the native people of the region.

1607: Popham's settlement at Sagahadoc established

This English colony was established for purposes of trade in skins and fish. Native people in the region soon became competitors to control this trade with the inland native people.

1607: Establishment of the settlement at Jamestown

The Jamestown colony succeeded in placating the powerful Powhatan for several years after its founding, but by 1622, the natives rose against the colonists in the first of two bloody attempts to drive the colonists out.

1608: Champlain and Lescarbot found Quebec City

This settlement became the locus of trade and diplomacy on the St. Lawrence, and provided a staging point for expeditions to the Huron and Great Lakes peoples.

1609: Henry Hudson explores New England and the Hudson River

The populous Mahican and Delaware first encountered English and Dutch explorers seeking trade near the mouth of the Hudson.

1610: Voyage of Adrien Block (Dutch) along New England coast

Block's maps of the area show many Indian communities, all of whom the Dutch attempted to engage in trade for skins and wampum.

1614: John Smith explores New England

Smith explored Cape Cod and the northern shore of Massachusetts Bay, where he found thirty or more communities, just prior to their destruction during the first of New England's epidemics.

1616–19: Epidemics ravage New England

The identity of the diseases that killed up to 90 percent of southern New England communities is unknown, but yellow fever or the bubonic plague are possibilities.

1620: Plymouth Colony established

The Separatists established an alliance with the Pokanoket paramount sachem, Massasoit, that remained intact for nearly fifty years.

1621–22: English-Powhatan War

The first war, organized by Powhatan's brother Opechancanough, led to the death of nearly half of the English settlers in the region.

1628: Salem founded

The Puritans who settled at Naumkeag and Salem, Massachusetts were the first of the "Great Migration" that flooded New England with English settlers during the 1640s and 1650s.

1630: Boston founded

Boston soon became the administrative center of Puritan New England, and saw the establishment of the United Colonies and Harvard College.

1636 : The Pequot War

The combined forces of the English, Narragansett, and Mohegan destroyed the fort at Mystic and killed all its inhabitants in a strike that ended Pequot hegemony in the region.

1644: Second Powhatan-English War

A well-executed attack, also killing many colonists but ultimately unsuccessful in ridding the region of the English, who retaliated brutally and quickly, eventually driving the surviving native combatants out of the peninsula and into the margins of their former territories.

1675–76: King Philip's War

Philip, or Metacom, son of the sachem Massasoit, grew increasingly dissatisfied with English repressive politics and organized a rebellion that briefly united many Indian groups of the region against the colonists. Defeated by the larger, better-organized English forces and their Mohawk allies, Philip was executed, and his family killed or deported.

1675: Bacon's Rebellion

Nathaniel Bacon led an uprising of disaffected colonists against friendly Indians, prompting retaliation from the colonial governor. Bacon was defeated and executed and his rebellion quelled, but the capital city of Jamestown was destroyed during the conflict.

1755–62: Seven Years' War

A conflict between French and British colonies in the New World over control of the fur trade, this war eventually spread to Europe.

1768: Treaty of Fort Stanwix

The treaty ceded significant portions of Iroquois-held land in Ohio to the British.

1769: Pontiac's Rebellion

Led by the native leader Pontiac against English forces at Detroit, this war had little effect on increasing European presence in the region.

1784: Treaty of Fort Stanwix

The second treaty ceded most of the remaining Ohio lands to the new federal government.

1797: Iroquois reservations established

Defeated in the Revolutionary War and stripped of most of their territories, some Iroquois communities were granted small reservations in western New York and Ontario.

1799: Handsome Lake's first visions

Cornplanter's brother Handsome Lake had a series of visions while ill that became the foundation for the Longhouse religion, still practiced in traditional Iroquois communities today.

1815: Death of Handsome Lake

1832: Black Hawk's War (Bad Axe Creek)

1834: Indian Removal Act passed

Many of the eastern Indians, including the Delaware and Shawnee, were sent west to Indian Territory in Oklahoma. Many lands in Iowa, Illinois, and the Great Lakes region were also ceded to the state and federal government in exchange for land or small allotments to surviving Indian communities.

1830–60: Period of Indian Removal

1842–57: Tonawanda Seneca settled claim against New York

1892: Settlement of Oneida land claims in Kansas

After the disastrous impact of the Allotment Act became clear, this act helped to reorganize eastern Indian communities and required that they establish elected councils.

1954: Menominee detribalization

1960: Kinzua Dam protests begin

Among the earliest native-organized protests against the federal government. The Seneca led the Kinzua Dam protest. It was ultimately unsuccessful, but raised consciousness about native rights.

1975: Mashpee land claims trial

Claiming reparation for illegally dispersed native lands, the Mashpee were unsuccessful in court, but the decision—*Mashpee vs. the New Seabrook*

Corporation — is a landmark case in tribal law. The Mashpee are currently appealing this decision.

1980: Narragansett federal recognition
The Narragansett received federal recognition in exchange for an agreement to refrain from establishing gaming on their small reservation lands in Charlestown, Rhode Island.

1980: *Passamaquoddy, Maliseet Penobscot land claims vs. the State of Maine*
The largest settlement in favor of an eastern tribe, this case set the stage for federal recognition and land claims cases throughout the Northeast.

1981: Gay Head federal recognition
After a preliminary negative finding, the Gay Head were successful in achieving federal recognition from the Bureau of Indian Affairs.

1984: Mashantucket Pequot federal recognition
The Mashantucket chose to achieve recognition legislatively, and were able to establish one of the most successful gaming establishments in the country as a result of their new sovereign status.

1994: Mohegan federal recognition
The Mohegan also received recognition via the BIA process, and are also successfully running a large gaming facility in their old reservation town of Montville, Connecticut.

Part IV

Resource Guide to Research
and Theory

Introduction

The Northeast culture area has attracted the attention of numerous scholars since the seventeenth century. Archaeologists, linguists, historians, anthropologists, ethnohistorians, and cultural critics have produced a rich body of literature and represent many different points of view concerning the region, its people, and its history. This section discusses a number of topics of current or enduring interest as they are reflected in the scholarly literature, with an annotated discussion of sources for the beginning or experienced student. In general, only the most comprehensive and/or most recent publications concerning each research subject are included. Exceptions are the "classics" in the literature on the Northeast, regardless of their date of publication, and some of the most important primary sources. Some of these topics are also addressed in part I, which concludes with an extensive list of references, many not duplicated in the following guide. Interested readers are advised to consult both parts. The reader is urged to consult the more recent publications listed for additional references concerning the topics discussed. The following discussion is organized by the type of resource, beginning with "primary sources," including archaeological data and human remains and their analyses, documentary sources, early linguistic records, and ethnographies. The second section focuses on secondary literature, and is organized by topic. The guide concludes with a brief survey of general reference works, and selected museum, media, archival, and electronic research resources.

Although the author has tried to make reference to most of the scholarly perspectives on the native people of the Northeast, the anthropological, ethnohistorical, and linguistic take precedence over the literary. Since this book focuses on the native people of the region, not on the history or perceptions of its non-Indian inhabitants, this preference seems justified. In keeping with a native-centered approach, this part begins with a list of native tribes and tribal organizations, some federally recognized and some not, who can be contacted for further information.

1. Indian Tribes

Agencies that administer Indian affairs and the tribes themselves can be sources of a wealth of information about history, government, and current events.

Administration of Indian Affairs

Bureau of Indian Affairs
1849 C Street, NW
Washington, DC 20240-0001

Federally Recognized Tribes

Federally recognized tribes have a government-to-government relationship with the United States, receive services administered by the Bureau of Indian Affairs, and enjoy limited sovereignty on their tribal land that is held in trust by the federal government. The following is a current listing of Indian tribes and tribal organizations of the Northeast. Not all are federally recognized; some are in the process of seeking recognition, and others are officially recognized only by the states or localities in which they reside.

CONNECTICUT

Eastern Pequot Reservation
Eastern Area Office
Roy Sebastian, Chairperson
North Stonington, CT 06359

Golden Hill Indian Reservation
Golden Hill Paugussett 3 Chief Government
Moonface Bear, Leader
95 Stanavage Road
Trumbull, CT 06415
(203) 377-4410

Mashantucket Pequot Tribal Nation
Eastern Area Office
Richard A. Hayward, Chairperson
P.O. Box 3060
Ledyard, CT 06339
(860) 572-6100

Mohegan Tribal Council
Eastern Area Office
Ralph W. Sturges, Chief
27 Church Lane
Uncasville, CT 06382

Paucatuck Eastern Pequot Tribe
Eastern Area Office
Roy Sebastian, Chairperson
935 Lantern Hill Road
Ledyard, CT 06339

Schaghticoke Tribal Nation of Kent
Schaghticoke Tribal Council
Richard Velky, Chairperson
605 Main Street
Monroe, CT 06468
(203) 459-2531

INDIANA

Indiana Miami Council
(not yet federally recognized)
641 Buchanan Street
Huntington, IN 46750

Miami Nation of Indians of Indiana Council
(not yet federally recognized)
P.O. Box 41
Peru, IN 46970
(317) 473-9631

Upper Kispoko Band of the Shawnee Nation
(not yet federally recognized)
Kokomo, IN 46901
(317) 457-5376

IOWA

Sac and Fox Tribe
Sac and Fox Tribal Council
Gailey Wanatee, Chief
349 Meskwaki Rd
Tama, IA 52399
(515) 484-4678

MAINE

Aroostook Band of Micmac Indians
Eastern Area Office
Roger Pictou, President
P.O. Box 772
Presque Island, ME 04769
(207) 764-1972

Houlton Band of Maliseet Indians
Eastern Area Office
Clair Sabattis, Chairperson
Route 3, P.O. Box 450
Houlton, ME 04730
(207) 532-4273

Indian Township Reservation
Indian Township Passamaquoddy Tribe
John Stevens, Tribal Governor
P.O. Box 301

Princeton, ME 04668
(207) 796-2301

Penobscot Reservation
Penobscot Tribal Council
Jerry Pardilla, Tribal Governor
Community Bldg., Indian Island
Old Town, ME 04468
(207) 827-7776

Pleasant Point Reservation
Pleasant Point Passamaquoddy Tribe
Cliv Dore, Tribal Governor
P.O. Box 343
Perry, ME 04667
(207) 853-2551

MASSACHUSETTS

Wampanoag Reservation
Wampanoag Tribal Council of Gay Head (Aquinnah)
Beverly Wright, Chairperson
20 Black Brook Road
Aquinnah, MA 02535
(508) 645-9265

MICHIGAN

Bay Mills Reservation
Bay Mills Executive Council
Jeff Parker, Chairperson
Route 1, Box 313
Brimley, MI 49715
(906) 248-3241

Grand Traverse Reservation
Grand Traverse Band Tribal Council
Joseph C. Raphael, Chairperson
2605 N.W. Bayshore Dr., P.O. Box 118
Suttons Bay, MI 49682
(616) 271-3538

Hannahville Indian Community
Michigan Agency
Kenneth Meshiguad, Chairperson
N14911 Hannahville B-1 Road
Wilson, MI 49896
(906) 466-2342

Isabella Reservation
Saginaw Chippewa Tribal Council
Gail George, Chief
7070 E. Broadway Road
Mt. Pleasant, MI 48858
(906) 632-6809

Lac Vieux Desert Band of Lake Superior Chippewa
Michigan Agency
John C. McGeshick, Chairperson
P.O. Box 249, Choate Road
Watersmeet, MI 49969
(906) 358-4577

L'Anse Reservation
Keweenah Bay Tribal Council
Frederick Dakota, Chairperson
Route 1, Box 45
Baraga, MI 49908
(906) 353-6623

Sault Ste. Marie Tribe of Indians Reservation
Sault Ste. Marie Chippewa Tribal Council
Bernard Bouschor, Chairperson
2218 Shunk Road
Sault Ste. Marie, MI 49783
(906) 635-6050

MINNESOTA

Fond Du Lac Reservation
Fond Du Lac Business Committee

Robert "Sonny" Peacock, Chairperson
105 University Road
Cloquet, MN 55720
(218) 879-4593

Grand Portage Reservation
Grand Portage Business Committee
Norman DesChampe, Chairperson
P.O. Box 428
Grand Portage, MN 55606
(218) 475-2279

Leech Lake Reservation
Business Tribal Council
Alfred "Tig" Pemberton, Chairperson
Route 3, Box 100
Cass Lake, MN 56633
(218) 335-8200

Lower Sioux Indian Community
Lower Sioux Indian Community Council
Joseph Goodthunder, President
R.R. 1, Box 308
Morton, MN 56270
(507) 697-6185

Mille Lacs Reservation
Mille Lacs Business Committee
Marjorie Anderson, Chairperson
HCR 67, Box 194
Onamia, MN 56359
(612) 532-4181

Minnesota Chippewa Tribe
Tribal Executive Committee
Darrell Wadena, President
P.O. Box 217
Cass Lake, MN 56633
(218) 335-8581

Nett Lake Reservation
Bois Forte Tribal Business Committee
Gary Donald, Chairperson
P.O. Box 16
Nett Lake, MN 55772
(218) 757-3261

Prairie Island Reservation
Prairie Island Community Council
Curtis Campbell Sr., President
1158 Island Blvd.
Welch, MN 55089
(612) 388-2554

Red Lake Reservation
Red Lake Tribal Council
Bobby Whitefeather, Chairperson
P.O. Box 550
Red Lake, MN 56671
(218) 679-3341

Skakopee Sioux Community
Shakopee Sioux Community Council
Stanley Crooks, Chairperson
2330 Sioux Trail, NW
Prior Lake, MN 55372
(612) 445-8900

Upper Sioux Indian Community
Upper Sioux Board of Trustees
Lorraine Gouge, Chairperson
P.O. Box 147
Granite Falls, MN 56241
(612) 564-2360

White Earth Reservation
White Earth Business Committee
Darrell Wadena, Chairperson
Hwy. 224, Box 418
White Earth, MN 56591
(218) 983-3285

NEW YORK

Cattaraugus Reservation
Seneca Nation Tribal Council
Dennis Bowen, President
1490 Route 438
Irving, NY 14081
(716) 532-4900

Cayuga Indian Nation
Cayuga Nation Tribal Council
Vernon Isaac, Chief
P.O. Box 11
Versailles, NY 14168
(716) 532-4847

Oil Spring Reservation
New York Liaison Office
Cuba Lake, NY 14727

Oneida Indian Nation of New York
New York Liaison Office
Ray Halbritter, Nation Representative
P.O. Box 1, West Road
Oneida, NY 13421
(315) 829-3090

Onondaga Reservation
Onondaga Nation Tribal Council
Leon Shenandoah Sr., Head Chief
R.R. 1, Box 270A
Nedrow, NY 13120
(716) 469-8507

Poosepatuck Reservation
Eastern Area Office
P.O. Box 86
Mastic, NY 11950
(516) 281-6464

Seneca Nation of Indians
Seneca Nation Tribal Council
P.O. Box 231
Salamanca, NY 14779
(716) 945-1790

St. Regis Mohawk Reservation
St. Regis Mohawk Council Chiefs
John Loran, Head Chief
R.R. 1, Box 14C
Hogansburg, NY 13655
(518) 358-2272

Tonawanda Reservation
Tonawanda Band of Senecas Council of Chiefs
Bernie Parker, Chief
7027 Meadville Road
Basom, NY 14013
(716) 542-4244

Tuscarora Reservation
Tuscarora Tribal Business Council
Arnold Hewitt, Head Chief
5616 Walmore Road
Lewiston, NY 14092
(716) 297-4990

RHODE ISLAND

Narragansett Reservation
Narragansett Indian Tribal Council
George H. Hopkins, Chief Sachem
P.O. Box 268
Charleston, RI 02813
(401) 364-1100

VIRGINIA

Cherokee Tribe of Virginia
Cherokee of Virginia Tribal Council

Samual W. Beeler Sr., Principal Chief
Route 1, Box 499
Rapidan, VA 22733
(703) 672-4841

Pamunkey Indian Reservation
Pamunkey Tribal Council
William P. Miles, Chief
Route 1, Box 2220
King William, VA 23086
(804) 843-3526

WISCONSIN

Bad River Reservation
Bad River Tribal Council
Elizabeth Drake, Chairperson
P.O. Box 39
Odanah, WI 54861
(715) 682-7111

Forest County Potawatomi Community
Forest County Potawatomi Executive Council
Hartford Shegonee, Chairperson
P.O. Box 340
Crandon, WI 54520
(715) 478-2903

Ho Chunk (Winnebago) Reservation
Wisconsin Ho Chunk Business Committee
Gordon Thunder, Chairperson
P.O. Box 667
Black River Falls, WI 54615
(715) 284-9343

Lac Courte Oreilles Reservation
Lac Courte Orielles Tribal Governing Board
Gaiashkibos, Chairperson
Route 2, Box 2700

Hayward, WI 54843
(715) 634-8934

Lac Du Flambeau Reservation
Lac Du Flambeau Tribal Council
Thomas Maulson, President
P.O. Box 67
Lac Du Flambeau, WI 54538
(715) 588-3303

Menominee Reservation
Menominee Tribal Legislature
Glenn Miller, Chairperson
P.O. Box 910
Keshena, WI 54135
(715) 799-5100

Oneida Reservation
Oneida Tribal Council
Deborah Doxtater, Chairperson
P.O. Box 365
Oneida, WI 54155
(414) 869-2214

Red Cliff Reservation
Red Cliff Tribal Council
Rose Gumoe, Chairperson
P.O. Box 529
Bayfield, WI 54814
(715) 779-3701

Sokaogon Chippewa Community
Sokaogon Chippewa Tribal Council
Arlyn Ackley, Chairperson
Route 1, Box 625
Crandon, WI 54520
(715) 478-2604

St. Croix Reservation
St. Croix Council

Lewis Taylor, Chairperson
P.O. Box 287
Hertel, WI 54845
(715) 349-2195

Stockbridge-Munsee Community
Stockbridge-Munsee Tribal Council
Laura Coyhis, Chairperson
8476 Moh He Con Nuck Road
Bowler, WI 54416
(715) 793-4111

2. Primary Sources and the Northeast

Archaeology, the Adoption of Agriculture, and the Rise of Complex Chiefdoms and Social Inequality in the Northeast

In 1978, Bruce G. Trigger listed a number of research issues of continuing interest to scholars working in the Northeast, many of which are concerned with regional patterns. These included the effects of contact on social complexity in the Northeast, and the possibilities for the identification of various subregional patterns, such as the "northern Algonquian foraging pattern" or the Mississippian pattern.

Disputes over the relative importance of the arrival of Europeans and their goods in the New World also continue. As Trigger remarks, even the state societies of the Mississippian period may have experienced decline due to the impact of diseases that spread inland in the fourteenth and fifteenth centuries A.D., long before Europeans themselves arrived in that area. The vacuum created by such a decline, or the breakdown of the complex chiefdoms or state societies of the Mississippian region would inevitably have had effects farther to the east, and a great deal of research remains to be done in order to determine exactly what those effects might have been. Dincauze and Hazenstab, for example, suggest that Mississippian expansion into Iroquoian territory indirectly impacted New England societies in the late fifteenth century, were perhaps a factor in the increasingly warlike nature of Iroquoian societies, and led to the proliferation of fortified sites and the subsequent raiding into New England for captives and slaves.

Among the most absorbing debates that bring together ethnographers and archaeologists are those concerning the rise of social complexity in societies around the world. In North America, the principal interest lies in determining the effects of the adoption of agriculture on "tribal" or "band-level" societies, the causes or conditions of the rise of complex chiefdoms or state-level societies during the Woodland period, and the effects of the arrival of Europeans, the trade in European-introduced objects, and the fur trade generally on social complexity in coastal groups. Legislation introduced in the 1970s as part of new cultural preservation measures required that all building projects using federal funds use some of those funds for archaeological mitigation. Since that time, hundreds of sites slated for destruction have been excavated and reported on, resulting in a huge increase in the amount of knowledge of late northeastern prehistory.

A larger question concerns the interconnections between the complex late Mississippian and Ohioan societies (Peregrine 1996) and the peoples in other parts of the Northeast (e.g., Griffin 1993). Traditional interpretations of the region have often emphasized the local diversity and relative isolation of the various Woodland peoples, and scholarly consensus has been that in situ development of most of the societies ancestral to the groups encountered by early European settlers was likely (Tuck 1978; Fitting 1978). New research that identifies intercultural interaction, including archaeological, linguistic, and ethnographic studies, suggest that peoples of the Northeast were not isolated from the socially complex polities to their west and south (Dincauze and Hasenstab 1987, Hasenstab 1990), and that an understanding of the effects of this contact and influence will be necessary to our understanding of native northeastern response to Europeans (Bragdon 1996).

Several issues need addressing. First, what does social complexity consist of? Cross-cultural studies of modern chiefdoms also suggest that these complex societies are quite variable, and that the seeds of social disparity are present even in cultures previously understood to be organized according to "egalitarian" principles. What would be the archaeological manifestations of social complexity? Recently, Timothy Earle has argued that the archaeological remains of chiefdoms may or may not reflect class distinctions (1987). Must complex societies be sedentary, or might sedentariness occur without the adoption of agriculture (Bennison 1997; Dimmick 1994)? Secondly, how would the adoption of agriculture and its attendant sedentariness, productivity, and work requirements affect previously mobile or semi-sedentary societies? Archaeologist Lynn Ceci argued that coastal societies of what is now New York, for example, were encouraged to adopt agriculture in order to permit year-round residence on the coast, to facilitate their access to European trade goods, and that the social complexity of these societies suggested in the early sources was in fact an artifact of contact (Ceci 1982). Finally, scholars debate the effects of European contact on the rise of complex societies, and whether tribal, chiefly, or state societies owe their origins to indigenous causes or to the stimulus of new trade goods or the threat of conquest. Increasingly, scholars lean toward the former explanation, arguing that the trend toward complexity existed in the Americas prior to the arrival of Europeans (Baker and Pauketat 1992; Potter 1993), although there are several documented examples of the reverse as well (e.g., Borque and White-head 1985).

Archaeologists also contribute to our understanding of the nature of chiefly societies and their range of variability. Studies of chiefdoms in the Southeast, for example, some of which survived into the contact period, demonstrate many variations in the trappings, privileges, and responsibilities of the elite, the role of women, specialization in the arts, and the nature of economic relations, trade, diplomacy, and warfare (see below). Another area of research identified by Trigger and others is the possibility of a pre-maize horticultural complex indigenous to the Eastern Woodlands, and the related possibility that such a complex might well form the basis for chiefly levels of social organization, such as that characterized the earlier Adena-Hopewell florescence, and which was apparently the case in the rise of complex societies in coastal regions of New England, New York, and the Mid-Atlantic. This issue, which received more attention from earlier generations of anthropologists, might well benefit from reconsideration in light of the great increase in archaeological data and the refinement of dating techniques that have characterized archaeological research since the 1970s. Archaeological data also has much to contribute to contemporary ethnological investigations. Topics such as the rise of social complexity, the contrasts between egalitarian and stratified societies in economy and worldview, and the nature of gender relations in these societies are all of great interest to contemporary scholars.

Sources

Baker, Alex W. and Timothy R. Pauketat, eds. 1992. *Lords of the Southeast: Social Inequality and the Native Elites of Southeastern North America.* Washington, D.C.: American Anthropological Association.

Although concerned with peoples outside the bounds of the Northeast culture area (with the exception of the Powhatan—see Rountree 1992, below), this volume contains several important articles that describe the rise of southeastern chiefdoms, the archaeological remains of such peoples, and theoretical issues involved in their study. The introduction also includes an important critique of previous archaeological studies of such peoples in native North America.

Benison, Chris. 1997. "Horticulture and the Maintenance of Social Complexity in Late Woodland Southeastern New England." *North American Archaeologist* 18(1): 1–17.

Part of the ongoing debate concerning the existence of complex societies in the Northeast, and the role agriculture played in their development.

Bourque, Bruce J. and Ruth H. Whitehead. 1985. "Tarrantines and the Introduction of European Trade Goods in the Gulf of Maine." *Ethnohistory* 32:327–41.

A thorough review of primary sources concerning Micmac (Tarrantine) traders and "big men" in coastal Maine during the early historic period, whose social and political status appears to have been enhanced through their role as middlemen.

Bragdon, Kathleen. 1996. *Native People of Southern New England, 1500–1650.* Norman: University of Oklahoma Press.

Contains a chapter reviewing the literature on chiefdoms, the archaeology of New England, and the likelihood that complex societies predated the establishment of agriculture in most of the region.

Ceci, Lynn. 1982. "Method and Theory in Coastal New York Archaeology: Paradigms of Settlement Pattern." *North American Archeologist* 3(1): 5–36.

A classic essay in which the author argues that social complexity and the establishment of permanent "year-round" villages in coastal regions was a response to the arrival of European traders.

Dimmick, Frederica R. 1994. "Creative Farmers of the Northeast: A New View of Indian Maize Horticulture." *North American Archaeologist* 15(3): 235–52.

Emphasizes the social processes of the adoption of agriculture, and the role of women in its adoption.

Dincauze, Dena and Robert J. Hasenstab. 1989. "Explaining the Iroquois: Tribalization on a Prehistoric Periphery." In *Centre and Periphery: Comparative Studies in Archaeology*, ed. T. C. Champion, 67–87. London: Unwin Hyman. Originally published in *Proceedings of the World Archaeological Congress*, September 1986, part 4.

A controversial essay that suggests that the Iroquois responded to pressure from Ohioan complex societies moving east, by themselves forming more centralized political organizations.

Earle, Timothy. 1987. "Chiefdoms in Archaeological and Ethnohistorical Perspective." *Annual Reviews in Anthropology* 16:279–308.

A comprehensive survey of the ethnological and archaeological literature on chiefdoms in North America and elsewhere.

Fitting, James E. 1978. "Regional Cultural Development, 300 B.C.–A.D. 1000." In *The Northeast*, ed, Bruce G. Trigger. Vol. 15 of *Handbook of North American Indians*, ed. William Sturtevant, 44–57. Washington, D.C.: Smithsonian Institution.

A thorough overview of the archaeological data available in 1978 on regional Woodland period cultures and their interrelationships.

Griffin, James B. 1993. "Cahokia Interaction with Contemporary Southeastern and Eastern Societies." *Midcontinental Journal of Archaeology* 18(1): 3–17.

A useful survey of the archaeological evidence for widespread interaction among Woodland cultures of the Northeast and elsewhere, and its social implications.

Hasenstab, Robert John. 1990. "Agriculture, Warfare, and Tribalization in the Iroquois Homeland of New York: A G.I.S. Analysis of Late Woodland Settlement." Ph.D. diss., University of Massachusetts.

A thorough archaeological investigation of late Woodland-period Iroquois development.

Peregrine, Peter. 1996. *Archaeology of the Mississippian Culture: A Research Guide*. New York: Garland.

A useful guide to recent studies of Mississippian complex societies and their impact on other Woodland peoples.

Potter, Stephen Robert. 1993. *Commoners, Tribute, and Chiefs: The Development of Algonquian Culture in the Potomac Valley*. Charlottesville: University Press of Virginia.

Potter reviews the literature on these poorly known chiefdoms of the Potomac region, which share developmental similarities with other coastal Algonquian societies.

Tuck, James A. 1978. "Regional Cultural Development, 3000 B.C. to 300 B.C." In *The Northeast*, ed. Bruce G. Trigger. Vol. 15 of *Handbook of North American Indians*, ed. William Sturtevant, 28–43. Washington, D.C.: Smithsonian Institution.

A thorough review of the literature and the accepted theories of cultural development in the Late Archaic and early Woodland period in the Northeast.

Turner, E. Randolph. 1985. "Socio-Political Organization Within the Powhatan Chiefdom and the Effects of European Contact, A.D. 1607–1646." In *Cultures in Contact: The European Impact on Native Cultural Institutions in Eastern North America, A.D. 1000–1800*, ed. William Fitzhugh. Washington, D.C.: Smithsonian Institution Press.

Turner argues that Powhatan's chiefdom was primarily of indigenous origin.

Physical Anthropology

The biological impact of European expansion and a number of issues regarding race have been the subject of several interesting studies, as well as the focus of furious debate within and outside of Indian communities. The recent advances in biological testing of human remains, including DNA testing, hold a great deal of potential for research in Native American history. However, these same advances coincided with the enactment of NAGPRA legislation (see below), so that the exhumation, examination, and scientific testing of human remains of native origin is surrounded with controversy. Of those studies recently completed, however, it has been possible to identify many details of prehistoric diet, health, and work patterns, differences in men's and women's diet and health that may have had social or cultural foundations, and important information about fertility and fecundity in precontact and postcontact populations. The study of interments is also very important to our understanding of social complexity, as burials and burial mounds, cemeteries, and ossuaries were often the locus of important ritual activity and frequently contain objects of great historic and artistic importance that provide crucial information about cultural contact, indigenous intellectual domains, and belief systems in the past.

Sources

Cook, S. F. 1970. *The Indian Population of New England in the Seventeenth Century*. Berkeley: University of California Press.

A landmark publication summarizing historical data concerning the effects of European-introduced diseases among the native peoples of southern New England.

Crosby, A. W. 1986. *Ecological Imperialism: The Biological Expansion of Europe, 900–1900*. New York: Cambridge University Press.

The award-winning study of the effects of European-introduced diseases, as well as the impact of animals and plants newly introduced into the New World.

Dobyns, H. F. 1983. *Their Number Become Thinned: Native American Population Dynamics in Eastern North America*. Knoxville: University of Tennessee Press.

A general study of population losses among the native peoples of North America following European colonization.

Ghere, David L. 1993. "The 'Disappearance' of the Abenaki in Western Maine: Political Organization and Ethnocentric Assumptions." *American Indian Quarterly* 17(2): 193–207.

Here and in the following article, Ghere argues in favor of a more balanced look at population loss, and suggests that claims of native "disappearance" have been exaggerated.

———. 1997. "Myths and Methods in Abenaki Demography: Abenaki Population Recovery, 1725–1750." *Ethnohistory* 44(3): 511–34.

Henige, David. 1986. "Primary Source by Primary Source: On the Role of Epidemics in New World Depopulation." *Ethnohistory* 33:293–312.

Henige challenges some of the estimates of population loss in Cook (1970) and Dobyns (1983).

Kelly, Marc A., Paul S. Sledzik, and Sean P. Murphey. 1987. "Health, Demographics, and Physical Constitution in Seventeenth-Century Rhode Island Indians." *Man in the Northeast* 34:1–25.

One of a series of studies of the Rhode Island 1000 contact period cemetery, documenting the effects of disease and stress on native population in the early historic period.

Larsen, Clark Spencer and George R. Milner. 1994. *In the Wake of Contact: Biological Responses to Conquest.* New York: Wiley-Liss.

A collection of essays by anthropologists, archaeologists, and physical anthropologists based on the analysis of human physical remains and documentary sources, investigating the biological consequences of colonization, including disease and changes in the demographic profiles of a number of Native American societies.

Mooney, James. 1928. "The Aboriginal Population of America North of Mexico." *Smithsonian Miscellaneous Collections* 80(7): 1–40.

The classic source, now considered to have seriously underestimated late prehistoric populations (and thus the effects of disease) in some regions.

Robinson, Paul, Marc Kelley, and Patricia Rubertone. 1985. "Preliminary Biocultural Interpretations from a Seventeenth-Century Narragansett Indian Cemetery in Rhode Island." In *Cultures in Contact: The European Impact on Native Cultural Institutions in Eastern North America, A.D. 1000–1800*, ed. William Fitzhugh, 107–30. Washington, D.C.: Smithsonian Institution Press.

Another article on the Rhode Island 1000 site, with an emphasis on the grave goods and their meaning.

Snow, Dean R. and Kim M. Lanphear. 1988. "European Contact and Indian Depopulation in the Northeast: The Timing of the First Epidemics." *Ethnohistory* 35:(1): 15–33.

A careful look at the primary sources for epidemics in New England.

Snow, John R. 1996. "Mohawk Demography and the Effects of Exogenous Epidemics on American Indian Populations." *Journal of Anthropological Archaeology* 15(2): 160–82.

A consideration of the effects of disease on Iroquoian populations, who, like other interior groups described in Larsen and Milner 1994, were also hard hit by European epidemics, sometimes before they encountered the Europeans themselves.

Starna, William A. 1992. "The Biological Encounter: Disease and the Ideological Domain." *The American Indian Quarterly* 16(4): 511–19.

A cross-cultural analysis of the social and ideological impact of epidemics. Starna suggests an increase in ritual activity is common in such situations.

First Impressions: Early Contact Period Documents

Among the earliest descriptions of the native people of the Northeast was Verrazano's 1524 report of his encounter with the people of what is now Narragansett Bay:

[June(?), 1524] We . . . proceeded to another place, fifteen leagues distant from the island [Block Island], where we found a very excellent harbor. Before entering it, we saw about twenty small boats full of people, who came about our ship, uttering many cries of astonishment, but they would not approach nearer than within fifty paces; stopping, they looked at the structure of our ship, our persons and dress, afterwards they all raised a loud shout together, signifying that they were pleased. By imitating their signs, we inspired them in some measure with confidence, so that they came near enough for us to toss to them some little bells and glasses, and many toys, which they took and looked at, laughing, and then came on board without fear. Among them were two kings more beautiful in form and stature than can possibly be described; one was about forty years old, the other about twenty-four, and they were dressed in the following manner; The oldest had a deer skin around his body, artificially wrought in damask figures, his head was without covering, his hair was tied back in various knots; around his neck he wore a large chain ornamented with many stones of different colors. The young man was similar in his general appearance. This is the finest looking tribe, the handsomest in their costumes, that we have found in our voyage. They exceed us in size, and they are of a very fair complexion; some of them incline more to a white, and others to a tawny color; their faces are sharp, and their hair long and black, upon the adorning of which they bestow great pains; their eyes are black and sharp; their expressions mild and pleasant, greatly resembling the antique. [Verrazano 1970:137–38]

This romantic portrayal of the natives of New England remarks upon their beauty, demeanor ("mild," "antique"), and innocence, and suggests that their society was organized in ways that Europeans could understand, as they, too, were ruled by kings

In the following century, several other descriptions—including the remarkable *Key Into the Language of America* by Roger Williams (1643), Edward Winslow's *Relation* (1624), and William Wood's *New England's Prospect (1634)*—provide important information about the people of southern New England and about the English settlers in that region, and although less idealized than that of Verrazano, these portraits compare the New England peoples favorably with Europeans.

Particularly after King Philip's War (1675–76), descriptions of Indians of New England come to emphasize what the English colonists saw as the cruelty and savagery of native character:

These parts were then covered with nations of barbarous indians and infidels, in whom the prince of power of the air did work as a spirit; nor could it be expected that the nations of wretches, whose whole religion was the most explicit sort of devil-worship, should not be acted by the devil to engage in some early and bloody action, for the extinction of a plantation so contrary to his interest, as that of New England was. [C. Mather 1702].

To later writers, Indians of the Northeast appeared to be a vanishing people. J. Hector St. John Crèvecoeur, who toured the eastern United States in 1782, wrote:

They are gone, and every memorial of them is lost; no vestiges whatever are left of those swarms which once inhabited this country. . . . They have all disappeared either in the wars which the Europeans waged against them, or else they have mouldered away, gathered in some of their ancient towns, in contempt and oblivion. . . .

Forty years after Crèvecoeur wrote this mordant passage, however, some New England Indians were beginning to speak for themselves. William

Apess, a Pequot minister, authored several books on New England native history and on the political issues of his own time, including his biography, *A Son of the Forest*, published in 1829. He wrote then:

> I presume that no person will doubt that great injustice has been done to the Indians, and I also think that no liberal mind will say that they are *only* savages. [Emphasis in original. O'Connell 1992:59]

Other important early sources on the native people of New England include Smith (1614), Morton (1646), Mourt's Relation (Heath 1969), and the writings of Dutch explorers in New Netherlands (Jameson 1909).

The principal early sources on the St. Lawrence Iroquoians, the Huron and their neighbors, and the Northern Iroquoians were written by French explorers such as Jacques Cartier, who explored Chaleur Bay and the Baie de Gaspé in 1534, and who enraged the local Stadacona by kidnapping two sons of their leader, Donnacona. Donnacona himself was later kidnapped and taken to France, where his meetings with Francis I sparked further attempts at colonization by the French (Trigger 1978:346). Samuel de Champlain, another prolific French explorer and the founder of Quebec, left accounts of his voyages in the Canadian Maritimes and along the St. Lawrence, as well as of his explorations of the New England coast ([1613] 1922). Champlain took part in several battles between various Indian groups of the region, and his information about the political ties, territorial bounds, and leadership of native communities from Stadacona on the St. Lawrence to Cape Cod are invaluable. Illustrations from his *Voyages* are among the earliest images of native people in the Northeast as well.

Vast amounts of information are available from the *Jesuit Relations*, an enormous collection of writings by early Jesuit missionaries about their trials in New France and the people they lived among (Thwaites 1959; Sagard-Theodat 1939). The Jesuit and Recollet missionaries were keen observers, spoke the languages of the people with whom they lived, and kept extensive records. From these we learn much about social organization, religion, economy, and politics of seventeenth-century northern Iroquoian and Algonquian-speaking peoples, along with a great deal of information about early Indian-white relations in the region.

The early source material for the coastal Algonquian of Virginia and North Carolina is especially rich. In 1585, English colonists at Roanoke (on the Pamlico River) included the skilled and sympathetic artist John White, whose watercolor illustrations of the people, animals, and plants of the re-

gion survived his return to England the next year, during which time the
colony itself disappeared. These drawings, along with several early and complete reports by John Smith, and William Strachey at the Jamestown colony,
bring these people and their languages to light far beyond what can be
known about other groups who met Europeans very early in the contact
period. Several early sources written by explorers of the Great Lakes region
are collected in Thwaites (1904–1907).

Aside from the *Jesuit Relations* mentioned earlier, a number of important
manuscripts and publications based on the writings of Recollet and Jesuit
missionaries in New France survive. These include translations of religious
writings into Montagnais, Cree, and Ojibwa, and the *Mot Loups* (Day
1975), the only known wordlist of the peoples of interior Vermont, New
Hampshire, and western Massachusetts, who were probably speakers of Western Abenaki.

Perhaps unique in North America is the remarkable collection of translations, descriptions, and related documents of the Protestant missions to the
Indians of southern New England. Funded by the Society for the Propagation for the Gospel, also known as the New England Company, missionaries
worked in southern New England until the Revolutionary War, and in Canada for more than a century thereafter. John Eliot, the teacher and minister
at Roxbury, Massachusetts, who had emigrated to the colonies after studying
at Cambridge University, took up a lifelong mission to the Indians in the
late 1640s. He, with the help of several native men, translated the entire
Bible into the Massachusett language. The first edition of the Bible was
published in 1663, and the second in 1685. Eliot also translated nearly a
dozen additional tracts, a psalter, a grammar, and two books on logic into
the Massachusett language. His writings about the mission fill a large volume, and he was also responsible for helping to launch the widespread
literacy in the native languages of eastern Massachusetts Bay and Plymouth
colonies. Many documents written by literate natives in their own languages
are collected in *Native Writings in Massachusett* (Goddard and Bragdon
1988).

Eliot was joined by missionaries elsewhere in the region, including James
Pierson, whose *Helpes to the Indians*, in the language of the Quiripi Indians
of Connecticut, preceded Eliot's grammar into publication. Other translations by Samuel Treat and Samuel Danforth, and especially Experience
Mayhew of Martha's Vineyard, provide additional information about the
native languages of the region. John Cotton of Plymouth and his son Josiah
took an interest in Indian languages. John Cotton's word list is based on his

brief stay on Martha's Vineyard in the 1660s, and Josiah's is based on his later experience with the Indians of Plymouth (Bragdon n.d.; Cotton 1820). The so-called "Indian Library" created by Eliot and others was also remarkable in that it contains the earliest books printed in North America, most produced in Cambridge by Nathaniel Green and his son-in-law, and many with the help of the Nipmuck Indian James Printer.

Elsewhere in southern New England, scattered writings by Indian converts survive, including the Latin essay of Tunxis native John Mettawun, now in the collections of the Society for the Propagation of the Gospel at the Guildhall, London. Johnathan Edwards, among his many writings, described the Indians of Stockbridge, of Mahican origin, and the Schaghticoke, who lived nearby. His prayer book in their language was also a significant addition to missionary literature on the southern New England Indians.

Another remarkable missionary effort, launched by the Moravians, focused on speakers of Onondaga, Delaware, and Mahican, as well as the Susquehannock of New York, New Jersey, and Pennsylvania. Among the most prominent of their missionaries, David Zeisberger compiled a spelling book in Delaware and English (1776), a dictionary in Onondaga and Delaware (1887), and a Mahican word list (Masthay 1990). His diaries, which have also been published, provide an important record of his missionary activities in western Pennsylvania.

Sources

Barlow, Arthur. [1584] 1981. "The First Voyage Made to the Coasts of America, with Two Barks . . ." In *Hakluyt's Voyages*, ed. Richard David, 445–53. Boston: Houghton Mifflin.

An important source for southern New England ethnohistory.

Beverley, Robert. 1705. *The History and Present State of Virginia*. London: R. Parker.

A primary source for the study of the Powhatan chiefdom.

Biggar, Henry P., ed. 1924. *The Voyages of Jacques Cartier: Published from the Originals with Translations, Notes and Appendices*. In "Notes and Appendices." Publications of the Public Archives of Canada, no. 11. Ottawa: F. A. Acland, printer.

An important early source of data on the St. Lawrence native populations.

Bogaert, Harmen Meyndertsz van den. [1895] 1991. *A Journey Into Mohawk and Oneida Country, 1634–1635: The Journal of Harmen Meyndertsz van den Bogaert.* Eds. Charles T. Gehring and William A. Starna. Iroquois and Their Neighbors Series. Reprint, Syracuse, N.Y.: Syracuse University Press.

An early source for southern New England and eastern New York.

Champlain, Samuel de. [1619] 1907. *Voyages of Samuel de Champlain, 1604–1618.* Ed. W. L. Grant. (Series: Original Narratives of Early American History.) New York: Scribner's.

A valuable source, including illustrations of many New England coastal societies.

Claus, Christian Daniel and Conrad Weiser. 1994. *The Journals of Christian Daniel Claus and Conrad Weiser: A Journey to Onondaga, 1750.* Ed. and trans. Helga Doblin and William A. Starna. Philadelphia: American Philosophical Society.

An early source on Iroquois ethnohistory.

Force, Peter, ed. [1836–46] 1947. *Tracts and Other Papers Relating Principally to the Origin, Settlement, and Progress of the Colonies in North America from the Discovery of the Country to the Year 1776.* 4 vols. Washington. P. Force. Reprint, Gloucester, Mass.: Peter Smith.

A useful compendium of early colonial period narratives.

Hakluyt, Richard. [1589] 1965. *The Principall Navigations, Voiages and Discoveries of the English Nation.* 2 vols. Eds. David B. Quinn and Raleigh A. Skelton. London: Cambridge University Press.

A classic collection of early contact narratives.

Hall, Clayton C., ed. 1910. *Narratives of Early Maryland, 1633–1684.* New York: Scribner's.

Hariot, Thomas. [1588] 1955. *A Briefe and True Report of the New Found Land of Virginia.* Reprinted in *The Roanoke Voyages, 1584–1590,* ed.

David B. Quinn. London: Cambridge University Press for the Hakluyt Society.

Hariot's gift for description and his intellectual curiosity about the native people he encountered makes his narrative a valuable one.

Hulton, Paul H. and David B. Quinn. 1964. *The American Drawings of John White, 1577–1590.* 2 vols. London: Trustees of the British Museum; Chapel Hill: University of North Carolina Press.

Important source of information on the material culture, costume, flora, and fauna of the Pamlico Sound region.

Jameson, J. Franklin. 1909. *Narratives of New Netherland, 1609–1664.* New York: Scribner's.

A standard source of Dutch exploration narratives.

Kellogg, Louise. 1917. *Early Narratives of the Northwest, 1634–1699.* New York: Scribner's.

Provides early glimpses of the "old northwest," including the Ohio Valley and the Great Lakes region.

La Salle, Nicolas de. 1901. *Relation of the Discoveries and Voyages of Cavelier de La Salle from 1679 to 1681, the Official Narrative.* Trans. Melville B. Anderson. Chicago: The Caxton Club.

An adventure story as well as an important source on the history and culture of peoples soon displaced by the fur trade.

Le Clercq, Chrétien. [1691] 1910. *New Relation of Gaspesia, with the Customs and Religion of the Gaspesian Indians.* Ed. and trans. W. F. Ganong. Toronto: The Champlain Society.

An important source on the native people of the maritime provinces.

Lederer, John. 1958. *The Discoveries of John Lederer, with Unpublished Letters by and About Lederer to Governor John Winthrop, Jr., and an Essay on the Indians of Lederer's Discoveries by Douglas L. Rights and William P. Cumming.* Ed. William P. Cumming. Charlottesville: University of Virginia Press.

Another important New England source.

Lescarbot, Marc. [1609] 1928. *Nova Francia, a Description of Acadia*. New York: Harper and Row.

Often-cited source on early New England and New France.

Lewis, C. M. and J. J. Loomie. 1953. *The Spanish Jesuit Mission in Virginia, 1570–1572*. Chapel Hill: Virginia Historical Society.

This short-lived mission is described in a narrative based on a number of early Spanish sources.

Lindeström, Peter. [1691] 1925. *Geographia Americae with an Account of the Delaware Indians Based on Surveys and Notes Made in 1654–1656*. Ed. Amandus Johnson. Philadelphia: The Swedish Colonial Society.

The Swedish colony's early interactions with the Delaware are the subject of this narrative.

McGhee, Robert. 1984. "Contact Between Native North Americans and the Medieval Norse." *American Antiquity* 49(1): 4–26.

A fascinating discussion of early Norse/native contacts based on archeological and Norse sources.

Morse, Jedidiah. 1822. *A Report to the Secretary of War of the United States, on Indian Affairs, Comprising a Narrative of a Tour Performed in the Summer of 1820, Under a Commission of the President of the United States, for the Purpose of Ascertaining for the Use of the Government the Actual State of the Indian Tribes in Our Country*. New Haven, Conn.: S. Converse.

A late but important body of data on native peoples remaining in the Northeast at the time of Removal.

Purchase, Samuel. [1625] 1905. *Hakluytus Posthumus or Purchas, His Pilgrimes*. 4 vols. London: Printed by W. Stansby for Henry Fetherstone. Reprint, Glasgow: J. MacLehose and Sons.

See Hakluyt, above.

Quinn, David. 1955. *The Roanoke Voyages, 1584–1590*. London: Cambridge University Press for the Hakluyt Society.

Includes all known descriptions of the ill-fated colony and its Indian neighbors.

———. 1977. *North America from Earliest Discovery to First Settlements: The Norse Voyages to 1612.* New York: Harper and Row.

Quinn's thorough search of the sixteenth-century literature turned up numerous important descriptions of European voyages to Roanoke, compiled here.

———. 1981. "Sources for the Ethnography of Northeastern North America to 1611." In *Canadian Ethnology Service Papers.* Mercury Series, no. 76. Ottawa: National Museum of Man.

Another important source of little-known early narrative accounts of northeastern native people.

Quinn, David and Allison M. Quinn, eds. 1983. *The English New England Voyages, 1602–1608.* London: Hakluyt Society.

Compiles a number of important sources for New England exploration and contact.

Sagard-Theodat, Gabriel. [1632] 1939. *Father Gabriel Sagard: The Long Journey to the Country of the Hurons.* Ed. George M. Wrong. Toronto: The Champlain Society.

The most important source on the Huron, and among the most detailed of all the Jesuit narratives.

Smith, John. 1986. *The Complete Works of Captain John Smith (1580–1631).* Ed. Philip L. Barbour. Chapel Hill: University of North Carolina Press for the Institute of Early American History and Culture, Williamsburg, Va.

Smith's narratives include much important data on the native peoples of the Atlantic coast.

Snow, Dean R., Charles Gehring, and William A. Starna. 1996. *In Mohawk Country: Early Narratives About a Native People.* 1st ed. Syracuse, N.Y.: Syracuse University Press.

The recently compiled body of descriptions is a boon to Iroquoian research.

Strachey, William. [1612] 1953. *The Historie of Travell Into Virginia Britania.* Ed. Louis B. Wright and Virginia Freund. (Works issued by Hakluyt Society, 2d ser., no. 103.) London: Hakluyt Society.

Strachey's narrative and word list are among the most important sources on the historic Powhatan.

Thwaites, Reuben G., ed. 1904–07. *Early Western Travels, 1748–1846: A Series of Annotated Reprints of Some of the Best and Rarest Contemporary Volumes of Travel.* 32 vols. Cleveland: A. H. Clark.

A valuable source of information on native peoples of the interior Northeast.

———. [1616] 1959. *The Jesuit Relations and Allied Documents: Travel and Explorations of the Jesuit Missionaries in New France, 1610–1791; the Original French, Latin, and Italian Texts, with English Translations and Notes.* 73 vols. Cleveland: Burrows Brothers, 1896–1901. Reprint, New York: Pageant.

An indispensable source for the early history of New France and the Jesuits' contacts with many native people of the Northeast.

Van den Bogaert, Harmen Meyndertsz. 1909. "Narrative of a Journey Into the Mohawk and Oneida Country, 1634–1635." In *Narratives of New Netherland, 1609–1664,* ed. J. Franklin Jameson, 135–62. New York: Scribner's.

Winslow, Edward. [1624] 1910. "Winslow's Relation." In *Chronicles of the Pilgrim Fathers,* ed. John Masefield. New York: E. P. Dutton.

An outstanding description of the complex societies of the southern New England coast.

Wood, William. [1634] 1977. *New England's Prospect.* Ed. Alden Baughan. Amherst: University of Massachusetts Press.

Describes the native people living near what is now Salem, Massachusetts.

Wroth, L. C. [1528] 1970. *The Voyages of Giovanni da Verrazzano: 1524–1528.* New Haven: Yale University Press.

A very early source on the coastal Algonquians of New England.

Captivity Narratives

Some of the best-known of the so-called "captivity narratives"—the unique literary genre comprised of stories of life among the Indians, written by those colonists who had been captured by Indians as children and adults—were written about native people in the Northeast. Perhaps the most enduring is that of Mary Rowlandson, who on the morning of February 10, 1657, was taken from her home in Lancaster, Massachusetts by Nipmuck Indians allied with King Philip. Rowlandson, like many who succeeded her, used her captivity and rescue as a metaphor for spiritual redemption, but her story makes a gripping tale. Forced to accompany her captors during their attack on Sudbury, she recorded:

Before they went to that fight, they got a company together to Powaw; the manner was as followeth. There was one that kneeled upon a Deerskin, with the company round him in a ring who kneeled, and striking upon the ground with their hands, and with sticks, and muttering and humming with their mouths; besides him who kneeled in the ring, there also stood one with a Gun in his hand: Then he on the Deer-skin made a speech, and all manifested assent to it; and so they did many times together. Then they bade him with Gun go out of the ring, which he did, but when he was out, they called him in again; but he seemed to make a stand, they called the more earnestly, till he returned again; Then they all sang. Then they gave him two Guns, in either hand one; and so on he on the Deerskin began again; and at the end of every sentence in his speaking, they all assented, humming or muttering with their mouths, and striking upon the ground with their hands. Then they bade him with the two Guns go out of the ring again, but he made a stand; so they called him with greater earnestness; but he stood reeling and wavering as if he know not whither he should stand or fall, or which way to go. Then they called him with exceeding great vehemency, all of them, one an another; after a little while he turned in staggering as he went, with his arms stretched out, in either hand a gun. As soon as he came in, they all sang and rejoyced exceedingly a while. And then he upon the Deerskin, made another speech unto which they all assented in a rejoicing manner; and so they ended their business and forthwith went to Sudbury-fight. [Rowlandson 1913:152–53]

Later narratives, such as Mary Jemison's description of her life among the Seneca Iroquois in the late eighteenth century, record details of domestic life:

> Our labor was not severe; and that of one year was exactly similar in almost every respect to that of others . . . notwithstanding the Indian women have all the fuel and bread to procure . . . their cares certainly are not half as numerous, nor as great [as those of white women]. In the summer season, we planted, tended, and harvested our corn, and generally had all our children with us . . . we could work as leisurely as we pleased. [Seaver 1992]

While captivity narratives offer the student interesting insights into the cultures of native people under siege, they are also of interest to cultural historians as examples of a unique American literary genre (see below).

Sources

Gyles, John. [1736] 1936. *Memoirs of Odd Adventures, Strange Deliverances, etc., in the Captivity of John Gyles, Esq., Commander of the Garrison on St. George's River: Written by Himself*. Photostat Americana, 2d ser., no. 7. Boston: Photostated at the Massachusetts Historical Society.

Gyles's famous narrative chronicles the hardships of the New England frontier for both natives and European settlers, from the unique perspective of a young Englishman taken captive by the Abenaki.

Rowlandson, Mary. [1682] 1913. "Narrative of the Captivity of Mrs. Mary Rowlandson." Reprinted in *Narratives of the Indian Wars, 1675–1699*, ed. Charles H. Lincoln, 107–67. New York: Scribner's.

Possibly the most famous captivity narrative of all times, Rowlandson's description of her captivity during King Philip's War is at once a gripping tale and a journey of self-revelation and redemption.

Seaver, James E. [1824] 1992. *A Narrative of the Life of Mrs. Mary Jemison*. Canandaigua, N.Y.: Bemis. Reprint, Norman: Oklahoma University Press.

Mary Jemison, an adopted Seneca of European descent, became an advocate for Indian rights after her return to white society late in her life.

Vaughan, Alden T. and Edward Clark, eds. 1981. *Puritans Among the In-dians: Accounts of Captivity and Redemption, 1676–1724.* Cambridge, Mass.: Belknap Press.

Ethnography

Among the best-known ethnographers in the world, Lewis Henry Morgan began his fieldwork with the Seneca Ely Parker (who was later Commissioner of Indian Affairs under Ulysses S. Grant). Morgan published his first ethnographic notes on the Iroquois in 1847, and his major study, *League of the Ho-de-no-sau-nee,* in 1851, still the best and most complete study of that people. The Bureau of American Ethnology was founded in 1879, and many of its staff ethnographers worked among northeastern peoples, including W. J. Hoffman, J. N. B. Hewitt, and Alice Fletcher. In Maine, Fannie Hardy Ekstorm worked for many years collecting data and stories from the Abenaki. Frank Speck, the dean of Woodlands ethnography in the early twentieth century, worked among nearly all the people, collecting data he thought reflected their traditional cultures. One of his students, Gladys Tantaquid-geon, was a Mohegan Indian of a respected old family, and her work in southern New England represents some of the earliest ethnography done by a New England native. William Fenton's long career as a student of Iro-quoian history and culture led him to fieldwork on all the Iroquoian reserves in New York and Canada. A pioneer of the technique known as "upstream-ing," Fenton has also made important contributions to the study of historic Iroquois cultures. Similarly, Elisabeth Tooker has made the development of the League of the Iroquois her special study. Irving Hallowell, who spent many years working with the Barren Ground Ojibwa, and Eleanor Burke Leacock, who worked with the Montagnais, both produced important eth-nographies of those people. Gordon M. Day did valuable fieldwork with the St. Francis Abenaki and documented their connections with southern New England Indians displaced during the seventeenth and eighteenth centuries.

In the Great Lakes region, Fred Eggan, Charles Callender, and Fred Gearing maintained a long tradition of examination of social organization, with extensive analyses of kinship and leadership that form the basis for modern understanding of Native American societies in the region. The Great Lakes is also important in the history of ethnographic research as that area where early land claims helped to establish the new field of ethnohistory in the 1950s. Erminie Wheeler Voegelin, and later Helen Tanner and Nancy Ostreich Lurie, have made many detailed studies of the postcontact history and movements of that complex region and its people. Paul Radin pioneered the biographical approach among the Winnebago, with whom George and Louise Spindler also did important work.

Sources

Callender, Charles. 1962. *Social Organization of the Central Algonkian Indians*. Publications in Anthropology 7. Milwaukee Public Museum.

One of Callender's many publications on Central Algonquian social organization, derived from his fieldwork with the Fox Indians and his associations with the "Chicago School" of social anthropology.

Cass, Lewis. 1823. *Inquiries Respecting the History, Traditions, Languages, Manners, Customs, Religion, etc. of the Indians Living Within the United States*. Detroit: Sheldon and Reed.

Part primary source, part early ethnography, a flawed but significant early source on the native people "behind the frontier."

Clifton, James. 1965. "Culture Change, Structural Stability and Factionalism in the Prairie Potawatomi Reservation Community." *Midcontinent American Studies Journal* 6:101–23.

One of Clifton's many publications on the Potawatomi, with an emphasis on identity politics.

Day, Gordon M. 1998. *In Search of New England's Native Past: Selected Essays of Gordon M. Day*, eds. Michael Foster and William Cowan. Amherst: University of Massachusetts Press.

A valuable collection of Day's many articles on the Western Abenaki, including analyses of fieldwork conducted with the St. Francis Abenaki.

Densmore, Francis. 1929. "Chippewa Customs." Bureau of American Ethnology Bulletin No. 86. Washington, D.C.: Government Printing Office.

Densmore's work provides valuable early ethnographic data on the Chippewa, particularly of the kind known as "memory ethnography."

Eckstorm, Fannie Hardy. 1904. *The Penobscot Man*. Boston and New York: Houghton Mifflin.

A prolific collector of folklore, Eckstorm collected much valuable information from the Eastern Abenaki (Penobscot) of Maine.

Eggan, Fred R. 1955. *Social Anthropology of North American Indian Tribes.* Chicago: Aldine.

A valuable synthesis of field data collected by several ethnologists associated with the University of Chicago's Department of Anthropology, with a focus on social and political organization.

Fenton, William N. 1941. "Tonawanda Longhouse Ceremonies: Ninety Years after Lewis Henry Morgan." Bureau of American Ethnology Bulletin 128(15): 140–66. Washington, D.C.: Government Printing Office.

One of Fenton's more than fifty publications on the Iroquois, with whom he has worked for more than half a century.

Gearing, Fred. 1970. *The Face of the Fox.* Chicago: Aldine.

A readable and important ethnography of contemporary Fox life.

Hallowell, A. Irving. 1946. "Some Psychological Characteristics of the Northeastern Indians." In *Man in Northeastern America* (vol. 3 of Papers of the Robert S. Peabody Foundation for Archaeology), ed. Frederick Johnson. Andover, Mass.: Phillips Academy, the Foundation.

This well-known article reflects Hallowell's interest in psychological anthropology and his fieldwork among various Ojibwa and Abenaki peoples.

Hewitt, J. N. B. 1899–1900, 1925–26. "Iroquoian Cosmology." Annual Reports of the Bureau of American Ethnology, 21:127–339 and 43:449-819. Washington, D.C.: Government Printing Office.

A tireless recorder of Iroquois life, Hewitt also published many articles on other northeastern peoples for the Bureau of American Ethnology.

Jenness, Diamond. 1935. "The Ojibway Indians of the Parry Sound, Their Social and Religious Life." Anthropological Series 17 (Bulletin no. 78). Ottawa: National Museum of Canada.

One of the many distinguished anthropologists employed by the Canadian Museum of Man (now the Canadian Museum of Civilization), Jenness conducted important research with several northeastern hunting peoples.

Johnson, Frederick. 1928. "The Algonquian at Golden Lake, Ontario." *Indian Notes* 5(2): 173–78. Museum of the American Indian, Heye Foundation.

Like many ethnologists of his day, Johnson published articles on a variety of subjects, including linguistics and archaeology.

Jones, William. 1939. "Ethnography of the Fox Indians." Ed. Margaret W. Fisher. Smithsonian Institution, Bureau of American Ethnology (Bulletin no. 125). Washington, D.C.: Government Printing Office.

Landes, Ruth. 1937. *Ojibwa Sociology*. Vol 29 of Columbia University Contributions to Anthropology. New York: Columbia University Press.

Landes's important research included some of the earliest work on Ojibwa gender roles.

Michaelson, Truman. 1927, 1930. *Contributions to Fox Ethnology*. Smithsonian Institution. Bureau of American Ethnology (Bulletin nos. 85, 95). Washington, D.C.: Government Printing Office.

A brilliant and prolific linguist, Michaelson also published many articles of ethnographic interest.

Mooney, James, et al. [1912] 1969. *Handbook of American Indians North of Mexico*. 2 vols. Ed. Frederick Hodge. Washington, D.C.: Government Printing Office. Reprint, Westport, Conn.: Greenwood.

Author of most of the entries in Hodge's *Handbook*, Mooney was an early pioneer in the discipline that came to be known as ethnohistory.

Morgan, Lewis Henry. [1851] 1962. *League of the Ho dé no sau nee or Iroquois*. Rochester, N.Y.: Sage. Reprinted as *League of the Iroquois*, New York: Corinth.

The most important source on traditional Iroquois culture, and among the first modern ethnographies.

Parker, Arthur C. 1913. "The Code of Handsome Lake, the Seneca Prophet." New York State Museum Bulletin No. 63. Albany.

Parker, himself a Seneca, published this significant version of the Code in cooperation with the New York State Museum.

Radin, Paul. 1929. *The Culture of the Winnebago: As Described by Themselves.* (Memoir 2 of Indiana University Publications in Anthropology and Linguistics.) Baltimore: Waverly Press.

Radin is best known for his interest in autobiographical and psychological approaches to the study of culture.

Rand, Silas. 1850. *A Short Statement of Facts Relating to the History, Manners, Customs, Language, and Literature of the Micmac Tribe of Indians, in Nova Scotia and Prince Edward Island.* Halifax, Nova Scotia: James Bowes and Son.

A significant source on the culture of the Micmac, with whom Rand lived for several decades.

Ritzenthaler, Robert E. 1953. "The Potawatomi Indians of Wisconsin." *Bulletin of the Public Museum of the City of Milwaukee* 19(4): 175–257.

Ritzenthaler produced this ethnography as part of the Milwaukee Public Museum's important research program.

Schoolcraft, Henry R. 1851. *Personal Memoirs of Residence of Thirty Years with the Indian Tribes on the American Frontiers: With Brief Notices of Passing Events, Facts, and Opinions, A.D. 1812 to A.D. 1842.* Philadelphia: Lippincott, Grambo.

A fascinating although sometimes unreliable early collection of folklore and ethnographic description.

Skinner, Alanson. 1923–25. "Observations on the Ethnology of the Sauk Indians." *Bulletin of the Public Museum of the City of Milwaukee* 5(1–3).

Like Ritzenthaler, Skinner conducted the fieldwork described in this volume under the auspices of the Milwaukee Public Museum.

Speck, Frank G. 1914. "The Family Hunting Band as the Basis of Algonkian Social Organization." *American Anthropologist* 17(2): 289–305.

This is one of nearly 100 articles and books published by Speck on the culture, language, and history of the native people of the Northeast. Speck was often concerned with demonstrating the persistence of "aboriginal" traits among twentieth-century native peoples, such as the family hunting grounds and bands. This notion, in particular, has been challenged by Eleanor Leacock (see below).

————. n.d. *Papers*. Philadelphia: American Philosophical Society.

One of the collections of Speck's large body of field notes, still only incompletely catalogued.

Spindler, George and Louise Spindler. 1971. *Dreamers Without Power: The Menomini Indians*. New York: Holt, Rinehart, and Winston.

A sensitive portrait of the modern Menominee.

Tantaquidgeon, Gladys. 1930. "Notes on the Gay Head Indians of Massachusetts." *Indian Notes* 7(1): 1–26. Museum of the American Indian, Heye Foundation.

Tantaquidgeon's interest, like that of Speck, was in documenting surviving traditions, especially folklore and herbal lore.

Tax, Sol. 1955. "The Social Organization of the Fox Indians." In *Social Anthropology of North American Indian Tribes*, ed. Fred Eggan, 243–82. Chicago: University of Chicago.

Another important study of Algonquian kinship organization.

Trowbridge, Charles C. 1972. "Account of Some of the Traditions, Manners, and Customs of the Lenee Lenaupaa or Delaware Indians." In *The Delaware Indians: A History by C. A. Weslager*, 473–500. New Brunswick, N.J.: Rutgers University Press.

A reprint of a nineteenth-century ethnography and history of the Delaware.

Language, Language Contact, and Early Linguistic Studies

Following the early work of Peter Stephen Du Ponceau and Albert Gallatin on the classification of Indian languages, James Pilling of the Bureau of American Ethnology began the task of collecting data on the vast number of documentary sources available on the languages of the Woodlands. His *Bibliography of Iroquoian Languages* (1888) and *Bibliography of Algonquian Languages* (1891) are remarkably timeless, and replete with fascinating bibliographic and historical information. James Hammond Trumbull, when health permitted, taught linguistics at Yale University; he took a special interest in the Massachusett or Natick language and other languages of southern New England, and published the *Natick-English Dictionary* in 1903.

Other Algonquian languages, includinged Fox, Unami, and Munsee, were studied by linguist Truman Michaelson, and Leonard Bloomfield's *Menominee Texts* (1928) set the standard for descriptive linguistics. Charles Hockett and Floyd Lounsbury continued this tradition with their exhaustive work with Proto-Algonquian and Iroquoian languages, respectively. Most recently, among the many fine linguists interested in northeastern languages, Ives Goddard of the Smithsonian Institution stands out with many publications.

Native languages and their speakers also underwent changes after the years of contact with Europeans. Changes included the development of pidgins, trade languages and lingua francas, and creoles. Some native people learned to read and write in their own languages, and others became linguists themselves. Finally, many languages have disappeared or are disappearing, while native people and linguists seek ways to prevent any further loss.

Descriptions of Native Languages

Data on languages is important in any understanding of the native peoples of the Northeast. Languages encompass information about subsistence, economy, social organization, and ideology. The study of languages can determine the history of a people and their movements through time. It also provides information about contact with peoples who spoke different languages, and the effects of such contact. Many early descriptions of the native people of the Northeast included data on their languages, and missionaries often made the study of native languages their principal goal. The following sources provide references to the hundreds of early sources on the native languages of the Northeast. A separate section, to follow, describes the results of modern studies of native languages and early language contact.

Sources

Boas, Franz. 1911. "Handbook of American Indian Languages." Pt. 1. Smithsonian Institution, Bureau of American Ethnology (Bulletin no. 40). Washington, D.C.: Government Printing Office.

A classic source on the native languages of North America, along with Boas's important introduction to the scientific study of these languages and their speakers.

Day, Gordon M. 1975. *The Mots Loups of Father Mathevet*. Ottawa: National Museums of Canada.

A thorough historical, ethnographical, and linguistic treatment of this important word list, one of the few representing languages of interior central New England.

Foster, Michael Kirk. 1996. "Language and the Culture History of North America." In *Languages and Language Families of North America*, ed. Ives Goddard. Vol. 17 of *Handbook of North American Indians*, ed. William Sturtevant, 64–110. Washington, D.C.: Smithsonian Institution.

A linguistic anthropologist's thoughtful discussion of patterns in language and culture.

French, David and Katherine S. French. 1996. "Personal Names." In *Languages and Language Families of North America*, ed. Ives Goddard. Vol. 17 of *Handbook of North American Indians*, ed. William Sturtevant, 200–21. Washington, D.C.: Smithsonian Institution.

A little-studied aspect of linguistic anthropology, thoroughly discussed in this interesting article.

Goddard, Ives. 1978. "Eastern Algonquian Languages." In *The Northeast*, ed. Bruce G. Trigger. Vol. 15 of *Handbook of North American Indians*, ed. William Sturtevant, 70–77. Washington, D.C.: Smithsonian Institution.

Based on Goddard's groundbreaking study of the characteristics of the Eastern Algonquian subfamily of the Algonquian language, this short but thorough review provides a useful overview of the Eastern Algonquian languages and their present status.

———. 1996. "The Classification of the Native Languages of North America." In *Languages and Language Families of North America*, ed. Ives Goddard. Vol. 17 of *Handbook of North American Indians*, ed. William Sturtevant, 290–323. Washington, D.C.: Smithsonian Institution.

An interesting review of the history of linguistic classification based on North American Indian languages.

————. 1996. "The Description of the Native Languages of North America Before Boas." In *Languages and Language Families of North America*, ed. Ives Goddard. Vol. 17 of *Handbook of North American Indians*, ed. William Sturtevant, 17–42. Washington, D.C.: Smithsonian Institution.

Goddard has made a study of research on northeastern languages, and provides an up-to-date review of the history of research here.

————, ed. 1996. *Languages and Language Families of North America*. Vol. 17 of *Handbook of North American Indians*, ed. William Sturtevant. Washington, D.C.: Smithsonian Institution.

The indispensable reference guide to American Indian languages, with sketches of languages and language families, a thorough bibliographic survey, and important interpretive and historical essays by leading scholars in the field.

Gray, Edward. 1998. *New World Babel*. Princeton: Princeton University Press.

Gray writes entertainingly about the way in which American Indian languages were linked to the study of Indian people, and to concepts of nationhood in the early Republic.

Hanzeli, Victor. 1969. *Missionary Linguistics in New France. A Study of Seventeenth and Eighteenth Century Descriptions of American Indian Languages*. Janua Linguarum, Series Maior 29. The Hague: Mouton.

An important early analysis of the science of linguistics in the New World.

Landar, Herbert J. 1996. "Sources." In *Languages and Language Families of North America*, ed. Ives Goddard. Vol. 17 of *Handbook of North American Indians*, ed. William Sturtevant, 721–61. Washington, D.C.: Smithsonian Institution.

A useful guide to important primary linguistic sources.

Miller, Wick R. 1996. "The Ethnography of Speaking." In *Languages and Language Families of North America*, ed. Ives Goddard. Vol. 17 of *Handbook of North American Indians*, ed. William Sturtevant, 222–43. Washington, D.C.: Smithsonian Institution.

An up-to-date discussion of the cultural and linguistic importance of speech in American Indian communities.

Mithun, Marianne. 1993. "Indian Languages: Iroquoian." In vol. 3 of *Encyclopedia of the North American Colonies*, ed. Jacob Ernest Cooke et al. New York: C. Scribner's Sons.

An expert on Iroquoian languages describes them briefly in this useful source.

———. 1996. "The Description of the Native Languages of North America: Boas and After." In *Languages and Language Families of North America*, ed. Ives Goddard. Vol. 17 of *Handbook of North American Indians*, ed. William Sturtevant, 43–63. Washington, D.C.: Smithsonian Institution.

The role of American Indian languages in the history of linguistic science is discussed here.

Pilling, James. 1888. *Bibliography of the Iroquoian Languages*. Smithsonian Institution, Bureau of American Ethnology (Bulletin no. 6). Washington, D.C.: Government Printing Office.

———. 1891. *Bibliography of the Algonquian Languages*. Smithsonian Institution, Bureau of American Ethnology (Bulletin no. 3). Washington, D.C.: Government Printing Office.

Pilling's exhaustive surveys enumerate many published and unpublished sources, including rare book manuscripts and fascinating historical essays on the history of language research in the Northeast.

Rudes, Blair R. 1994. "John Napoleon Brinton Hewitt: Tuscarora Linguist." *Anthropological Linguistics* 36(4): 466–81.

This article reviews the linguistic work of a native speaker of Tuscarora.

Salmon, Vivian. 1992. "Thomas Harriot (1560–1621) and the English Origins of Algonkian Linguistics." *Historiographia Linguistica* 19(1): 25–56.

Salmon's fascinating research on early linguistic studies links the Old World and the New.

Sapir, Edward S., and William Bright. 1990. *American Indian Languages.* Vol. 1. New York: Mouton de Gruyter.

These two volumes are new editions, with many improvements, of Sapir's classic studies of American Indian languages. Both are important sources for students of American Indian languages.

Sapir, Edward S., and Victor Karl Golla. 1991. *American Indian Languages.* Vol. 2. New York: Mouton de Gruyter.

Singerman, Robert. 1996. *Indigenous Languages of the Americas: A Bibliography of Dissertations and Theses.* Lanham, Md.: Scarecrow.

A crucial source for any serious survey of American Indian language research.

Pidgins, Jargons, and Creoles

Among the many important changes brought about by the coming of Europeans was the development of "mixed" languages for trade and diplomacy, sometimes called "pidgins" or "jargons," and newly minted languages that emerged out of pidgins, known as "creoles." Pidgins and creoles are interesting sources of information about the date and type of contact between speakers of different languages, and their development is common in contact situations. Since the development of such languages is a sign of widespread contact between people of different backgrounds, some scholars argue that jargons and creoles may predate the arrival of Europeans in the New World, and stem from the wide-ranging contacts between allies in late Woodland period "state societies," which survived into the fifteenth century. In addition, some scholars are interested in the way in which pidgins and creoles reflect the earliest stages of language formation, and suggest that all exhibit characteristics of universal linguistic structures.

Sources

Bartelt, Hans Guillermo. 1991. "American Indian English: A Phylogenetic Dilemma." In *Development and Structure of Creole Languages: Essays in Honor of Derek Bickerton,* eds. Francis Byrne and Thom Heubner, 29–39. Amsterdam: Benjamins.

This essay considers American Indian languages in light of theories of language origin and change.

Callaghan, Catherine A. and Geoffrey Gamble. 1996. "Borrowing." In *Languages and Language Families of North America,* ed. Ives Goddard. Vol. 17 of *Handbook of North American Indians,* ed. William Sturtevant, 111–16. Washington, D.C.: Smithsonian Institution.

This interesting subject is thoroughly discussed in light of American Indian language data.

Goddard, Ives. 1999. "Early Pidgins and Creoles." In *Language Encounter in the Americas, 1492–1800: A Collection of Essays,* eds. Edward Gray and Norman Fiering, 61–80. John Carter Brown Library. New York: Berghahn.

A fascinating review of the linguistic details of trade jargons of the Atlantic coast.

Gray, Edward and Norman Fiering, eds. 2000. *Language Encounter in the Americas, 1492–1800: A Collection of Essays.* New York: Berghahn.

A collection of essays that focus on the impact of languages and their speakers on one another in the early contact period.

Silverstein, Michael. 1996. "Dynamics of Language Contact." In *Languages and Language Families of North America,* ed. Ives Goddard. Vol. 17 of *Handbook of North American Indians,* ed. William Sturtevant, 117–36. Washington, D.C.: Smithsonian Institution.

Silverstein provides an insightful and thorough review of this complex issue.

Waldman, Carl and Molly Braun. 1994. *Word Dance: The Language of Native American Culture.* New York: Facts on File.

This readable book for the nonspecialist surveys the contributions of Indian languages to American culture.

Writing Systems and Literacy

Although no indigenous writing systems developed in the Northeast prior to the arrival of Europeans, a number of Indian communities were introduced to literacy subsequently, and numerous works were produced in their languages for religious or secular instruction. The adoption of literacy often leads to other changes in native society or is a reflection of such changes, but recent studies of literate communities in the Northeast suggest that many native literary traditions survived the transition to the written word.

Sources

Goddard, Ives. 1990. "Some Literary Devices in the Writings of Alfred Kiyana." In *Papers of the Twenty-First Algonquian Conference*, ed. William Cowan, 158–71. Ottawa, Ontario: Carleton University.

> A native consultant to linguist Truman Michaelson, and a skilled linguist himself, Kiyana produced many important vernacular texts in the Fox language.

Goddard, Ives and Kathleen J. Bragdon. 1988. *Native Writings in Massachusett*. Memoir Series 185. Philadelphia: American Philosophical Society.

> Includes translations and transcriptions of a large body of vernacular writings of Massachusett-speaking people produced in the seventeenth and eighteenth centuries.

Mason, Roger Burford. 1994. "The Sound of Innovation: James Evans's Syllabic Alphabet." *Queen's Quarterly* [Canada] 101(4): 848–53.

> Evans's syllabary adapted the sounds of Cree to a writing system that was widely used in the Northeast and elsewhere.

Walker, Willard. 1996. "Native Writing Systems." In *Languages and Language Families of North America*, ed. Ives Goddard. Vol. 17 of *Handbook of North American Indians*, ed. William Sturtevant, 158–84. Washington, D.C.: Smithsonian Institution.

> Walker summarizes the types of systems known in the New World and their origins, in this thorough review of the subject.

Language Loss

Although the processes by which languages go out of use are still unclear, a number of languages in the Northeast are no longer spoken, and linguists continue to search for the reasons in the hope, in particular, that remaining languages might survive.

Sources

Rees-Miller, Janie. 1998. "Stages in the Obsolescence of Certain Eastern Algonquian Languages." *Anthropological Linguistics* 40(4): 535–69.

A linguist's view of the patterned grammatical and semantic change in Algonquian languages.

Rhodes, Richard A. 1992. "Language Shift in Algonquian." In *Language Obsolescence, Shift, and Death in Several Native American Communities*, ed. Allan R. Taylor, 87–92. New York: Mouton de Gruyter.

Rhodes's detailed knowledge of several northeastern Algonquian languages makes his analysis of the processes of change both convincing and informative.

3. Current Issues in Northeast Research

Early Encounters: The Impact of Colonization

In the postcolonial modern world, many scholars have taken as their subject the impact of European colonization on the indigenous peoples of the world, and there is a large body of such scholarship for the Northeast. Among the topics of interest are the effects of the encounter with New World people on Old World science, politics, and literature; the development of colonial society and its relationship to native peoples; and the "clash" of different cultures in the New World. Additional topics of concern to anthropologists are the impact of European society on native economy, spirituality, and social structure.

Sources

Axtell, James. 1985. *The Invasion Within: The Contest of Cultures in Colonial North America*. New York: Oxford University Press.

An innovative treatment of colonial history that seeks to balance the perspectives of both Indians and Europeans.

Brasser, T. J. 1978. "Early Indian-European Contacts." In *The Northeast*, ed. Bruce G. Trigger. Vol. 15 of *Handbook of North American Indians*, ed. William Sturtevant, 78–88. Washington, D.C.: Smithsonian Institution.

A succinct and thought-provoking survey of general patterns of culture contact in eastern North America.

Burton, William and Richard Lowenthal. 1974. "The First of the Mohegans." *American Ethnologist* 1:589–99.

A provocative analysis of the rise of the Mohegan people, in particular their leader Uncas, out of the ashes of the Pequot War.

Conkey, Laura, Ethel Boissevain, and Ives Goddard. 1978. "Indians of Southern New England and Long Island: Late Period." In *The Northeast*, ed. Bruce G. Trigger. Vol. 15 of *Handbook of North American Indians*, ed. William Sturtevant, 177–89. Washington, D.C.: Smithsonian Institution.

A thorough and scholarly summary of the history and culture of the Indians of southern New England in the late seventeenth through the twentieth centuries.

Grumet, Robert S. 1995. *Historical Contact: Indian People and Colonists in Today's Northeastern United States in the Sixteenth Through the Eighteenth Centuries.* Norman: University of Oklahoma Press.

A survey of archaeological resources for the study of the contact period, mostly protected or curated by the National Park Service.

Hagedorn, Nancy Lee. 1995. "'A Friend to Go Between Them': Interpreters Among the Iroquois, 1664–1775." Ph.D. diss., College of William and Mary.

This important dissertation is one of the few studies to focus on the role of interpreters in Indian-white relations during the early historic period.

Hamell, George R. 1992. "The Iroquois and the World's Rim: Speculations on Color, Culture, and Contact." *American Indian Quarterly* 16(4): 451–69.

———. 1987. "Mythical Realities and European Contact in the Northeast During the Sixteenth and Seventeenth Centuries." *Man in the Northeast* 33:63–87.

Hamell's provocative research is concerned with the ontology and cosmology of native people, and the impact of European goods on native cosmological beliefs.

Hantman, Jeffrey L. 1990. "Between Powhatan and Quirank: Reconstructing Monacan Culture and History in the Context of Jamestown." *American Anthropologist* 92(3): 676–90.

Hantman uses archaeological and documentary data to reconstruct the culture of the little-known Iroquoian speakers whose territories bounded the Powhatan chiefdom to the west.

Kaplan, Susan. 1985. "European Goods and Socio-Economic Change in Early Labrador Inuit Society." In *Cultures in Contact: The European Impact on Native Cultural Institutions in Eastern North America, A.D. 1000–1800*, ed. William Fitzhugh, 45–70. Washington, D.C.: Smithsonian Institution Press.

An archaeological and documentary study of the impact of the early trade in European goods in Labrador, documenting the depth of the so-called "contact period" in the New World.

King, J. C. H. 1982. *Thunderbird and Lightning: Indian Life in Northeastern North America, 1600–1900*. London: British Museum Publications.

A museum catalogue for an exhibit of the same title, describing and illustrating many interesting objects and works of art reflecting or produced during three centuries of northeastern native history.

McGee, Harold Franklin. 1974. "Ethnic Boundaries and Strategies of Ethnic Interaction: A History of Micmac-White Relations in Nova Scotia." Ph.D. diss., Southern Illinois University.

A thorough review of the history of Indian-white relations on the northeasternmost frontier of the Northeast culture area.

Pendergast, James F. 1991. *The Massawomeck: Raiders and Traders Into the Chesapeake Bay in the Seventeenth Century*. Transactions of the American Philosophical Society, vol. 81, pt. 2. Philadelphia: American Philosophical Society.

An ethnohistorical survey of Massawomeck culture history, drawn from the scattered sources concerning this little-known people.

———. 1994. "The Kakouagoga or Kahkwas: An Iroquoian Nation Destroyed in the Niagara Region." *Proceedings of the American Philosophical Society* 138(1): 96–143.

A creative use of historical sources to reconstruct the history and culture of another little-known Iroquoian group.

Rountree, Helen C. 1989. *The Powhatan Indians of Virginia: Their Traditional Culture*. Norman: University of Oklahoma Press.

Rountree provides a thorough summary of the remarkably rich documentary sources available for study of the Powhatan paramount chiefdom.

Salisbury, Neal. 1982. *Manitou and Providence: Indians, Europeans, and the Making of New England, 1500–1634*. New York: Oxford University Press.

This important study attempts to explain New England colonial history in light of the interactions between Indians and English settlers.

———. 1996. "Native People and European Settlers in Eastern North America, 1600–1783." In *North America*, eds. Bruce G. Trigger and Wilcomb E. Washburn. Vol. 1 of *The Cambridge History of the Native Peoples of the Americas*, eds. Bruce G. Trigger, Wilcomb E. Washburn, and Richard E. W. Adams, 349–460. New York: Cambridge University Press.

A valuable summary of recent historical research on the contact period in the Northeast.

Sleeper-Smith, Susan. 1994. "Silent Tongues, Black Robes: Potawatomi, Europeans, and Settlers in the Southern Great Lakes, 1640–1850." Ph.D. diss., University of Michigan.

This dissertation surveys the complicated history of interaction between the Potawatomi and other Great Lakes people, and the explorers and settlers of many backgrounds.

Tanner, Helen Hornbeck, ed. 1987. *Atlas of Great Lakes Indian History.* Norman: University of Oklahoma Press.

This invaluable resource helps to sort out the tangled threads of native history and movement in the historic period through a series of maps reflected their locations at various times. Complete with an extensive narrative and bibliography, this volume supersedes all others as a source on Great Lakes Indian history.

Trelease, Allen W. 1997. *Indian Affairs in Colonial New York: The Seventeenth Century.* 2nd ed. Lincoln: University of Nebraska Press. Originally published 1960.

Still considered among the most important surveys of Indian-white relations in colonial New York.

Trigger, Bruce G. 1976. *Children of Ataentsic: A History of the Huron People to 1660.* 2 vols. Montreal: McGill-Queen's University Press.

Trigger's monumental study of the Huron set the standard for ethnohistorical reconstruction.

———. 1985. *Natives and Newcomers: Canada's "Heroic Age" Reconsidered.* Montreal: McGill-Queen's University Press.

A remarkable history of Indian-white relations in the seventeenth century, applying theoretical perspectives drawn from sociology and anthropology and demonstrating a command of the large body of primary sources available for the early colonial period.

Wolf, Eric R. 1982. *Europe and the People Without History.* Berkeley: University of California Press.

A fascinating and persuasive survey of the impact of the expansion of European societies on indigenous peoples, written by a prominent anthropologist.

4. Spirituality and Worldview

Traditional Spirituality

The subject of American Indian spirituality is as absorbing as it is controversial. Early descriptions, as well as early ethnographic accounts of native cosmological beliefs, remain some of the most important sources of information on this subject. The disruption of native communities in the wake of contact and colonization, conversion, and the suppression of or contempt shown for native beliefs soon drove their expression "underground." Recently, NAGPRA legislation (see below) and the return of objects of religious significance to Indian communities havea contributed to the controversies surrounding the subject. Ironically, the popular interest in native spirituality has increased in recent decades, so that publications on native cosmology continue to appear.

Sources

Carpenter, Roger Merle. 1999. "The Renewed, the Destroyed, and the Remade: The Three Thought Worlds of the Iroquois and the Huron, 1609–1650." University of California–Riverside.

Based on the early reports of Jesuit missionaries, this thesis describes the symbolic underpinnings of Huron traditional religion.

Hallowell, A. Irving. 1960. "Ojibwa Ontology, Behavior, and World View." In *Culture in History: Essays in Honor of Paul Radin*, ed. Stanley Diamond, 19–52. New York: Columbia University Press.

Hallowell's research on the psychological characteristics of the northern hunting people with whom he worked remain provocative and intriguing approaches to cultural analysis.

Hamell, George R. 1987. "Mythical Realities and European Contact in the Northeast During the Sixteenth and Seventeenth Centuries." *Man in the Northeast* 33:63–87.

Hammel's many publications, including this and the one following, focus on the way in which European trade goods were incorporated into native ritual and symbolic systems, and have shed light on the relevance of color in northeastern cosmology.

————. 1992. "The Iroquois and the World's Rim: Speculations on Color, Culture, and Contact." *American Indian Quarterly* 16(4): 451–69.

Hirschfelder, Arlene and Paulette Fairbanks Molin. 1991. *Encyclopedia of American Indian Religions.* New York: Facts on File.

Simmons, William S. 1976. "Southern New England Shamanism: An Ethnographic Reconstruction." In *Papers of the Seventh Algonquian Conference,* ed. William Cowan, 217–56. Ottawa.

Simmons's comprehensive and informed analysis of New England shamanism is a good starting place for research on this topic.

Tooker, Elisabeth. 1979. *Native North American Spirituality of the Eastern Woodlands.* New York: Paulist.

A thorough summary of scholarship on Eastern Woodlands spirituality, focusing on early or primary sources.

Underhill, Ruth. 965. *Red Man's Religion: Beliefs and Practices of the Indians North of Mexico.* Chicago: University of Chicago Press.

A classic survey, still a useful summary of continentwide patterns in native spirituality and cosmology.

Wallace, Anthony. 1958. "Dreams and Wishes of the Soul: A Type of Psychoanalytic Theory Among the Seventeenth-Century Iroquois." *American Anthropologist* 60(2): 234–48.

This remarkable study highlights the connections between Iroquoian dream interpretation and modern psychoanalytic practice.

Changing Native American Religions

Paradoxically, although ambiguity about the nature of traditional native spirituality continues and questions about the ethics of research and publication on native religion are on the increase, research into changes in native religious beliefs remains an important focus of recent scholarship. Topics include the social and economic effects of missions and missionaries on native people, the impact of conversion on native women, and the nativistic or revitalistic movements among native people "behind the frontier." Below is a collection of articles and books that concern themselves with the history of religious change in a number of northeastern native communities.

Sources

Abler, Thomas S. 1992. "Protestant Missionaries and Native Cultures: Parallel Careers of Asher Wright and Silas T. Rand." *American Indian Quarterly* 16(1): 25–37.

Barton, Lois. 1990. *A Quaker Promise Kept: Philadelphia Friends' Work with the Allegany Senecas, 1795–1960.* Norman: University of Oklahoma Press.

Bragdon, Kathleen J. 1991. "Native Christianity in Eighteenth-Century Massachusetts: Ritual as Cultural Reaffirmation." In *New Dimensions in Ethnohistory*, eds. Barry Gough and Christie Laird, 117–26. Papers of the Second Laurier Conference on Ethnohistory and Ethnology. Hull, Quebec: Canadian Museum of Civilization.

———. 1991b. "Vernacular Literacy and Massachusett World View 1650–1750." *Annual Proceedings (Dublin Seminar for New England Folklife)* 16:26–34.

Dauria, Susan R. 1994. "Kateri Tekakwitha: Gender and Ethnic Symbolism in the Process of Making an American Saint." *New York Folklore* 20(3–4): 55–73.

Devens, Carol. 1992. *Countering Colonization: Native American Women and Great Lakes Missions, 1630–1900.* Berkeley: University of California Press.

Goode, Richard C. 1995. "The Only and Principal End: Propagating the Gospel in Early Puritan New England." Ph.D. diss., Vanderbilt University.

Green, Debra Kathryn. 1996. "The Hymnody of the Seneca Native Americans of Western New York." Ph.D. diss., University of Cincinnati.

Hankins, Jean Fittz. 1993. "Bringing the Good News: Protestant Missionaries to the Indians of New England and New York, 1700–1775." Ph.D. diss., University of Connecticut.

Harp, Maureen Anna. 1996. "Indian Missions, Immigrant Migrations, and Regional Catholic Culture: Slovene Missionaries in the Upper Great Lakes, 1830–1892." Ph.D. diss., University of Chicago.

Hart, William Bryan. 1998. "For the Good of Our Souls: Mohawk Authority, Accommodation, and Resistance to Protestant Evangelism, 1700–1780." Ph.D. diss., Brown University.

Hauptman, Laurence M. and L. Gordon McLester III, eds. 1999. *The Oneida Indian Journey: From New York to Wisconsin, 1784–1860.* Madison: University of Wisconsin Press.

Jacobs, Lyn Richard. 1995. "Native American Prophetic Movements of the Eighteenth and Nineteenth Centuries." *Social Science Review* [Syracuse University] 70(3–4): 243.

Kasprycki, Sylvia S. 1996. "Matters of Faith: Notes on Missionaries and Material Culture." *European Review of Native American Studies* [Germany] 10(2): 45–50.

Knapp, Henry M. 1998. "The Character of Puritan Missions: The Motivation, Methodology, and Effectiveness of the Puritan Evangelization of the Native Americans in New England." *Journal of Presbyterian History* 76(2): 111–26.

Moore, Cynthia Marie. 1999. "'Rent and Ragged Relation[s]': Puritans, Indians, and the Management of Congregations in New England, 1647–1776." Ph.D. diss., State University of New York at Stony Brook.

Patrick, Christine Sternberg. 1993. "The Life and Times of Samuel Kirkland, 1741–1808: Missionary to the Oneida Indians, American Patriot, and Founder of Hamilton College." Ph.D. diss., State University of New York at Buffalo.

Pflug, Melissa Ann. 1990. "Contemporary Revitalization Movements Among the Northern Great Lakes Ottawa (Odawa) Indians: Motives and Accomplishments." Ph.D. diss., Wayne State University.

———. 1992. "Politics of Great Lakes Indian Religion." *Michigan Historical Review* 18(2): 15–31.

Reid, John G. 1990. "Mission to the Micmac." *Beaver* [Canada] 70(5): 15–22.

Richter, Daniel K. 1992. "'Some of Them . . . Would Always Have a Minister With Them:' Mohawk Protestantism, 1683–1719." *American Indian Quarterly* 16(4): 471–84.

Rountree, Helen C. 1992. "Powhatan Priests and English Rectors: Worldviews and Congregations in Conflict." *American Indian Quarterly* 16(4): 485–500.

Sagard-Theodat, Gabriel. [1632] 1939. *Father Gabriel Sagard: The Long Journey to the Country of the Hurons.* Ed. George M. Wrong. Toronto: The Champlain Society.

Salisbury, Neal. 1982. *Manitou and Providence: Indians, Colonists, and the Making of New England.* London: Cambridge University Press.

———. 1992. "Religious Encounters in a Colonial Context: New England

and New France in the Seventeenth Century." *American Indian Quarterly* 16(4): 501–509.

Sleeper-Smith, Susan. 1994. "Silent Tongues, Black Robes: Potawatomi, Europeans, and Settlers in the Southern Great Lakes, 1640–1850." Ph.D. diss., University of Michigan.

Speck, Frank G. and Alexander General. 1995. *Midwinter Rites of the Cayuga Longhouse.* Lincoln: University of Nebraska Press.

Steckley, John. 1992. "The Warrior and the Lineage: Jesuit Use of Iroquoian Images to Communicate Christianity." *Ethnohistory* 39(4): 478–509.

Sturtevant, William. 1984. "A Structural Sketch of Iroquois Ritual." In *Extending the Rafters: Interdisciplinary Approaches to Iroquoian Studies,* eds. Michael K. Foster, Jack Campisi, and Marianne Mithun, 133–52. Albany: State University of New York Press.

Thwaites, Reuben G., ed. [1616] 1959. *The Jesuit Relations and Allied Documents: Travel and Explorations of the Jesuit Missionaries in New France, 1610–1791; the Original French, Latin, and Italian Texts, with English Translations and Notes.* 73 vols. Cleveland: Burrows Brothers, 1896–1901. Reprint, New York: Pageant.

Tooker, Elisabeth. 1970. *The Iroquois Ceremonial of Midwinter.* Syracuse, N.Y.: Syracuse University Press.

———. 1979. *Native North American Spirituality of the Eastern Woodlands.* New York: Paulist.

Trigger, Bruce G. 1985. *Natives and Newcomers: Canada's "Heroic Age" Reconsidered.* Montreal: McGill-Queen's University Press.

———. 1991. "The Jesuits and the Fur Trade." In *Sweet Promises: A Reader on Indian-White Relations in Canada,* ed. J. R. Miller, 3–18. Ontario: University of Toronto Press.

Van Lonkhuyzen, Harold W. 1990. "A Reappraisal of the Praying Indians: Acculturation, Conversion, and Identity at Natick, Massachusetts 1646–1730." *New England Quarterly* 63(3): 396–428.

Wallace, Anthony. 1969. *The Death and Rebirth of the Seneca.* New York: Knopf.

———. 1978. "Origins of the Longhouse Religion." In *The Northeast,* ed. Bruce G. Trigger. Vol. 15 of *Handbook of North American Indians,* ed. William Sturtevant, 442–48. Washington, D.C.: Smithsonian Institution.

Walsh, Martin W. 1992. "The 'Heathen Party': Methodist Observation of the Ohio Wyandot." *American Indian Quarterly* 16(2): 189–211.

Willig, Timothy D. 1996. "Prophetstown on the Wabash: The Native Spiritual Defense of the Old Northwest." *Michigan Historical Review* 23(2): 115–58.

Zeisberger, David. 1885. *Diary of David Zeisberger, a Moravian Missionary Among the Indians of Ohio, 1781–1798*. 2 vols. Ed. and trans. Eugene R. Bliss. Cincinnati: Robert Clarke.

5. Politics and Economy

Economy and Subsistence, Then and Now

A traditional topic of ethnographic research, native economy and subsistence continue to intrigue researchers, both those whose interest is in reconstructing past lifeways and those who are concerned with the impact of colonization on traditional economies. Recent research also focuses on the ways in which governmental policies and programs had a continued, often negative effect on native economy and subsistence in the eighteenth and nineteenth centuries. Finally, much recent research concerns modern economic development among Indian communities of the Northeast.

Sources

Anderson, Terry L., ed. 1992. *Property Rights and Indian Economies*. Lanham, Md.: Rowman and Littlefield.

A recent summary of a large body of research concerned with the nature of native property rights as these affect economic development.

Barker, Alex W. 1992. "Powhatan's Pursestrings: On the Meaning of Surplus in a Seventeenth-Century Algonkian Chiefdom." In *Lords of the Southeast: Social Inequality and the Native Elites of Southeastern North America*, eds. Alex W. Barker and Timothy R. Pauketat, 61–80. Washington, D.C.: American Anthropological Association.

Historical reconstruction of the economy of the Powhatan paramount chiefdom, with a materialist interpretation of Powhatan society and hierarchy.

Bennett, M. K. 1955. "The Food Economy of the New England Indians, 1605–1675." *The Journal of Political Economy* 63:360–96.

A classic of ethnohistorical research. Bennett combed early sources to determine the seasonal subsistence round and diet of the southern New

England natives, documenting the importance of domesticated crops and other vegetable foods in their diet.

Bourque, Bruce J. 1973. "Aboriginal Settlement and Subsistence on the Maine Coast." *Man in the Northeast* 6:3–20.

A competent summary based on archaeological and ethnohistorical sources of seasonal subsistence of the coastal natives of Maine.

Bragdon, Kathleen. 1996. *Native People of Southern New England, 1500– 1650.* Norman: University of Oklahoma Press.

An historical ethnography for southern New England native cultures in the early contact period.

Brown, Judeth Kredel. 1990. "Economic Organization and the Position of Women Among the Iroquois." In *Iroquois Women: An Anthology,* ed. William G. Spittal. Ohsweken, Ontario: Iroqrafts.

One of the topics of interest in the Northeast is the relationship between women's economic role and their overall status within their societies. Iroquois women, whose labor produced the bulk of Iroquois food and who, in a matrilineal society, were thought to enjoy a prominent social and political status as well, have been the subject of a great deal of feminist scholarship as well (see below).

Ceci, Lynn. 1975. "Fish Fertilizer: A Native North American Practice?" *Science* 188(4183): 26–30.

In this article, Ceci argued, based on documentary sources, that the practice of fertilizing corn hills with fish introduced to the Pilgrims by Squanto was actually an English practice that Squanto learned about while held captive among them prior to the founding of Plymouth Plantation. This article sparked a decade or more of debate about native economy, and the effect of colonization on native subsistence and settlement pattern.

———. 1990. "Wampum as a Peripheral Resource in the Seventeenth-Century World System." In *The Pequots in Southern New England: The Fall and Rise of an American Indian Nation,* eds. Laurence M. Hauptman and James D. Wherry, 48–65. Norman: University of Oklahoma Press.

Ceci's research on the production of wampum suggests that political centralization in southern New England coastal societies was accelerated by their control over the production of wampum, the currency of the fur trade in the early contact period.

Cronon, William. 1983. *Changes in the Land: Indians, Colonists, and the Ecology of New England.* New York: Hill and Wang.

An innovative and persuasive study of the impact of English settlement on the ecology of New England, and the way in which native people's traditional way of life was made impossible there by the incompatibility of Indian broad-based strategies and English practices. Cronon advocates understanding ecologies as economic/social systems as well, and focuses on the consequences to human societies of ecological change.

Flannery, Regina. 1946. "The Culture of the Northeastern Indian Hunters: A Descriptive Survey." In *Man in Northeastern America* (vol. 3 of Papers of the Robert S. Peabody Foundation for Archaeology), ed. Frederick Johnson. Andover, Mass.: Phillips Academy, the Foundation.

A still useful summary of a wide variety of cultural "traits" as described in early sources. A good place to begin historical investigation of any number of native practices and beliefs.

Guillemin, Jeanne. 1975. *Urban Renegades: The Cultural Strategies of American Indians.* New York: Columbia University Press.

This unique book looks at Indians in an urban setting, particularly the Micmac community in Boston, Massachusetts. The economic and social characteristics of displaced Indian communities in the Northeast deserve further consideration.

Herrick, James W. and Dean R. Snow. 1995. *Iroquois Medical Botany.* 1st ed. Syracuse, N.Y.: Syracuse University Press.

A survey and analysis of the numerous descriptions of Iroquois plant use, useful to historians, ethnologists, and archaeologists.

Leacock, Eleanor B. 1954. "The Montagnais 'Hunting Territory' and the Fur Trade." *Memoirs of the American Anthropological Association* 78.

The classic critique of Frank Speck's theory of family-owned hunting territories. Speck's argument that the private ownership of property was aboriginal was successfully countered by Leacock's use of documentary sources.

McBride, Kevin A. 1991. "'Ancient and Crazie': Pequot Lifeways During the Historic Period." *Annual Proceedings (Dublin Seminar for New England Folklife)* 16:63–75.

One of the few archaeologists to study southern new England native life during the eighteenth and nineteenth centuries, McBride demonstrates the continued distinctiveness of native life "behind the frontier."

McConnell, Michael Norman. 1992. *A Country Between: The Upper Ohio Valley and Its Peoples, 1724–1774.* Lincoln: University of Nebraska Press.

An innovative regional history that looks at economic and social interaction between Indians and settlers in the decades preceding the Revolution.

Nanepashemet. 1991. "It Smells Fishy to Me: An Argument Supporting the Use of Fish Fertilizer by the Native People of Southern New England." *Annual Proceedings (Dublin Seminar for New England Folklife)* 16:42–50.

Wampanoag historian Nanepashemet's critique of Lynn Ceci's theory that fish fertilizer was European in origin.

Porter, Frank, III, ed. 1987. *Strategies for Survival: American Indians in the Eastern United States.* Westport, Conn.: Greenwood.

A collection of essays by anthropologists and historians, and one of the few that looks at eastern Indian communities in the recent past.

Richards, Patricia B. 1993. "Winnebago Subsistence: Change and Continuity." *Wisconsin Archeologist* 74(1–4): 272–89.

A useful discussion of the ways in which these upper Great Lakes people have maintained a distinctive economy throughout their history.

Roback, Jennifer. 1992. "Exchange, Sovereignty, and Indian-Anglo Relationship." In *Property Rights and Indian Economies,* ed. Terry L. Anderson, 5–26. Lanham, Md.: Rowman and Littlefield.

Reciprocity and exchange, central to economic and social relations in native communities in the Northeast, have been misunderstood by contemporaries and modern historians as well.

Rogers, Edward S. 1994. "The Algonquian Farmers of Southern Ontario, 1830–1945." In *Aboriginal Ontario: Historical Perspectives on the First Nations,* eds. Edward S. Rogers and Donald B. Smith, 122–66. Toronto: Dundurn Press.

An interesting study of the largely unsuccessful attempt to encourage farming among the Woodlands people of the St. Lawrence lowlands.

Rountree, Helen C. 1990. *Pocahontas's People: The Powhatan Indians of Virginia Through Four Centuries.* Norman: University of Oklahoma Press.

An overview of the history of the many native communities of Virginia, focusing on changing economy, social relations, and relations with the state and federal government.

———. 1992. "Indian Virginians on the Move." In *Indians of the Southeastern United States in the Late Twentieth Century*, ed. J. Anthony Paredes, 9–28. Tuscaloosa: University of Alabama Press.

An interesting review of the choice made by many Virginian Indians, in the face of racist state policies, to emigrate to other regions while keeping in contact with their families and communities in Virginia.

Speck, Frank. 1940. *Penobscot Man: The Life History of a Forest Tribe in Maine.* Philadelphia: University of Pennsylvania Press.

An important ethnographic portrait of the Penobscots in the early twentieth century, with an emphasis on their "traditional" culture.

Squire, Mariella Rose. 1996. "The Contemporary Western Abenakis: Maintenance, Reclamation, and Reconfiguration of an American Indian Ethnic Identity." Ph.D. diss., State University of New York at Albany.

This remarkable dissertation, written by a woman of Western Abenaki descent, while largely concerned with the nature of contemporary Abenaki "ethnicity," provides a wealth of fascinating detail about contemporary Indian life in the Northeast.

Strong, John A. 1996. *"We are still here!": The Algonquian Peoples of Long Island Today.* Interlaken, N.Y.: Empire State.

A brief introduction to the history and culture of the Long Island native peoples, and their contemporary concerns.

Weinstein, Laurie, ed. 1994. *Enduring Traditions: The Native Peoples of New England.* Westport, Conn.: Bergin and Garvey.

A collection of important articles by native and non-native scholars concerning the contemporary politics and economics of southern New England Indians.

Wright, Mary C. 1981. "Economic Development and Native American Women in the Early Nineteenth Century." *American Quarterly* 33:525–36.

> One of a number of important articles in this collection of historical studies of Indians and their contribution to American history.

Warfare, Diplomacy, and Frontier Studies

Surely among the most enduring of interests to historians are the relationships between colonial powers and the various Indian groups who stood in the way of frontier expansion. A review of the literature on Indian wars, and warfare in general, demonstrates the evolving understanding of Indian-white relations from one in which Indians played little or no lasting role in American history to one in which their involvement appears crucial. A second interest among scholars of several disciplines is the nature of Indian war practices, from scalping to the torture of captives to the taking of hostages. Finally, several historians have looked at the role of Indians in the evolution of European and Euro-American military tactics.

Sources

Axelrod, Alan. 1993. *Chronicle of the Indian Wars: From Colonial Times to Wounded Knee.* New York: Prentice Hall.

> A useful starting place for those interested in the history of warfare between Native Americans and various colonial and federal forces.

Benn, Carl. 1998. *The Iroquois in the War of 1812.* Toronto: University of Toronto Press.

> A look at a period in Iroquois history that has received less attention than it deserves.

Brandao, Jose Antonio. 1997. *"Your Fyre Shall Burn No More": Iroquois Policy Toward New France and Its Native Allies to 1701.* Lincoln: University of Nebraska Press.

> A recent analysis of the role played by the powerful Iroquois in colonial politics in the seventeenth century.

Calloway, Colin G. 1990. "Sentinels of the Revolution: Bedel's New Hamp-

shire Rangers and the Abenaki Indians on the Upper Connecticut."
Historical New Hampshire 45(4): 270–95.

Calloway's many studies of the Abenaki peoples and their ongoing significance to colonial history include this and the following entries.

―――. 1991. "New England Algonkians in the American Revolution." *Annual Proceedings (Dublin Seminar for New England Folklife)* 16:51–62.

―――, ed. 1997. *After King Philip's War: Presence and Persistence in Indian
New England.* Hanover, N.H.: University Press of New England.

Carter, Harvey. 1987. *The Life and Times of Little Turtle, First Sagamore of
the Wabash.* Urbana: University of Illinois Press.

A sympathetic portrait of Little Turtle, war chief of the Miami, who
successfully defended his people against American-led expeditions until
their defeat at Fallen Timbers.

Demos, John. *The Unredeemed Captive: A Family Story from Early America.*
New York: Knopf.

An interesting study by a prominent historian of the experiences of
colonists captured by Indians in the colonial period.

Dennis, Matthew. 1993. *Cultivating a Landscape of Peace: Iroquois–European Encounters in Seventeenth-Century America.* Ithaca, N.Y.: Cornell
University Press.

A study that contrasts with Brandao's (above.)

Densmore, Christopher. 1999. *Red Jacket: Iroquois Diplomat and Orator.*
Syracuse, N.Y.: Syracuse University Press.

This important Seneca orator participated in nearly all diplomatic negotiations between his people and the U.S. government between 1780
and 1820. His goal, to maintain a united Iroquois front in negotiations,
was foiled by the decentralized and factionalized politics of the formerly
powerful League.

Edmunds, R. David and Peyser, Joseph L. 1993. *The Fox Wars: The Mesquakie Challenge to New France.* (Vol. 211 of the Civilization of the
American Indian Series.) Norman: University of Oklahoma Press.

A thorough study of the period during which the Mesquakie defended
their position in the fur trade between Green Bay and the Mississippi
River.

Engelbrecht, William. 1985. "New York Iroquois Political Development." In *Cultures in Contact: The Impact of European Contacts on Native American Cultural Institutions, A.D. 100–1800*, ed. William Fitzhugh, 163–86. Washington, D.C.: Smithsonian Institution Press.

A review of the archaeological data reflecting the relationships among various northern Iroquoian peoples in the early contact period.

Fausz, Frederick J. 1985. "Patterns of Anglo–Indian Aggression and Accommodation Along the Mid-Atlantic Coast, 1584–1634." In *Cultures in Contact: The European Impact on Native Cultural Institutions in Eastern North America, A.D. 1000–1800*, ed. William Fitzhugh, 225–70. Washington, D.C.: Smithsonian Institution Press.

Fausz is one of the few scholars to study the significant role of the Catholics of Maryland in Anglo-Indian conflict in the early colonial period.

Gleach, Frederic W. 1997. *Powhatan's World and Colonial Virginia: A Conflict of Cultures.* Lincoln: University of Nebraska Press.

Gleach's interesting analysis of relations between the Powhatan chiefdom and the early English settlers of Virginia focuses on the meaning of war in Powhatan culture.

Graymont, Barbara. 1991. "The Six Nations Indians in the Revolutionary War." In *Sweet Promises: A Reader on Indian-White Relations in Canada*, ed. R. J. Miller, 93–104. Toronto: University of Toronto Press.

This veteran of Iroquois history summarizes the role of the Six Nations in the Revolution.

Hauptman, Laurence M. 1993. *The Iroquois in the Civil War: From Battlefield to Reservation.* Syracuse, N.Y.: Syracuse University Press.

Hauptman specializes in the later history of the Iroquois, in this case, their participation in the Civil War and its effect on their communities. An interesting counterpoint to the ethnographic analysis provided by Lewis Henry Morgan's *League of the Ho dé No Sau Ne*, published in 1851.

Igneri, David Sebastian. 1992. "Sir William Johnson's Influence on the Iroquois and Other Indians Which Affected the Outcome of the French and Indian War." Ph.D. diss., Union Institute (Cincinnati).

This dissertation, and the one that follows, summarize important information about Iroquois warfare and their involvement in colonial politics.

Keener, Craig Scott. 1998. "An Ethnohistoric Perspective on Iroquois Warfare During the Second Half of the Seventeenth Century (A.D. 1649–1701)." Ph.D. diss., Ohio State University.

Leach, Douglas. [1958] 1992. *Flintlock and Tomahawk: New England in King Philip's War.* New York: Macmillan. Reprint, East Orleans, Mass.: Parnassus.

Still the classic study of the war and its participants.

LePore, Jill. 1998. *The Name of War: King Philip's War and the Origins of American Identity.* New York: Knopf.

A literary analysis of the many works in English regarding King Philip's War, with an emphasis on the resulting conceptualization of Indian people in popular culture.

Malone, Patrick M. 1993. *The Skulking Way of War: Technology and Tactics Among the New England Indians.* Baltimore: Johns Hopkins University Press.

A study of the contrasts between native and English warfare, and the changes that resulted among both people's practice as a result of their encounter.

Mintz, Max M. 1999. *Seeds of Empire: The Revolutionary Conquest of the Iroquois.* New York: New York University Press.

The drama of the Iroquois involvement in the Revolutionary War as allies of the British revisited.

Parker, Arthur C. 1998. *Red Jacket, Seneca Chief.* Lincoln: University of Nebraska Press.

Parker's study of Red Jacket, the Seneca leader, is among the many publications of this prolific scholar on the Seneca, and the Iroquois generally, in the early part of the century.

Parmenter, Jon William. 1997. "Pontiac's War: Forging New Links in the Anglo–Iroquois Chain, 1758–1766." *Ethnohistory* 44(4): 617–54.

An analysis of Iroquois warfare and diplomacy on their western borders.

———. 1999. "At the Wood's Edge: Iroquois Foreign Relations, 1727–1768." Ph.D. diss., University of Michigan.

A study of colonial politics from the Iroquois point of view.

Pendergast, James F. 1991. *The Massawomeck: Raiders and Traders Into the Chesapeake Bay in the Seventeenth Century*. Transactions of the American Philosophical Society Series, vol. 81, pt. 2. Philadelphia: American Philosophical Society.

An ethnohistorical reconstruction of a little-known Algonquian people and their role in early Anglo-Indian competition.

———. 1994. "The Kakouagoga or Kahkwas: An Iroquoian Nation Destroyed in the Niagara Region." *Proceedings of the American Philosophical Society* 138(1): 96–143.

In the chaotic early years of the fur trade, a number of presumably Iroquoian-speaking peoples were destroyed or displaced. This study gathers information about one such group.

Prins, Harald and Bruce Bourque. 1987. "Norridgewock: Village Translocation on the New England–Acadian Frontier." *Man in the Northeast* 33:137–58.

The history of Anglo-French-Indian relations in Maine and New France is complex and undeservedly neglected. This study summarizes much interesting data from the Abenaki point of view.

Rountree, Helen C. 1993. *Powhatan Foreign Relations, 1500–1722*. Charlottesville: University Press of Virginia.

A thorough review of historical accounts of Powhatan relations with Europeans explorers and settlers, as well as with other native groups.

Sims, Catherine A. 1992. *Algonkian–British Relations in the Upper Great Lakes Region: Gathering to Give and to Receive Presents, 1815–1843*. London: University of Western Ontario [Canada].

An important analysis of the later history of British-native relations and trade in the upper Great Lakes.

Stanley, George F. G. 1991. "The Indians in the War of 1812." In *Sweet*

Promises: A Reader on Indian-White Relations in Canada, ed. J. R. Miller, 105–24. Toronto: University of Toronto Press.

Another look at this neglected period in northeastern Native history.

Stewart-Smith, David. 1998. "The Pennacook Indians and the New England Frontier, Circa 1604–1733." Ph.D. diss., Union Institute, School of Interdisciplinary Arts and Sciences (Cincinnati).

An important study of the complex interrelations among the Pawtucket, Pennacook, and Western Abenaki in the frontier regions of New England and New France.

Wallace, Anthony F. 1990. *King of the Delawares: Teedyuscung, 1700–1763.* Syracuse, N.Y.: Syracuse University Press.

Wallace brings his formidable talents as an anthropologist and a writer to the story of the Delaware leader of the Delaware "Five Nations," who, during the Seven Years' War, raided territories swindled from the Delaware as part of the infamous "Walking Purchase." Later persuaded to accept cash in settlement for the fraudulent deal, Teedyuscung was murdered, and his negotiations failed to protect his people.

Washburn, Wilcomb. 1978. "Colonial Indian Wars." In *The Northeast,* ed. Bruce G. Trigger. Vol. 15 of *Handbook of North American Indians,* ed. William Sturtevant, 89–100. Washington, D.C.: Smithsonian Institution.

A survey and analysis of early colonial wars, with an emphasis on the conflicting motives of the Indians and colonists.

Iroquois Politics, the League, and the Origins of the Constitution

Judging by the number of publications concerning it, the history and influence of the League of the Iroquois ranks among the most controversial topics of the past several decades. This important native confederacy, with all its many diplomatic, symbolic, and ideological outgrowths, remains one of the most remarkable political institutions known in native North America, and well deserves the respect and interest of scholars. Two principal issues emerge from the literature: first, what are the origins of the League? Did it precede the arrival of Europeans, as the Iroquois themselves claim, or was it at least in part a response to the nascent fur trade, the new availability of European trade goods, and the pressures of intercolonial rivalry in North America? Second, what was the influence, if any, of the League on the framers of the U.S. Constitution? Many scholars have suggested that the founders of the new republic took as their model the organization of the League, with its egalitarian representation and its grand council. These two questions strike at the heart of profound concerns: did complex native institutions precede European influence, and did native institutions in turn contribute to American culture more generally? Many native people argue that both were so.

Sources

Aquila, Richard. 1997. *The Iroquois Restoration: Iroquois Diplomacy on the Colonial Frontier, 1701–1754.* Lincoln: University of Nebraska Press.

Barreiro, Jose Antonio. 1992. *Indian Roots of American Democracy.* Ithaca, N.Y.: Akwe'kon Press, Cornell University.

———. 1997. *"Your Fyre Shall Burn No More": Iroquois Policy Toward New France and Its Native Allies to 1701.* Lincoln: University of Nebraska Press.

Brandao, J. A. and Willliam A. Starna. "The Treaties of 1701: A Triumph of Iroquois Diplomacy." *Ethnohistory* 43(2): 209–44.

Campisi, Jack and William A. Starna. 1995. "On the Road to Canandaigua: The Treaty of 1794." *American Indian Quarterly* (1995) 19(4): 467–90.

Engelbrecht, William. 1985. "New York Iroquois Political Development." In *Cultures in Contact: The Impact of European Contacts on Native American Cultural Institutions, A.D. 1000–1800,* ed. William Fitzhugh, 163–86. Washington, D.C.: Smithsonian Institution Press.

Fenton, William N. 1998. *The Great Law and the Longhouse: A Political History of the Iroquois Confederacy.* Civilization of the American Indian Series, no. 223. Norman: University of Oklahoma Press.

Foster, Michael K., Jack Campisi, and Marianne Mithun, eds. 1984. *Extending the Rafters: Interdisciplinary Approaches to Iroquoian Studies.* Albany: State University of New York Press.

Goldenweiser, Alexander A., Hanni Woodbury, John Arthur Gibson, Reginald Henry, and Harry Webster. 1992. *Concerning the League: The Iro-*

quois League Tradition as Dictated in Onondaga by John Arthur Gibson.
Winnipeg: Algonquian and Iroquoian Linguistics.

Grinde, Donald A. and Bruce E. Johansen. 1991. *Exemplar of Liberty: Native America and the Evolution of Democracy.* Los Angeles, Calif.: American Indian Studies Center, University of California.

Jennings, Francis. 1984. *The Ambiguous Iroquois Empire: The Covenant Chain Confederation of Indian Tribes with English Colonies from Its Beginnings to the Lancaster Treaty of 1744.* New York: Norton.

Jennings, Francis, William Fenton, and Mary Druke, eds. 1985. *The History and Culture of Iroquois Diplomacy: An Interdisciplinary Guide to the Treaties of the Six Nations and Their League.* Syracuse, N.Y.: Syracuse University Press.

Johansen, Bruce Elliot. 1990. "Native American Societies and the Evolution of Democracy in America, 1600–1800." *Ethnohistory* 37(3): 279–90.

———. 1996. "Debating the Origins of Democracy: Overview of an Annotated Bibliography." *American Indian Culture and Research Journal* 20(2): 155–72.

———. 1997. *Debating Democracy: The Iroquois Legacy of Freedom.* Santa Fe, N.M.: Clear Light.

———. 1999. *Native America and the Evolution of Democracy: A Supplementary Bibliography.* Westport, Conn.: Greenwood, xix, 160.

Johansen, Bruce E. and Donald A. Grinde Jr. 1990. "The Debate Regarding Native Precedents for Democracy: A Recent Historiography." *American Indian Culture and Research Journal* 14(1): 61–88.

Richter, Daniel K. 1992. *Ordeal of the Longhouse: The Peoples of the Iroquois League in the Era of European Colonization.* Chapel Hill: University of North Carolina Press for the Institute of Early American History and Culture, Williamsburg, Va.

Starna, William A. and George R. Hamell. 1996. "History and the Burden of Proof: The Case of Iroquois Influence on the U.S. Constitution." *New York History* 77(4): 427–52.

Tooker, Elisabeth. 1978b. "The League of the Iroquois: Its History, Politics, and Ritual." In *The Northeast,* ed. Bruce G. Trigger. Vol. 15 of *Handbook of North American Indians,* ed. William Sturtevant, 418–41. Washington, D.C.: Smithsonian Institution.

———. 1990a. "Rejoinder to Johansen." *Ethnohistory* 37(3): 291–97.

———. 1990b. "The United States Constitution and the Iroquois League."

In *The Invented Indian: Cultural Fictions and Government Policies*, ed. James A. Clifton, 107–28. New Brunswick, N.J.: Transaction.

The Middle Ground

Historian Richard White's examination of the politics, economy, and society of the "Middle Ground"—the interdependency of the peoples of the Great Lakes region in the eighteenth century, when Indians and settlers reached a kind of balance from which both benefited for a time—has been an influential concept among historians, who appreciate White's attempt to re-create, in the manner of the French *annalists*, a picture of the frontier culture of the region that was neither wholly Indian nor wholly European. Although increasing English settlement and more repressive military policies eventually tipped the balance in favor of the Europeans, future research in other frontier regions where Indians and non-Indians came together would undoubtedly reveal similar examples. This promising approach also allows a focus on the region, rather than a particular ethnic/racial/colonial entity, thus freeing the analyst and the reader from the necessity to "take sides."

Sources

McConnell, Michael Norman. 1992. *A Country Between: The Upper Ohio Valley and Its Peoples, 1724–1774*. Lincoln: University of Nebraska Press.

White, Richard. 1991. *The Middle Ground: Indians, Empires and Republics in the Great Lakes Region, 1650–1815*. London: Cambridge University Press.

6. Women in Native America

Historical and anthropological studies of women in Native America have advanced greatly since the 1970s. With the increasing realization by archaeologists and ethnographers that women's contributions to economics were poorly understood, many new studies of women as farmers and foragers have been initiated. Other work concerns women's status in traditional and contact-period Indian communities. Initial formulations by Leacock (1978)—for example, suggesting that "separate spheres" characterized the

work of men and women in many native societies in the New World and
elsewhere—have been questioned for many parts of North America. Gender
relations in the Northeast, among matrilineal societies such as the Iroquois,
Mahican, and Delaware as well as in patrilineal and bilateral systems, are
unsurprisingly more complex than either historical sources reveal or ethnographic analogy implies. Indian women, for good or ill, frequently served
as mediators or "brokers" between their communities and encroaching settlers. Contemporary native women are also a source of interest to researchers,
as many have been at the forefront of native cultural renaissance and political
resistance.

Sources

Anderson, Karen Lee. 1990. *The Subjugation of Women in Seventeenth-
Century New France*. London, New York: Routledge.

A provocative study of the ways in which French colonization nega-
tively impacted native women.

Bataille, Gretchen Mueller. 1993. *Native American Women: A Biographical
Dictionary*. New York: Garland.

Summarizes the numerous writings on the lives of Native American
women from the contact period to the present.

Bataille, Gretchen Mueller and Kathleen Mullen Sands. 1991. *American
Indian Women: A Guide to Research*. New York: Garland.

Another useful review of literature and research issues focusing on Indian women.

Bragdon, Kathleen. 1996. "Gender as a Social Category in Native Southern
New England." *Ethnohistory* 43(4): 573–92.

Argues that in coastal New England societies, rank and status were more
relevant social categories than gender.

Brown, Judeth Kredel. 1990. "Economic Organization and the Position of
Women Among the Iroquois." In *Iroquois Women: An Anthology*, ed.
William G. Spittal, 182–98. Ohsweken, Ontario: Iroqrafts.

A review of the contributions of Iroquois women to their traditional
society, and the implications for social organization.

Claassen, Cheryl and Rosemary A. Joyce. 1997. *Women in Prehistory: North America and Mesoamerica*. Philadelphia: University of Pennsylvania Press.

A fascinating collection of articles using archaeological and documentary data to address the specifics of women's contributions to economy, society, and ideology in the period prior to contact with Europeans.

Dauria, Susan R. 1994. "Kateri Tekakwitha: Gender and Ethnic Symbolism in the Process of Making an American Saint." *New York Folklore* 20(3–4): 55–73.

Among the many studies of the seventeenth-century Mohawk woman, with a focus on the politics of sainthood.

Devens, Carol. 1992. *Countering Colonization: Native American Women and Great Lakes Missions, 1630–1900*. Berkeley: University of California Press.

Another important issue in studies of Native American woman is whether they constituted a conservative force or "resisted" colonization and acculturation. This study takes the position that women of the Great Lakes played the latter role.

Earle, Thomas. 1996. *The Three Faces of Molly Brant: A Biography*. Kingston, Ontario: Quarry.

Mohawk Molly Brant and her complicated relationships with Sir William Johnson, her brother Joseph Brant, and her own people continues to fascinate scholars and readers.

Etienne, Mona and Eleanor Burke Leacock, eds. 1980. *Women and Colonization: Anthropological Perspectives*. New York: Praeger Scientific.

This important collection of articles looks specifically at women's role in colonization worldwide (but with a focus on North America). Leacock suggests that native women's status generally declines in colonial contexts.

Fisher, Lillian M. 1996. *Kateri Tekakwitha: The Lily of the Mohawks*. Boston: Pauline.

A focus on Tekakwitha's life as a devout Catholic convert.

Grumet, Robert. 1980. "Sunksquaws, Shamans, and Tradeswomen: Middle

Atlantic Coastal Algonkian Women During the Seventeenth and Eighteenth Centuries." In *Women and Colonization: Anthropological Perspectives*, eds. Mona Etienne and Eleanor Burke Leacock, 43–62. New York: Praeger.

Grumet cites several examples of native women in roles more commonly occupied by men.

Hewitt, J. N. B. 1990. "Status of Women in Iroquois Polity Before 1784." In *Iroquois Women: An Anthology*, ed. William G. Spittal, 53–68. Ohsweken, Ontario: Iroqrafts.

A classic essay on this topic of current interest.

Jaimes, Marie Annette and Theresa Halsey. 1992. "American Indian Women: At the Center of Indigenous Resistance in Contemporary North America." In *The State of Native America: Genocide, Colonization, and Resistance*, ed. Annette M. Jaimes, 311–44. Boston: South End.

An interesting look at the contemporary political activism of native women in many communities.

Kidwell, Clara Sue. 1992. "Indian Women as Cultural Mediators." *Ethnohistory* 39(2): 97–107.

Kidwell surveys the early historical literature in this useful discussion of women as intermediaries.

Klein, Laura F. and Lillian A. Ackerman, eds. 1995. *Women and Power in Native North America*. Norman: University of Oklahoma Press.

An important collection of essays concerning women's status in native North America, drawn from documentary and ethnographic sources.

Koehler, Lyle. 1997. "Earth Mothers, Warriors, Horticulturists, Artists, and Chiefs: Women Among the Mississippian and Mississippian–Oneota Peoples, A.D. 1000 to 1750." In *Women in Prehistory: North America and Mesoamerica*, eds. Cheryl Claassen and Rosemary A. Joyce, 211–26. Philadelphia: University of Pennsylvania Press.

Koehler focuses on the creative role of women farmers in the late Woodland period.

La Fromboise, Teresa Davis, Anneliese M. Heyle, and Emily J. Ozer. 1994.

"Changing and Diverse Roles of Women in American Indian Cultures: Transformation from Headquarters City to Community." In *Native American Resurgence and Renewal: A Reader and Bibliography*, ed. Robert N. Wells Jr., 464–94. Lanham, Md.: Scarecrow.

Another in a growing list of studies of contemporary native women as political activists.

Landes, Ruth. [1938] 1997. *The Ojibwa Woman*. Vol. 31 of Columbia University Contributions to Anthropology. New York: Columbia University Press. Reprint, Lincoln: University of Nebraska Press.

This undeservedly neglected book, now reprinted with an introduction by Sally Cole, is a sympathetic study of the ways in which the Ojibwa women from whom Landes collected life histories understood and interpreted their own lives as structurally distinct from those of Ojibwa men.

Leacock, Eleanor. 1978. "Women's Status in Egalitarian Society: Implications for Social Evolution." *Current Anthropology* 19:247–55, 268–75.

Leacock writes eloquently about the ways in which European institutions have oppressed women in formerly egalitarian societies.

Lurie, Nancy O. 1961. *Mountain Wolf Woman: The Autobiography of a Winnebago Indian*. Ann Arbor: University of Michigan Press.

This famous autobiography details the fascinating life of Mountain Wolf Woman, whose life covers the period during which the Winnebago lived lives typical of other Great Lakes people but were coming under the influence of Protestant missionaries.

McBride, Bunny. 1996. "Walking the Medicine Line: Molly Ockett, a Pigwacket Doctor." In *Northeastern Indian Lives, 1632–1816*, ed. Robert Grumet, 321–48. Boston: University of Massachusetts Press.

An interesting study of this itinerant midwife and healer, whose travels took her to many parts of east-central New England during the late eighteenth and early nineteenth centuries. Ockett became an important folk hero in the region, and lives in local legend to this day.

Miller, Bruce G. 1994. "Contemporary Native Women: Role Flexibility and Politics." *Anthropologica* 36(1): 57–72.

The consensus of modern scholarship that native women play important roles in contemporary politics is here treated from a theoretical
point of view.

Mossiker, Frances. 1996. *Pocahontas: The Life and the Legend.* 1st ed. New
York: Da Capo.

A useful survey of the life of Matoaka, or Pocahontas, one of the many
children of Powhatan, who married the Englishman John Rolfe and
died a convert in England.

Nash, Alice N. 1997. "The Abiding Frontier: Family, Gender, and Religion
in Wabanaki History, 1600–1763." Ph.D. diss., Columbia University.

This dissertation looks again at the native people of Maine, now known
as Wabanaki, from the perspective of social relations and gender roles.

Plane, Anne. 1995. "The Examination of Sarah Ahaton: The Politics of
Adultery in an Indian Town of Seventeenth-Century Massachusetts."
In *Major Problems in American Women's History: Documents and Es-
says,* 2nd ed., eds. Mary B. Norton and Ruth M. Alexander, 14–25.
Lexington, Mass.: D. C. Heath.

Plane's dynamic examination of the role of a woman torn between
traditional life and the politics of native "praying towns" on the eve of
King Philip's War.

———. "Putting a Face on Colonization: Factionalism and Gender Politics
in the Life History of Awashonks, the 'Squaw Sachem' of Saconnet."
In *Northeastern Indian Lives, 1632–1816,* ed. Robert Grumet, 140–65.
Amherst: University of Massachusetts Press.

Plane uses the life-history approach to examine the dilemmas faced by
native leaders in seventeenth-century southern New England.

Rountree, Helen. 1998. "Powhatan Indian Women: The People Captain
John Smith Barely Saw." *Ethnohistory* 45(1): 1–29.

Rountree uses ethnographic analogy and experimental reconstructions
of Powhatan women's work to round out the picture of Powhatan life
provided by early English explorers and settlers.

Seaver, James E. [1824] 1992. *A Narrative of the Life of Mrs. Mary Jemison.*

Canandaigua, N.Y.: Bemis. Reprint, Norman: Oklahoma University Press.

This reprint makes accessible the famous story of Mary Jemison, captured as a teenager by the French and Shawnee and later married to a Seneca man. Jemison spent the remainder of her life with the Seneca, and became an advocate for the Iroquois in the years following the Revolutionary War.

Spittal, William G. 1990. *Iroquois Women: An Anthology*. Oshweken, Ontario: Iroqrafts.

A useful collection of classic and contemporary studies of Iroquois women.

Tooker, Elisabeth. 1984. "Iroquois Women." In *Extending the Rafters: Interdisciplinary Approaches to Iroquoian Studies*, eds. Michael K. Foster, Jack Campisi, and Marianne Mithun, 109–24. Albany: State University of New York Press.

Tooker takes a conservative position with respect to the status of Iroquois women, based on her analysis of the early documentary sources.

Wilson, Diane E. 1997. "Gender, Diet, Health, and Social Status in the Mississippian Powers Phase Turner Cemetery Population." In *Women in Prehistory: North America and Mesoamerica*, eds. Cheryl Claassen and Rosemary A. Joyce, 119–35. Philadelphia: University of Pennsylvania Press.

Recent work suggests that native men's and women's differing status and work led to differing health, as revealed by scientific analysis of human remains.

Wright, Mary C. 1981. "Economic Development and Native American Women in the Early Nineteenth Century." *American Quarterly* 33:525–36.

Indian women have played important roles in providing for their own families as native people struggle to survive in the modern world.

Zawicki, Kathy Ann. 1991. "A Material Strong Enough to Encompass Our Lives: Mohawk Women and the Gambling Dispute." Ph.D. diss., University of Iowa.

This dissertation looks at the contemporary issue of gaming (see below) and the political and social role of women in the controversy.

7. Ecological Indians?

William Cronon's influential discussion of ecological change in colonial New England was premised on the notion that the effects of germs, intro-duced plants and animals, and other changes in the way the land was used were part of a complex system in which both Indians and non-Indians par-ticipated (1982). Cronon documented changes in both English and Indian economies as a result of the way in which their traditional ways of life were transformed in the New World environment, and the way in which their mutual interdependence led to mutual alteration. Until recently, most re-search has focused on the negative impact of the imported dairy/farming complex on native seasonal hunting and foraging patterns, the devastating effect on them of the continuous expansion of English settlement into their traditional territories, and the decline in native biota due to overhunting, injudicious timber use, and overuse of fragile salt marsh and estuarine re-sources.

Recently, however, Shepard Krech has focused attention on the long-term ecological effects of native land use (1998). These obviously were ex-aggerated after the introduction of trade in furs, but significant potential exists for research in the specific impact of each adaptation, especially the increased production of skins for trade in the northernmost regions of the area.

Sources

Cronon, William. 1983. *Changes in the Land: Indians, Colonists, and the Ecology of New England.* New York: Hill and Wang.
Krech, Shepard, III. 1997. *The Ecological Indian: Myth and History.* New York: Norton.
————, ed. 1981. *Indians, Animals, and the Fur Trade: A Critique of Keepers of the Game.* Athens: University of Georgia Press.
Martin, Calvin. 1978. *Keepers of the Game: Indian-Animal Relationships and the Fur Trade.* Berkeley: University of California Press.
Thomas, Peter. 1976. "Contrastive Subsistence Strategies and Land Use as

Factors for Understanding Indian-White Relations in New England."
Ethnohistory 23(1): 1–18.

8. Racial Politics

Although race itself is an extremely problematic category, one rejected as
imprecise and politicized by most anthropologists, its centrality in Indian
history and contemporary Indian politics cannot be denied. Tribal blood
quantum requirements imposed by the federal and state governments, anti-
miscegenation legislation, and restrictions on citizenship rights are all the
outcome of racial politics and the racist treatment of native people. In addition, the eugenics movement of the early twentieth century led some state
governments, most notably Virginia's, to enforce segregationist treatment of
all people labeled "colored" or "Negro," a category that by law included
Indians, until 1969 (Moretti-Langholtz 1995).

Sources

Blu, Karen I. [1980] 2001. *The Lumbee Problem: The Making of an American
Indian People.* New York: Cambridge University Press. Lincoln: University of Nebraska Press (with new afterword by author).

Although concerned with a people traditionally associated with the
Southeast culture area, Blu's landmark volume raises many important
issues concerning the nature of people of mixed ethnic heritage. The
Lumbee, like many such groups, consider themselves to be Indians,
and Blu's analysis of how their identity is formed and expressed is an
important contribution to the study of race and culture.

Bourne, Russell. 1990. *The Red King's Rebellion: Racial Politics in New
England, 1675–1678.* New York: Atheneum.

Bourne takes the position that King Philip's War was motivated on both
sides by increasing tension between the natives of the region and the
English and Anglo-American settlers.

Feest, Christian. 1990. "Pride and Prejudice: The Pocahontas Myth and the
Pamunkey." In *The Invented Indian: Cultural Fictions and Government*

Policies, ed. James A. Clifton, 49–70. New Brunswick, N.J.: Transaction.

The peculiar place of Pocahontas and her descendants within the racialized politics of traditional Virginia society is discussed here.

Kupperman, Karen. 1980. *Settling with the Indians: The Meeting of English and Indian Cultures in America, 1580–1640.* Lanham, Md.: Rowman and Littlefield.

This fine book was among the first to consider the impact of the Native American on European and Euro-American conceptions of humanity through a close examination of early English descriptions of American Indians. Kupperman argued that English treatment of Indians derived from their ideas about social order, rather than race.

Mandell, Daniel R. 1998. "Shifting Boundaries of Race and Ethnicity: Indian-Black Intermarriage in Southern New England, 1760–1880." *Journal of American History* 85(2): 466–501.

Indian people became enmeshed in racial politics throughout the nineteenth century, and this is reflected in patterns of marriage with non-Indians and the ways in which each native community attempted to maintain its identity.

Moretti-Langholtz, Danielle. 1998. "Other Names I Have Been Called: Political Resurgence Among Virginia Indians in the Twentieth Century." Ph.D. diss., Department of Anthropology, University of Oklahoma.

Moretti-Langholtz's important dissertation reveals the shocking story of the eugenics movement in Virginia, as applied to its native people, and its effect on contemporary Indian politics and identity.

Rountree, Helen C. 1990. *Pocahontas's People: The Powhatan Indians of Virginia Through Four Centuries.* Norman: University of Oklahoma Press.

An overview of Indian history, with some attention paid to the controversial subject of African-Indian relations through time.

Thomas, G. E. 1975. "Puritans, Indians, and the Concept of Race." *New England Quarterly* 48(1): 3–27.

Like Karen Kupperman, Thomas considers the problem of cultural differences between Indians and Puritans in light of modern concepts of race.

9. Land Claims, Resistance, Sovereignty, and Federal Recognition

Although not a subject of traditional research, the history of resistance by native people of the Northeast is one of great significance, both theoretically and as it directly affects the lives of contemporary Indians. The large number of articles and books now available concerning these subjects suggests that this research topic will continue to interest scholars, natives, and general readers alike. The following is a selected list of references to recent protests, land claims cases, and federal recognition disputes.

Sources

Alfred, Gerald R. 1995. *Heeding the Voices of Our Ancestors: Kahnawake Mohawk Politics and the Rise of Native Nationalism*. Toronto, New York: Oxford University Press.

Annette, James M. and Ward Churchill, eds. 1992. *The State of Native America: Genocide, Colonization, and Resistance*. Boston: South End.

Begin, P. W. Woss and P. Niemczak. 1990. *The Land Claim Dispute at Oka*. Ottawa: Library of Parliament, Research Branch.

Berkey, Curtis. 1993. "The Legal Basis for the Iroquois Land Claims." *Akwe'kon Journal* 10(1): 23–25.

Bilharz, Joy Ann. 1998. *The Allegany Senecas and Kinzua Dam: Forced Relocation Through Two Generations*. Lincoln: University of Nebraska Press.

Brodeur, Paul. 1985. *Restitution: The Land Claims of the Mashpee, Passamaquoddy and Penobscot Indians of New England*. Boston: Northeastern University Press.

Campisi, Jack. 1984. "National Policy, States' Rights, and Indian Sovereignty: The Case of the New York Iroquois." In *Extending the Rafters: Interdisciplinary Approaches to Iroquoian Studies*, eds. Michael K. Foster, Jack Campisi, and Marianne Mithun, 95–108. Albany: State University of New York Press.

———. 1990a. "The Emergence of the Mashantucket Pequot Tribe, 1637–

1975." In *The Pequots in Southern New England: The Fall and Rise of an American Indian Nation*, eds. Laurence M. Hauptman and James D. Wherry, 117–40. Norman: University of Oklahoma Press.

————. 1990b. "The New England Tribes and Their Quest for Justice." In *The Pequots in Southern New England: The Fall and Rise of an American Indian Nation*, eds. Laurence M. Hauptman and James D. Wherry, 179–93. Norman: University of Oklahoma Press.

————. 1991. *The Mashpee Indians: Tribe on Trial*. Syracuse, N.Y.: Syracuse University Press.

Ciborski, Sara. 1990. *Culture and Power: The Emergence and Politics of Akwesasne Mohawk Traditionalism*. Albany: State University of New York.

Deloria, Vine Jr. 1992. "The Application of the Constitution to American Indians." In *Exiled in the Land of the Free: Democracy, Indian Nations, and the U.S. Constitution*, eds. Oren R. Lyons and John C. Mohawk, 282–315. Santa Fe, N.M.: Clear Light.

Doherty, Robert. 1990. *Disputed Waters: Native Americans and the Great Lakes Fishery*. Lexington: University Press of Kentucky.

French, Laurence-Armand. 1994. *The Winds of Injustice: American Indians and the U.S. Government*. New York: Garland.

Goodleaf, Donna K. (Kahenrakwas). 1995. *Entering the War Zone: A Mohawk Perspective on Resisting Invasions*. 1st ed. Penticton, British Columbia: Theytus.

Goodman-Draper, Jacqueline. 1994. "The Development of Underdevelopment at Akwesasne: Cultural and Economic Subversion." *American Journal of Economics and Sociology* 53(1): 41–56.

Gosse, Richard, James Youngblood Henderson, Roger Carter, and J. R. Miller. 1994. "The Historical Context of the Drive for Self-Government." In *Continuing Poundmaker and Riel's Ouest: Presentations Made at a Conference on Aboriginal Peoples and Justice*. Proceedings of "Getting It Together" conference held in Saskatoon, Sask., 15–18 September 1993. Saskatoon: Purich Publishing for College of Law, University of Saskatchewan.

Grossman, Mark. 1996. *The ABC-CLIO Companion to the Native American Rights Movement*. Santa Barbara, Calif.: ABC-CLIO, x, 498.

Hauptman, Laurence M. 1986. *The Iroquois Struggle for Survival: World War II to Red Power*. Syracuse, N.Y.: Syracuse University Press.

————. 1991. "Compensatory Justice: The Seneca Nation Settlement Act." *National Forum* 71(2): 31–33.

Holt, H. Barry and Gary Forrester. 1990. *Digest of American Indian Law: Cases and Chronology.* Littleton, Colo.: F. B. Rothman, x, 138.

Horn, Kahn-Tineta. 1991. "Beyond Oka: Dimensions of Mohawk Sovereignty." *Studies in Political Economy* [Canada] (35): 29–41.

Landsman, Gail H. 1988. *Sovereignty and Symbol: Indian-White Conflict at Ganienkeh.* Albuquerque: University of New Mexico Press.

Lewis-Lorentz, Alexandra Jane. 1990. "From Gannagaro to Ganondagan: A Process and Reality of Seneca-Iroquois Identity." Ph.D. diss., University of Washington.

Lyons, Oren, ed. 1992. *Exiled in the Land of the Free: Democracy, Indian Nations, and the U.S. Constitution.* 1st ed. Santa Fe, N.M.: Clear Light.

Lyons, Oren and John C. Mohawk. 1994. "Sovereignty and Common Sense." *Cultural Survival Quarterly* 17(4): 58–60.

MacLaine, Craig, Michael Baxendale, and Robert Galbraith. 1990. *This Land Is Our Land: The Mohawk Revolt at Oka.* Montreal: Optimum.

Maine Indian Tribal State Commission Task Force on Tribal State Relations. 1997. "At Loggerheads: The State of Maine and the Wabanaki: Final Report of the Task Force on Tribal-State Relations." Hallowell: Maine Indian Tribal-State Commission, 74.

Oreskov, Claus. 1990. "Eleven Weeks that Shook Canada." *IWGIA Newsletter* 62:53–56.

Pertusati, Linda. 1997. *In Defense of Mohawk Land: Ethnopolitical Conflict in Native North America.* Albany: State University of New York Press.

Shattuck, George C. 1991. *The Oneida Land Claims: A Legal History.* Syracuse, N.Y.: Syracuse University Press.

Squire, Mariella Rose. 1996. "The Contemporary Western Abenakis: Maintenance, Reclamation, and Reconfiguration of an American Indian Ethnic Identity." Ph.D. diss., State University of New York at Albany.

Thompson, William Norman. 1996. *Native American Issues: A Reference Handbook.* Santa Barbara, Calif.: ABC-CLIO.

U.S. House. 1991. Committee on Interior and Insular Affairs. *To Provide for the Renegotiation of Certain Leases of the Seneca Nation: Hearing Before the Committee on Interior and Insular Affairs, House of Representatives, One Hundred First Congress, Second Session, on H.R. 5367; Hearing Held in Washington, D.C., September 13, 1990.* Washington, D.C.: Government Printing Office.

U.S. Senate. 1994. Select Committee on Indian Affairs. *Pokagon Band of Potawatomi Indians Act and the Little Traverse Bay Bands of Odawa Indians and the Little River Band of Ottawa Indians Act: Hearing Before the Committee on Indian Affairs, United States Senate, One Hundred Third Congress, Second Session, on S. 1066, to Restore Federal Services to the Pokagon Band of Potawatomi Indians and S. 1357, to Reaffirm and Clarify the Federal Relationships of the Little Traverse Bay Bands of Odawa Indians and the Little River Band of Ottawa Indians as Distinct Federally Recognized Indian Tribes, February 10, 1994.* Washington, D.C.: Government Printing Office.

U.S. Senate. 1995. Select Committee on Indian Affairs. *Federal Recognition Administrative Procedures Act: Hearing Before the Committee on Indian Affairs, United States Senate, One Hundred Fourth Congress, First Session, on S. 479, to Provide for Administrative Procedures to Extend Federal Recognition to Certain Indian Groups, July 13, 1995.* Washington, D.C.: Government Printing Office.

10. Gaming

Another controversial topic is gaming—its pros, cons, and effects on Indian communities. Frequently linked with the federal recognition process, gaming has been a significant factor in the economic and social renaissance of many eastern Indian groups.

Sources

Anders, Gary Carson. 1999. "Indian Gaming: Financial and Regulatory Issues." In *Contemporary Native American Political Issues,* ed. Troy Johnson, 163–73. Walnut Creek, Calif.: Alta Mira.

Hill, Richard. 1994. "The Future of Indian Gaming." *Cultural Survival Quarterly* 17(4): 61.

Jorgensen, Joseph G. 1998. "Gaming and Recent American Indian Economic Development." *American Indian Culture and Research Journal* 22(3): 157–72.

Lane, Ambrose I. 1995. *Return of the Buffalo: The Story Behind America's Indian Gaming Explosion.* Westport, Conn.: Bergin and Garvey, xx, 190.

Ribis, Nicholas and Michelle Traymar. 1996. "'Raising the Stakes' Raises the Issues." Indian Gaming Conference sponsored by Cultural Survival. *Cultural Survival Quarterly* 19(4): 10–11.

11. Native American Graves Protection Act (NAGPRA)

This controversial legislation, which protects native graves from desecration, also provides for the return of objects of sacred significance to the Indian communities whose ancestors or contemporaries produced them. NAGPRA regulations have impacted American museums, whose collections include such objects, and contemporary archaeological research on Native American sites. Native people argue that human remains are inappropriately or disrespectfully treated; scientists claim that much knowledge about the past can be derived from the analysis of such remains. Many concerns regarding the curation of repatriated items, the suppression of research, and the identity of prehistoric populations have been raised by natives and non-natives alike, but it has succeeded in raising consciousness about native sovereignty and religious freedom in a way that little other legal action has done.

Sources

Rose, Jerome C., Thomas J. Green, and Victoria D. Green. 1996. "NAGPRA is Forever: Osteology and the Repatriation of Skeletons." Palo Alto, Calif.: *Annual Reviews of Anthropology* 25:81–103.

Russell, Steve. 1995. "The Legacy of Ethnic Cleansing: Implementation of NAGPRA in Texas." *American Indian Culture and Research Journal* 19(4): 193–211.

Schermer, Shirley J., William Green, et al. 1998. *NAGPRA Inventory and Consultation: Human Remains and Funerary Objects in the Charles R. Keyes Collection.* Iowa City: Office of the State Archaeologist, University of Iowa, iv, 356.

Stone, Pamela Kendall, Venture R. Perez, and Debra Marin. 1998. "Science or Sacrilege: Native Americans, Archaeology and the Law." *American Anthropologist* 100(4): 1022–24.

Tooker, Elisabeth J. 1998. "A Note on the Return of Eleven Wampum Belts to the Six Nation Iroquois Confederacy on the Grand River, Canada." *Ethnohistory* 45(2): 219–36.

12. Postmodern Critique and Cultural Studies

A peripheral area of research in the Northeast is the postmodern concern with contact-period literature and its ethnographic analysis. An additional issue concerns the "invention" of contemporary Indian culture and ethnicity, seen by scholars primarily in political terms. A selected number of such studies are included below.

Sources

Arnold, Laura K. 1995. "Crossing Cultures: Algonquian Indians and the Invention of New England." Ph.D. diss., University of California–Los Angeles.

Feest, Christian. 1990. "Pride and Prejudice: The Pocahontas Myth and the Pamunkey." In *The Invented Indian: Cultural Fictions and Government Policies*, ed. James A. Clifton, 49–70. New Brunswick, N.J.: Transaction.

Fisher, Marvin. 1990. "Seeing New Englandly: Anthropology, Ecology, and Theology in Thoreau's *Week on the Concord and Merrimack Rivers*." *Centennial Review* 34(3): 381–94.

Green, Rayna D. 1992. "Mythologizing Pocahontas." In *Musical Repercussions of 1492: Encounters in Text and Performance*, ed. Carol E. Robertson. Washington, D.C.: Smithsonian Institution Press.

Gross, Judith. 1999. "Molly Brant: Textual Representations of Cultural Midwifery." *American Studies* 40(1): 23–40.

LePore, Jill. 1998. *The Name of War: King Philip's War and the Origins of American Identity*. New York: Knopf.

McMullen, Ann. 1996. "Culture by Design: Native Identity, Historiography, and the Reclamation of Tradition in Twentieth-Century Southeastern New England." Ph.D. diss., Department of Anthropology, Brown University.

13. Cultural Renaissance

A number of factors have contributed to the exciting cultural renaissance among Indian peoples of the Northeast, including: important new legislation that allows additional autonomy and provides funds for economic development and cultural programming; native population growth; funds provided by gaming; federal recognition; and an increasing interest in and respect for native culture and history among the general population. Among the many areas of growth are language revitalization projects and the arts.

Language Revitalization

Sources

Broadwell, George Aron. 1995. "1990 Census Figures for Speakers of American Indian Languages." *International Journal of American Linguistics* 61(1): 145–49.

Hoover, Michael L. 1992. "The Revival of the Mohawk Language in Kahnawake." *Canadian Journal of Native Studies* 12(2): 269–87.

Leavitt, Robert M. and David A. Francis. 1984. *Kolusuwakonol: Peskotomuhkati-Wolastoqewi naka Ikolisomani Latuwewakon; Philip S. Lesourd's English and Passamaquoddy-Maliseet Dictionary*, ed. and rev. Robert M. Leavitt and David A. Francis. Fredericton, N.B.: Micmac-Maliseet Institute, University of New Brunswick.

Little Doe, Jessie. 1998. "Report on the Wampanoag Dictionary Project." Paper presented at the annual meetings of the Algonquian Conference, Boston.

Maracle, David R., ed. 1990. *Iontewennaweienhstáhkwa': Mohawk Language Dictionary*. Belleville, Ontario: Mika.

Mithun, Marianne and Wallace Chafe. 1987. "Recapturing the Mohawk Language." In *Languages and Their Status*, ed. Timothy Shopen, 3–34. Philadelphia: University of Pennsylvania Press.

Rhodes, Richard. 1993. *Eastern Ojibwa-Chippewa-Ottawa Dictionary*. Berlin: Mouton de Gruyter.

Skinner, Linda. 1991. "Teaching Through Traditions: Incorporating Native Languages and Cultures Into Curricula: Indian Nations at Risk." [Papers commissioned by task force.] Washington, D.C.: United States Department of Education, Indians at Risk Task Force, 2.

Strong Woman and Moondancer. 1998. "Bringing Back Our Lost Language." *American Indian Culture and Research Journal* 22(3): 215–22.

U.S. Congress. 1992. *Native American Languages Act of 1992*. Washington, D.C.: Government Printing Office.

U.S. Senate. 1992. *Assisting Native Americans in Assuring the Survival and Continuing Vitality of Their Languages: Report (to Accompany S. 2044)*. Select Committee on Indian Affairs. Washington, D.C.: Government Printing Office, 2.

The Arts

Sources

Abbot, Larry. 1995. "Between Heaven and Earth: The Art of Alex Jacobs."
    Studies in American Indian Literatures 7(3): 39–49.
Dufrene, Phoebe Mills. 1991. *Contemporary Powhatan Art and Culture: Its
    Link with Tradition and Implications for the Future.* Ottawa, Ontario:
    Carleton University Press.
Grant, E. 1995. "He Walks in Two Worlds: A Visit with Maurice Kenny."
    Studies in American Indian Literatures 7(3): 17–27.
Hawley, Carolyn T. 1990. "A New School of Iroquois Sculpture." *American
    Indian Art Magazine* 15(2): 48–57.
Ryan, Allan J. 1994. "I Enjoy Being a Mohawk Girl: The Cool and Comic
    Character of Shelley Niro's Photography." *American Indian Art Mag-
    azine* 20(1): 44–53.

14. Telling Their Own Story

Biographies and Autobiographies

Areas of recent interest among scholars include native biographies and autobiographies, and some from the Northeast are collected in Robert Grumet's *Northeastern Indian Lives, 1632–1816* (1996), and in the *Encyclopedia of American Indians* (Hoxie 1996). The complete writings of William Apess, collected in the volume *On Our Own Ground*, edited by Barry O'Connell, include Apess's autobiography, the earliest ever published by a Native American (1992:xxxix). Arnold Krupat's books, especially his *Critical Bibliography of American Indian Autobiographies*, include several written by native people of the Northeast.

Sources

Bruchac, Joseph. 1990. "The Unbroken Circle: Contemporary Iroquois Sto-
    rytelling." *Northeast Indian Quarterly* 7(4): 13–16.
Brumble, H. David, III. 1981. *An Annotated Bibliography of American In-
    dian and Eskimo Autobiographies.* Lincoln: University of Nebraska
    Press.

Crozier-Hogle, Lois and Darryl Babe Wilson, eds. 1997. *Surviving in Two Worlds: Contemporary Native American Voices.* Austin: University of Texas Press.

Dixon-Kennedy, Mike. 1996. *Native American Myth and Legend: An A–Z of People and Places.* London: Blandford, 88.

Hirschfelder, Arlene. 1995. *Native Heritage: Personal Accounts by American Indians, 1790 to the Present.* New York: Macmillan, 38–40.

Jemison, Peter G. 1997. "Who Owns the Past?" In *Native Americans and Archaeologists: Stepping Stones to Common Ground,* eds. Kurt E. Swindler, Roger Anyon Dongoske, and Alan S. Downer, 57–63. Walnut Creek, Calif.: Alta Mira.

Johansen, Bruce E. and Donald A. Grinde, eds. 1998. *The Encyclopedia of Native American Biography: Six Hundred Life Stories of Important People, from Powhatan to Wilma Mankiller.* 1st ed. New York: Da Capo.

Landsman, Gail-Heidi. 1992. "Representation and Politics: Contesting Histories of the Iroquois." *Cultural Anthropology* 7(4): 425–47.

MacLeod, D. Peter. 1992. "The Anishinabeg Point of View: The History of the Great Lakes Region to 1800 in Nineteenth-Century Mississauga, Odawa and Ojibwa Historiography." *Canadian Historical Review* 73(2): 194–210.

Malinowski, Sharon and Simon Glickman, eds. 1996. *Native North American Biography.* New York: UXL.

Obomsawin, Alanis, director. 1993. *Kanehsatake—270 Years of Resistance.* A National Film Board production. Produced by Wolf Koenig and Alanis Obomsawin. Distributed by National Film Board of Canada, Ottawa.

Peattie, Lisa R. 1960. "Being a Mesquakie Indian." In *Documentary History of the Fox Project, 1948–1959,* eds. Frederick O. Gering, Robert McNetting, and Lisa R. Peattie, 39–62. Chicago: University of Chicago Press.

Phillips, Ruth B. 1993. "'Messages from the Past': Oral Traditions and Contemporary Woodlands Art." In *In the Shadow of the Sun: Perspectives on Contemporary Native Art,* ed. The Canadian Museum of Civilization, 233–55. Hull, Quebec: Canadian Museum of Civilization.

Rice, Brian D. 1999. "The Rotinonshonni: Through the Eyes of Teharonhia: Wako and Sawiskera. A Traditional Iroquoian History for Modern Times." Ph.D. diss., California Institute of Integral Studies.

Skinner, Linda. 1991. "Teaching Through Traditions: Incorporating Native
    Languages and Cultures Into Curricula: Indian Nations at Risk." [Paper
    commissioned by task force.] Washington, D.C.: United States De-
    partment of Education, Indians at Risk Task Force, 32.
Slapin, Beverly and Doris Seale. 1992. *Through Indian Eyes: The Native
    Experience in Books for Children.* Philadelphia: New Society.
Squire, Mariella Rose. 1996. "The Contemporary Western Abenakis: Main-
    tenance, Reclamation, and Reconfiguration of an American Indian
    Ethnic Identity." Ph.D. diss., State University of New York at Albany.

15. General Works

Encyclopedias, Compendia, Dictionaries

There are several published guides to the Northeast culture area that are
good starting places for research. Of these, the most significant is *The Northeast,* volume 15 of the *Handbook of North American Indians.* Published in
1978, this fine volume includes chapters on all major tribal groups in the
region, with additional essays on historiography, archaeology, linguistics, and
the early contact period. Many of the chapters were authored by scholars
who have made important contributions to the research they describe. Maps,
illustrations, synonymies, summaries of important historical sources, and a
comprehensive bibliography make this a valuable and enduring resource.
However, a great deal of additional research on the Northeast has been done
since the publication of the *Handbook,* and the political and economic
changes among Indian communities in the last thirty years also demand
attention. Several collected volumes of essays on the history and culture of
native peoples of the region are now available, including *Raising the Rafters*
(Foster and Mithun) and *The History and Culture of Iroquois Diplomacy:
An Interdisciplinary Guide to the Treaties of the Six Nations and Their League*
(Jennings et al. 1985). *Powhatan's Mantle: Indians in the Colonial Southeast*
(Wood et al. 1989) includes several chapters about the Virginia and North
Carolina Algonquians and their neighbors. A number of important collec-
tions of archaeological essays that link historic communities to Woodland
period chiefdoms and states have been produced, including *Women in Pre-
history* (Claassen and Joyce 1996), and *Lords of the Southeast* (Barker and
Pauketat).

Another important and often overlooked resource is doctoral dissertations,
obtained through University Microfilms. Among the most important recent

dissertations on the Northeast are Robinson (1990), Johnson (1992), Chilton (1996), Drake (1995), Ghere (1992), and Squires (1995).

Sources

Bataille, Gretchen Mueller. 1993. *Native American Women: A Biographical Dictionary.* New York: Garland, 353.

Brumble, H. David, III. 1981. *An Annotated Bibliography of American Indian and Eskimo Autobiographies.* Lincoln: University of Nebraska Press.

Davis, Mary B. 1996. *Native America in the Twentieth Century: An Encyclopedia.* New York: Garland, xxxvii, 787.

Gallay, Alan. 1996. *Colonial Wars of North America, 1512–1763: An Encyclopedia.* New York: Garland.

Gibbon, Guy and Kenneth M. Ames. 1998. *Archaeology of Prehistoric Native America: An Encyclopedia.* New York: Garland.

Goddard, Ives, ed. 1996. *Languages and Language Families of North America.* Vol. 17 of *Handbook of North American Indians,* ed. William C. Sturtevant. Washington, D.C.: Smithsonian Institution.

Haas, Marilyn L. 1994. *The Seneca and Tuscarora Indians: An Annotated Bibliography.* Lanham, Md.: Scarecrow.

Heard, J. Norman. 1990. *The Northeastern Woodlands.* Vol. 2 of *Handbook of the American Frontier: Four Centuries of Indian-White Relationships.* Lanham, Md.: Scarecrow.

Hirschfelder, Arlene and Paulette Fairbanks Molin. 1991. *Encyclopedia of American Indian Religions.* New York: Facts on File, xiii, 367.

Hoxie, Fred, ed. 1996. *Encyclopedia of North American Indians.* Boston: Houghton Mifflin.

Johansen, Bruce E. 1996. "Debating the Origins of Democracy: Overview of an Annotated Bibliography." *American Indian Culture and Research Journal* 20(2): 155–72.

Klein, Barry T. 1998. *Reference Encyclopedia of the American Indian.* 8th ed. Nyack, N.Y.: Todd, ii, 727.

Malinowski, Sharon and Anna Sheets, eds. 1998. *Northeast, Southeast, Caribbean.* Vol. 1 of *The Gale Encyclopedia of Native American Tribes,* ed. Sharon Malinowski et al. Detroit: Gale, 199–204.

Marino, Cesare. 1995. *The American Indian: A Multimedia Encyclopedia.* CD-ROM, version 2.0 for Windows and DOS. New York: Facts on File.

McBride, Kevin A., Nanepashemet, Neal Salisbury, Neal McMullen, and
    Ann McMullen, comps. 1991. "Selected Bibliography of Algonkian
    Peoples in New England." *Annual Proceedings (Dublin Seminar for
    New England Folklife)* 16:144–51.
Singerman, Robert. 1996. *Indigenous Languages of the Americas: A Bibli-
    ography of Dissertations and Theses*. Lanham, Md.: Scarecrow.
Thompson, William Norman. 1996. *Native American Issues: A Reference
    Handbook*. Santa Barbara, Calif.: ABC-CLIO.
Tooker, Elisabeth. 1978a. *The Indians of the Northeast: A Critical Bibliog-
    raphy*. Bloomington: Published for the Newberry Library by Indiana
    University Press.
Trigger, Bruce G., ed. 1978. *The Northeast*. Vol. 15 of *Handbook of North
    American Indians*, ed. William C. Sturtevant. Washington, D.C.:
    Smithsonian Institution.
Wells, Robert N., ed. 1994. *Native American Resurgence and Renewal: A
    Reader and Bibliography*. Lanham, Md.: Scarecrow.
Whittaker, David J. 1996. *United States Government Policies Toward Native
    Americans, 1787–1990: A Guide to Materials in the British Library*.
    London: Eccles Centre for American Studies.

16. Film

Much of the film material available on native people in the Northeast is
an outgrowth of earlier dramatic treatments of such subjects as King Philip,
who became a celebrated topic of discussion after the publication of Washington Irving's reappraisal of King Philip's War (*History of New York*, 1809),
and especially during the long and successful run of the play *Metamora*,
which also cast Philip in the role of hero. Buffalo Bill Cody's Wild West
Show enjoyed great popularity in the Northeast, attracting large audiences
of Indians and non-Indians alike. Buffalo Bill visited the grave of the Mohegan sachem Uncas on one of his tours through New England, and he is
credited with encouraging the spread of pan-Indian consciousness through
the Northeast (see part II). James Fenimore Cooper's *Last of the Mohicans*
and *Drums Along the Mohawk* were both successfully adapted as films, the
former remade three times. Less well known, but important in the history
of filmmaking nonetheless, Plymouth Plantation's film *The Peach Gang*
(PBS 1975) dramatized the trial and eventual execution of three men who
robbed and killed a Narragansett Indian in the seventeenth century. The
disturbing film *Black Robe* signaled a new popular interest in historical dra-

mas, this one with accurate portrayals of Algonquian and Iroquoian societies in New France and their relationships with Jesuit missionaries. *The Witness*, produced by the Mashantucket Pequot Museum, dramatically reenacts the events of the massacre of 400 Pequot men, women, and children at Mystic Fort in 1636. This film includes dialogue in several of the native languages of the region, as do *The Peach Gang, Black Robe*, and *Last of the Mohicans*. Most recently, the popular film *Smoke Signals* addressed contemporary issues common to Indians in all parts of the United States and Canada. In addition to these widely distributed films, there are numerous short-subject films produced by museums and private film companies that explore such issues as land claims, sovereignty, and fishing rights. Many films also document traditional skills such as canoe manufacture, trapping and fishing techniques, basketry and pottery making, quillwork and beading. Finally, many Indian communities have commissioned or produced films featuring traditional stories and storytelling and the biographies of important figures in their communities.

Sources

Chan-Marples, Lan. 1992. "Our Own Stories and Our Own Realities: Canada's First Nations Speaking Out Through Films." *Canadian Journal of Education* 19(1): 123–37.

Fast, Robin Riley. 1996. "Resistant History: Revising the Captivity Narrative in 'Captivity' and 'Blackrobe: Isaac Jogues.'" *American Indian Culture and Research Journal* 23(1): 69–86.

17. Museums and the Northeast

The most important collections of northeastern native arts and manufactures reside in a number of museums in the region. These museums also fund important ethnographic and archaeological research in the Northeast, and their collections often include the notes and papers of the scholars in their employ. Some museums hold important collections of historic documents and photographs relating to Indians of the Northeast as well.

Prior to the establishment of the first academic programs in anthropology or Native American Studies, the Peabody Museum at Harvard and the Peabody Museum at Phillips Academy in Andover, Massachusetts supported archaeological and ethnographic research in the Northeast. Frederick Putnam at Harvard and Warren K. Moorehead at Phillips Academy were accomplished archaeologists whose research focused on the Archaic and Woodland peoples of the Northeast, and whose excavations yielded the first important and systematically collected data available for study. The publications of these museums remain valuable resources concerning their collections, some of which have since been returned to descendant communities as part of NAGPRA repatriation. Both the Harvard Peabody and the museum at Phillips maintain educational exhibits concerning the cultures of the Northeast, and continue to support archaeological and ethnographic research and teaching.

The Rochester Museum of Science contains a large collection of materials relating to Iroquoia, as well as some of the papers and collections of Lewis Henry Morgan, also based on his work with the Iroquois and the basis for the celebrated *League of the Ho-de-no-sau-nee or Iroquois*, the first modern work of ethnography, published in 1851.

The Canadian Museum of Civilization (formerly the Museum of Man) supported important research on Woodland and Subarctic peoples, including the important research of linguist Edward Sapir and ethnologist and linguist Gordon Day. Many of Day's field notes and recordings are also housed at the museum at Dartmouth College. Other important university museums include the museum at Bowdoin, the Haffenreffer Museum of Anthropology at Brown, and the Museum of Anthropology at the University of Pennsylvania. The Carnegie Museum in Pittsburgh has supported archaeological research in the Northeast since the beginning of the twentieth century.

In New York City, the American Museum of Natural History and the Heye Foundation house significant archaeological and ethnographic collections relating to the Northeast. Much of the latter's have become part of the holdings of the National Museum of the American Indian in Washington, D.C., although the large documentary holdings remain at the foundation's library in the Bronx.

Indian Notes and Monographs, published by the Heye Foundation, contain many important studies of northeastern languages and cultures.

Two of the largest and oldest American ethnographic collections are housed at the Field Museum in Chicago and at the Bureau of American Ethnology, whose collections are now held by the Smithsonian's Museum of Natural History in Washington, D.C. These museums, along with the Peabody at Harvard, employed teams of anthropologists and archaeologists who, in the late nineteenth and early twentieth centuries, worked with many northeastern people, studying their languages and customs and collecting archaeological and ethnographic materials for study and exhibition. Both these museums have extensive documentary holdings and produced publication series containing significant research results, especially the important Annual Reports, and Bulletins of the Bureau of American Ethnology. The Smithsonian also produced the Handbook of North American Indians, the original series published between 1907 and 1910 by Frederick Hodge, and the entirely new series, edited by William C. Sturtevant, curator of North American Ethnology. The handbook will have 20 volumes when complete; thus far, 11 have been published.

Of an entirely different order are "living" or "outdoor" museums, which present past lifeways to the public through third-person and first-person interpretation, in reconstructed settings. Plymouth Plantation's Hobbomok's Campsite, part of their larger research and exhibit program, interprets the summer camp where Hobbomok, emissary of the Pokanoket (Wampanoag) paramount sachem Massasoit was said to live. All aspects of native economy, social life, and cosmology are discussed by interpreters, many of whom are descendants of native people of the region. This living exhibit is further enhanced by interpretations presented in the Plantation's museum. Similarly, the Indian village at Jamestown Settlement presents a reconstructed Powhatan village based on early seventeenth-century descriptions and archaeological research. The museum at Prophetstown, the location of Tenskwatawa's settlement, interprets the experiences and events of Tecumseh's rebellion and the teachings and legacy of the Prophet.

Two museums developed by Indian tribes—the Ganondagan Museum, devoted to a reconstruction of Iroquois life and located near Buffalo, New York; and the Mashantucket Pequot Museum in Ledyard, Connecticut—take different approaches to the treatment of the native past. Ganondagan's exhibits are part of extensive nature trails, while the Mashantucket museum has extensive exhibit space devoted to reconstructed environments. The Museum of Iroquois Art, developed in cooperation with Iroquois communities, showcases the work of contemporary Iroquois artists.

Sources

Metz, Elizabeth. 1995. *Sainte Marie Among the Iroquois: A Living History Museum of the French and the Iroquois at Onondaga in the Seventeenth Century.* Syracuse, N.Y.: Printed by Quartier (Liverpool, N.Y.), distributed by Friends of Historic Onondaga Lake, 18.

18. Electronic Resources

Sources

Polly, Jean Armour. 1998. "Standing Stones in Cyberspace: The Oneida Indian Nation's Territory on the Web." *Cultural Survival Quarterly* 21(4): 37–41.

Akwesasne Task Force on the Environment Home Page
http://www.slic.com/atfe/atfe.htm

> Akwesasne Task Force on the Environment (ATFE) is a grass-roots organization designed to confront environmental issues in a Mohawk community. Their Web site provides information on their history, mission, projects, and environmental concerns as well as links to sites on regional Indians and environmental resources.

American Indian Library Association Home Page
http://www.nativeculture.com/lisamitten/aila.html

> American Indian Library Association is an affiliate of the American Library Association. This site provides links, indexes, bibliographies, and information about accessing their electronic resources on a wide range of American Indian issues. It contains a page with links to language centers, databases, and advocate groups.

American Native Press Archives Home Page
http://anpaserever.ualr.edu/

> The American Native Press Archives is a clearinghouse for information on American Indian and Alaska native newspapers and periodicals. This site includes indexes and bibliographies for the holdings and information about gaining access.

American Indian Resource and Referral Database
http://www.airr.net/non/default.asp

> The American Indian Resource and Referral Database is designed to help native people and social service workers find native cultural and social services in the Minneapolis/St. Paul area. The system currently lists more than 230 organizations designed to assist native people.

North American Indian Rights Fund Home Page
http://www.narf.org/

The North American Indian Rights Fund (NARF) is a nonprofit organization that provides legal representation and technical assistance to Indian tribes, organizations, and individuals nationwide. Their Web site provides information on breaking news, publications, calendar, and access to the National Indian Law Library.

Anishinabek Nation Home Page
http://www.anishinabek.ca/

The Anishinabek Nation maintains this Web site, which includes history of the Anishinabek, stories from the *Anishinabek News*, events calendar, tribal contacts, and community issues.

Assembly of First Nations Home Page
http://www.afn.ca/

The Web site of the Assembly of First Nations (AFN) provides resources for Canadian Indians on a wide range of issues, including education, health, economic development, housing, land rights, treaties, and language, as well as links to related sites.

Bureau of Indian Affairs Home Page
http://www.doi.gov/bureau-indian-affairs.html

This is the Web site of the the Bureau of Indian Affairs of the Department of the Interior. It includes information on hot issues, reports and statistics, tribal contact information, and BIA organizational information.

Casinos: Is Gaming the New Buffalo?
http://indy4.fdl.cc.mn.us/~isk/games/gaming.html

This Web site explores the controversial issue of gaming, and includes editorials, news stories, and links to related sites, casinos, and gaming tribes.

College of Menominee Nation Library Home Page
http://www.menominee.edu/library/home.html

This site provides information about library resources and provides online access to electronic resources.

Dakota Ojibway Tribal Council Home Page
http://www.dotc.mb.ca/

This site provides tribal and governmental contacts, but also includes links, resources, and programs available for tribal members.

Daybreak Farming and Food Project Home Page
    http://www.acsu.buffalo.edu/~ydb/dayweb2.html

The Daybreak Farming and Food Project is an organization that supports, encourages, and promotes traditional native farming within the Iroquois Six Nations, as well as the marketing of its products. This site provides project information, recipes, and discussions of the cultural significance of particular foods.

Delaware Tribe of Indians Home Page
    http://www.delawaretribeofindians.nsn.us/

This site documents the history of the Delaware and discusses aspects of traditional Delaware society, such as dress, humor, sports, dance, and language.

Delaware Tribe of Western Oklahoma Home Page
    http://www.westerndelaware.nsn.us/

This site provides historic information about the Delaware.

First Nations Home Page
    http://www.dickshovel.com/

First Nations is dedicated to informing the public of injustices committed against American Indians. This site provides mostly historic information and editorial discussions of such issues. It also boasts an impressive amount of links to related sites and topics.

Foxwoods Resort Casino Home Page
    http://www.foxwoods.com/

This is the Web site of the Pequot-run Foxwoods Resort Casino. It provides casino and hotel entertainment information.

Great Lakes Intertribal Council Home Page
    http://www.glitc.org/

Great Lakes Intertribal Council is a resource for American Indian communities and events in Wisconsin. This site provides information about community events, cultural communication activities, accommodations, and attractions in Wisconsin's Indian country for tourists.

Great Lakes Regional American Indian Network Home Page
http://www.glrain.net/

Great Lakes Regional American Indian Network is dedicated to assisting native people to acquire, train, and utilize telecommunications technologies. It includes links to native sites.

Huntington Free Library and Reading Room Home Page
http://www.binc.org/hfl/

The Huntington Free Library and Reading Room is a privately endowed library in the Bronx open to the public. It has two separate noncirculating collections, one of which is a research collection on the native peoples of the Western Hemisphere. The collection includes books, manuscripts, photographs, periodicals, bibliographies, and genealogical information.

The Illini Confederation Home Page
http://members.tripod.com/~RFester/

This Web site is dedicated to preserving the history of the Illinois Confederation. It discusses the history, geography, customs, and cultures of the Confederation, and also includes links to sites concerned with native issues.

Index of Native American Language Resources
http://hanksville.org/NAresources/indices/NAlanguage.html

Index of Native American Language Resources on the Internet, maintained by an individual. It is constructed primarily to provide information resources to the Native American community and only secondarily to the general community. It provides an immense number of links to sites on the topic of language.

Indian Circle Web Ring Home Page
http://www.indiancircle.com/links.shtml

Indian Circle Web Ring is a great place to begin. This site provides links to federally recognized tribes, American Indian newspapers, and discussions of hot topics.

Indian Country Home Page
http://www.indiancountry.com

Indian Country is the widest-circulating American Indian newspaper.

California Indian Gaming News Home Page
http://www.pechanga.net/

This is the premiere Web site for gaming information. The title is misleading, as gaming all over the United States is discussed. The site consists of news articles, chat rooms, archives, and gaming links.

Indians of the Eastern USA Home Page
http://www.hi.is/~baldurs/ind_links.html

Indians of the Eastern USA provides links to tribal and reservation Web sites in addition to histories of American Indians.

Indianz.com Home Page
http://www.indianz.com/

Indianz.com is a native electronic newspaper discussing not only politics and hot topics but also Indian life, entertainment, relationships, and money.

Introduction to Ojibway Culture and History Home Page
http://www.geocities.com/Athens/Acropolis/5579/ojibwa.html

Introduction to Ojibway Culture and History is a detailed and documented discourse on Ojibway culture and history. It contains links and a bibliography of suggested readings.

Kahon'wes's Mohawk and Iroquois Index
http://www.kahonwes.com

This site provides links, paintings, bibliographies, and articles on the history and culture of the Iroquois, with a particular emphasis on language.

Labriola National American Indian Data Center Home Page
http://www.asu.edu/lib/archives/labriola.htm

Labriola National American Indian Data Center, at the University of Arizona, is a collection of resources on American Indians. This site contains the collection's catalog, access information, and links to related sites.

Mashantucket Pequot Museum and Research Center Home Page
http://www.mashantucket.com/

This site contains the card catalog, contact information, and information about educational and arachaeological programs.

The Massachusetts State Archives Microfilm Index of Native Americans
http://www.geocities.com/Athens/Oracle/7595/http://
www.geocities.com/Athens/Oracle/7595/

This site contains the card index for the Archives' microfilm collection.

Mattaponi Indian Reservation Home Page
http://www.baylink.org/mattaponi/

This site provides basic information on the Mattaponi Indian Reservation located in Virginia's Tidewater. This includes information on the mission, goals, reservation history, and government of the Mattaponi, as well as the Mattaponi Fish Hatchery and Marine Science Center.

Menominee Tribe of Wisconsin Home Page
http://www.menominee.nsn.us/

The Menominee Tribe of Wisconsin maintains this Web site with tribal information such as a calendar of public and social services, events, tribal officials, and minutes from committee meetings.

Miami Nation Home Page
http://www.geocities.com/RainForest/7156/

This site consists of pre-Removal language and treaty information compiled by representatives of the Miami Tribe of Oklahoma and the Miami Nation of Indiana. It includes links to both tribes.

Mille Lacs Band of Ojibwa Home Page
http://www.millelacsojibwe.org/

This site provides tribal, cultural, casino, educational, and historic information about the Ojibwa, as well as a calendar of events.

Mingo-EGADS Home Page
http://fife.speech.cs.cmu.edu/egads/mingo/

The Mingo-EGADS site is dedicated to the preservation and revitalization of Unyœœshœötká', the language of the West Virginia Mingo.

It includes phrases, stories, grammar, dictionary, and links to other language sites.

Mohegan Sun Casino Home Page
http://www.mohegansun.com/

The Web site of the Mohegan Sun Casino provides travel, tourist, and entertainment information for Connecticut.

Mohegan Tribe Home Page
http://www.mohegan.nsn.us/

Outreach Web site for the Mohegan Tribe, with basic information on history, culture, religion, and upcoming events.

Mohican.com
http://www.mohican.com/

Mohican.com is a tribal site with news, history, and casino information.

The National Congress of American Indians Home Page
http://www.ncai.org/

The Web site of the National Congress of American Indians (NCAI) provides organizational materials such as resolutions, officers, mission, calendar, and history, and contains an issue page with information on fundamental issues.

The National Indian Gaming Association
http://www.indiangaming.org/

The National Indian Gaming Association (NIGA) is a clearinghouse for educational, legislative, and public policy resources for tribes, policy makers, and the public on Indian gaming issues and tribal community development. This site contains forums, calendars, and tribal contacts, as well as seminar and roundtable information.

The National Indian Gaming Commission Home Page
http://www.nigc.gov/

The National Indian Gaming Commission (NIGC) is an independent federal regulatory group created by the Indian Gaming Regulatory Act (IGRA). Their Web site includes testimony, newsletters, laws, and press releases relating to gaming.

Native American Authors Online Home Page
http://www.hanksville.org/storytellers/

Native American Authors Online promotes the rich tradition of American Indian storytelling. This site contains the prose and poetry of current Indian authors as well as traditional oral tales.

Native American Indian Resources Home Page
http://cs.fdl.cc.mn.us/risk/

Native American Indian Resources is no longer updated but provides links to more than 300 native sites dealing with tribal history, traditional tales, recipes, herbal knowledge, astronomy, crafts, leaders, gaming, and current fiction.

Native American Links Home Page
http://dent.edmonds.wednet.edu/imd/nativeamerican.html

This site provides an incredible amount of links to sites concerned with many aspects of American Indian culture, including art, society, politics, literature, education, government, and history.

Native American Sites Home Page
http://www.nativeculture.com/lisamitten/indians.html

Truly impressive, Native American Sites is one of the best survey Web sites that provide an overview of Internet resources for and about American Indians. It is likely the most comprehensive survey site, and provides links to sites concerned with virtually every aspect of American Indian culture and society.

Native American Indian Treaty Library Home Page
http://www.councilfire.com/treaty/index.html

Native American Indian Treaty Library is a wonderful site providing full-text treaties. More than 350 treaties during the period 1778–1868 are included, along with lists of the signatories.

Native Americans of the Northeast and the Environment Home Page
http://conbio.rice.edu/nae/internet.html

Native Americans of the Northeast and the Environment is maintained by Dr. Alex Dark, an anthropologist who studies the politics of land and treaty rights. His work focuses on the negotiation of treaties in

British Columbia and the environmental politics of First Nations land rights. His site provides links and information on a wide variety of environmental, conservation, and management issues.

NativeNet Home Page
http://cs.fdl.cc.mn.us/natnet/

NativeNet facilitates communications of native peoples around the world and focuses on the problems that confront them, particularly environmental issues. This site provides links, forums, and information on a variety of issues.

Native Web Home Page
http://www.nativeweb.org/

Native Web is an electronic news source for worldwide native peoples.

Newberry Library Home Page
http://www.newberry.org

The Newberry Library is an independent research library in Chicago noted for its American Indian and contact-period collection. Privately funded, but free and open to the public, it houses an extensive noncirculating collection of rare books, maps, and manuscripts. This site provides access and resource information.

Occaneechi Band of the Saponi Nation Home Page
http://www.occaneechi-saponi.org/

This is the site of the Occaneechi Band of the Saponi Nation, located in North Carolina. It provides history of the Saponi and information on current events.

Official Web Page of the Southern Band Tuscarora Indian Tribe
http://www.crosswinds.net/~sbtuscarora/

This is a tribal site with information on history, leadership, announcements, obituaries, and community projects.

Oneida Indian Nation Home Page
http://www.oneida-nation.net/

This site provides information on the culture, history, land claims, economic opportunities, and government of the Oneida.

Oneida Nation of Wisconsin Home Page
http://www.oneidanation.org/

This site provides information on the culture, history, government, news, and events of the Oneida of Wisconsin.

Pamunkey Indian Tribe Home Page
http://www.baylink.org/pamunkey/

This site includes history of the Pamunkey, as well as information about the Pamunkey fishery, museum, and pottery.

Passamaquoddy Tribe at Pleasant Point Home Page
http://www.wabanaki.com/

Passamaquoddy Tribe at Pleasant Point is a tribal page with information about Passamaquoddy government, history, culture, land claims, language, crafts, economic opportunities, and artifacts.

Peoria Tribe of Indians of Oklahoma Home Page
http://www.peoriatribe.com/

This is the news and update site for members of the tribe. It includes political information, a calendar of events, and information about federal programs and government policies.

Petun Research Institute Home Page
http://www.ukans.edu/kansas/wn/petun/

Petun Research Institute is a registered charitable foundation that conducts and publishes scholarly research on the Petun-Wyandot people. The institute conducts archaeological excavations, maintains an Artifact Repository, provides research facilities to accredited scholars, conducts and supports interdisciplinary studies, and advises and assists researchers. This site also includes links to other native resources.

Pokagon Band of Potawatomi Indians Home Page
http://www.pokagon.com/

This site provides tribal contact information.

Powhatan Renape Nation Home Page
http://www.powhatan.org/

This site provides information about the Powhatan Rankokus Reservation. Information on the museum and history is included, as well as calendar of events and friends programs.

Red Lake Band of Chippewa Indians Tribal Council Home Page
http://www.redlakenation.org/

This site provides contact, powwow, casino, and social services information.

Sac and Fox Nation Home Page
http://www.cowboy.net/native/sacnfox.html

The Web site of the Sac and Fox Nation provides a brief historic description of their peoples and several links.

St. Croix Casino at Turtle Lake, Wisconsin, Home Page
http://www.stcroixcasino.com/

This site provides information about events, entertainment, dining, and accommodations at the casino.

Sandy Lake Band of Ojibwa Home Page
http://www.mlecmn.net/˜skinaway/

This site provides maps, history, treaties, photos, and links to related topics.

Sault-Ste. Marie Tribe of Chippewa Indians Home Page
http://www.sootribe.org/

This is a tribal site providing government, contact, health, and historical information, as well as links to local casinos and tribal reports.

Seneca Nation of Indians Home Page
http://www.sni.org/

This site provides basic information about government, history, treaty, education, health care, government programs, and contacts for additional information.

Stockbridge-Munsee Tribe of Mohican Indians Home Page
http://unr.edu/homepage/shubinsk/mohican1.html

This site provides information about the history, culture, language, archaeology, and society of the Mohican. It also includes contact information and a discussion of James Fenimore Cooper.

Traditional Abenaki of Mazipskwik and Related Bands Home Page
http://hmt.com/abenaki/

This site provides information about the complex historical role of
Abenaki in northern New England and includes discussions of Abenaki
culture, customs, and language, as well as links to related topics and
the Abenaki Law Library.

Turning Stone Casino Resort Home Page
http://www.turning-stone.com/

This site includes information about entertainment, events, dining, accommodations, and conferences at the casino.

Turtle Island News Home Page
http://www.turtleislandnews.on.ca/

The Web site of *Turtle Island News* provides news and information
about the Six Nations of the Grand River Territory. It also includes chat
rooms, forums, and links.

Tuscarora and Six Nations Home Page
http://tuscaroras.com/index.shtml

This an electronic news and information site, with current events,
sports, and community and entertainment news, as well as information
on history, treaties, books, and environment.

United Tribe of Shawnee Indians Home Page
http://home.att.net/~hdqrs/

This site provides biographical information on Tecumseh as well as
treaties and government documents that impacted of the Shawnee during the eighteenth and nineteenth centuries. Links to other American
Indian sites are included.

Unofficial Pamunkey Indian Home Page
http://home.earthlink.net/~pamunkey/

The Unofficial Pamunkey Indian site.

Virginia Council on Indians Home Page
http://indians.vipnet.org/

This site provides organizational, member, and mission information as
well as links to the home pages of Virginia's Indians.

Wampanoag Tribe of Gay Head Home Page
  http://www.wampanoagtribe.net/

Wisconsin Gaming Directory
  http://www.wisconsingaming.com/

  This site includes links to Wisconsin native-run casinos and travel information.

Woodland Cultural Centre Home Page
  http://www.woodland-centre.on.ca/

  The Woodland Cultural Centre is located in Ontario on the land of the Six Nations. It promotes community awareness of culture, history, and heritage, and recognizes that contemporary Indian lifestyles are rooted in ancient traditions. The center maintains a museum and research library, and also focuses on language.

Wyandot Nation of Kansas Home Page
  http://www.sfo.com/~denglish/wynaks/

  The historical focus of this site is extensive. It includes the reproduction of various treaties, letters, and excerpts from famous works, and also has discussions of language issues, historic missions, and sites sacred to the Wyandot.

Wyandotte Nation of Oklahoma Home Page
  http://www.ukans.edu/kansas/wn/oklahoma/

  This site provides tribal contact information and several links.

Conclusion

Some of the topics discussed in part IV represent areas of enduring research interest among scholars working in the Northeast. Others reflect the interests of native people, some of whom are scholars themselves. Still other topics, such as the debates over the possible contributions of the League of the Iroquois to the development of the U.S. Constitution, are included because they reflect current debates of broader scholarly or popular interest. In fact, some topics, such as "Captivity Narratives," were chosen because of the sheer number of recent articles devoted to them. Each researcher will bring his or her own interests to the broad culture area of the Northeast as well. The materials reviewed here can serve as the basis for more detailed research.

Index